Dancing in
Two Realms

A LOVE STORY BEYOND DEATH

Anne Marie Higgins

This is a work of creative nonfiction. The events are portrayed
to the best of my memory with added benefit of daily journaling
and audio recording of some conversations. While all of the stories
in this book are true, some names and identifying details have
been changed to protect the privacy of the people involved.

Cover Design: Sarah Treanor is an artist and widow with a focus on
grief-centered work. After the sudden death of her fiancé in 2012, she
created a year-long photographic self portrait series entitled "Still, Life"
in order to explore and record her own grief journey and continues this
theme throughout her work today. Along with her photography, she
writes a blog, hosts presentations and writes essays on the topics of grief
and creativity. You can view her work or contact her at streanor.com
The cover background photo was the last Lake Ontario
sunset photo taken by Tim Higgins before his diagnosis and
death. It was chosen for the cover for it's ethereal quality.

Book Design: Tim Atseff served as the book's designer. Atseff is a
widower and an artist who brought his design skills and sensibilities
to the project. He retired after a 46 year career as a designer, political
cartoonist and managing editor of a daily newspaper and was
the creator, designer and editor of three regional magazines.

ISBN-13: 978-1514207987
First Printing, 2015
Printed in the United States
Published by Timmy Hawk Press

DEDICATION

To my beloved Tim.

As I soar above her car, I feel an overwhelming urge to save
her from this grief and pain but it's not in my power.

I can only watch and let her know I am here.

I will always be here. I wish I could be with her in the
physical realm. I long for her and yet I have her. She is just a
breath away in a dimension of time and space I no longer
share. I'm on a different journey now but we're still united in
our eternal bond of love.

It's been five months since I left my body, and she has to
have eye surgery without me. She is frightened but I must
make her aware I am here watching over her.

I will protect her.

As I swoop down toward her car window, I am filled with
joy. She'll know it's me when she sees my blue eyes.

—Timmy Hawk, March 27, 2010

PREFACE

There is no greater agony than bearing an untold story inside you.

— Maya Angelou

Some may find my story unbelievable. Initially, I found it that way too. I'm a nurse practitioner and family therapist, a believer in science, research and human relationships. I knew nothing about after-death relationships until my beloved husband, Tim, started coming to me after he died.

Before this all began, Tim and I were both extremely happy with our lives. We had careers that were busy and fulfilling; Tim was a city court judge and I worked in a hospital-based genetics practice. We shared our dedication for hard work and public service, but our deepest passion was being with each other, enjoying life and celebrating our love. There were hardships along the way, but we weathered our storms in each other's protective arms.

We had dreams for our future, but the year before Tim was to retire, the rug was ripped out from under us. Just 18 days after being diagnosed with leukemia, Tim died and my world was shattered. But when he found ways to let me know he was still with me, a strange, new world was revealed.

I almost didn't tell my story for fear of being called crazy. Grief alone is enough to make you crazy. Add communication from my deceased husband to the mix and I felt like one of my psychotic patients seeing and hearing things that weren't real.

My training and life experience had not prepared me for this; there is no way to prepare. I had to figure it out as I traveled an unfamiliar terrain of signs from the beyond. As much as I wanted to accept that Tim was here, I questioned each time he came to me. Then, when his messages became too numerous to be ignored, I accepted that what was happening was real.

I kept Tim's signs to myself for a while and wrote each one down when they happened so none would be forgotten. This was our intimate secret that brought a measure of hope to my grief-filled existence. As I started telling my story to family and trusted friends, I began to emerge from the depths of sorrow.

I decided to write this memoir because, if sharing helped me, perhaps it would help others grieving a loss or those curious about connecting with another realm. Please, dear reader, keep your mind open and if our story helps you on your path, then sharing it has been an honor.

EYES FILLED
WITH TEARS

1

Let your tears come.
Let them water your soul.

— Eileen Mayhew

On October 20, 2009, when my office phone rang at 2:30pm, my trembling hand picked up the receiver and out came a voice I did not expect.

"Anne Marie? It's Sean."

"Sean?" I was surprised to hear our internist's voice instead of Darci's, the nurse practitioner who'd seen Tim that morning because symptoms from stubbing his toe had gotten worse.

My mind raced back to the unpleasant experience we'd had at the doctor's office three hours earlier. After a brief examination of Tim's right leg and toe, Darci recommended a compression bandage. But I thought he needed more.

As Darci rumbled through the exam room's drawers looking for God-knows-what, I said, "Tim stubbed his right toe nine days ago; blood clotted in the toenail and it was drained by our podiatrist yesterday. Then because his right leg was swollen, he did an ultrasound of Tim's femoral artery to make sure there was no blockage. The ultrasound was fine. But today, Tim's other leg is swollen, he's exhausted, he had a nosebleed this past weekend and has a small hemorrhage in his left eye."

"Honey," my husband interrupted, "I've had many nosebleeds and my eye has had blood in it before."

"I know Tim, but you're so tired and it looks like you have petechiae on both legs. See those tiny red spots all over?" I was shocked at how many different things had happened to his body in a little over a week.

Darci looked more carefully at both legs, "Anne Marie, what are

2

you thinking?"

Pissed off that I had to be the nurse practitioner instead of the spouse in this situation, I said, "I'm concerned there's something wrong with his platelets or I don't know. What do *you* think?"

"You want me to draw blood?"

Without expressing my true feelings ('Are you fucking dense?'), I answered, "*Ah, yeah! Definitely!* Tim has to be in court this afternoon but I have no patients so call me with the results as soon as you get them."

Zooming back to the present, Sean did not mince words, "Anne Marie, Tim has leukemia."

A scream rose from my throat. I saw the phone receiver hit the floor as my boss rushed into my office with a startled look on his face. I glanced up at him then stared at my empty hand, suspended in the air, and said, "Grab my hand." He grasped it and squeezed tightly. I reached down with my other hand, picked up the phone and looked at it like it was a strange object from another world. A concerned voice was coming out of one end, repeating my name over and over. A deep sigh escaped my lungs and I finally drew the handset to my ear, "Okay Sean, tell me what we have to do."

"This is an emergency. Where's Tim? I need to see him as soon as possible."

"He's in court but he'll be finished about 3:30."

"Fine. Just get him here."

I have no memory of what I did waiting for the time to pass. When Tim called me at 3:28pm, I somehow calmly said, "Hi honey, Sean wants you to come to his office."

"That doesn't sound very good."

"I'll meet you there."

The office staff was alerted; we didn't even sign in at the desk before being whisked into an exam room. Sean immediately appeared and without hesitation said, "Tim, you have leukemia. You have to go to the emergency room. There is no time to go home. You need a procedure called leukapheresis right away to remove the high numbers of abnormal white blood cells that are crowding out the normal cells in your bone marrow."

As we tried to grasp the enormity of Sean's words, Tim haltingly said, "Wow, I guess I'm really becoming a patient."

When Tim was diagnosed, neither of us could have imagined the horrendous journey we were about to endure. Tim's parents had each survived and even thrived after adulthood cancer and chemo, so we naively believed this was a temporary annoyance in our lives.

The head oncologist, Dr. Greg White, met us in the ER. I thought this sandy-haired man with a warm smile was the hospital chaplain until he introduced himself as Tim's physician. Dr. Greg was direct, clear and held our hands as he explained that an inpatient 10-day chemotherapy "induction" would be followed by a month-long treatment.

Tim calculated the days. He told me to call his secretary to ask his colleagues for court coverage and to get an absentee ballot so he could vote in the local election.

"You've just been diagnosed with leukemia and you're worried about work and voting?" I said with raised eyebrows.

"What about St. Bart's? My hospital treatment will be done just before Thanksgiving. We're due to leave on vacation three days later."

"Honey, we'll just take it day by day. St. Bart's will give us something to look forward to," I said, willing the calendar to magically jump ahead.

The whirlwind first 24 hours in the hospital included the insertion of an intravenous line into Tim's arm and another into the femoral vein in his groin for the emergency leukapheresis, a bone marrow aspiration, and placement of a port-a-catheter under the skin in Tim's chest for chemotherapy and blood draws.

"They poked me full of holes, but the local anesthetics helped," Tim said while I smoothed lotion on his arms, anxious to soothe him.

"I'm glad it didn't hurt, Boo." I smiled while secretly cringing at the sight of Tim with multiple plastic tubes connected to his body.

We settled into a routine on the oncology floor. Then, on day three, Tim started bleeding around his groin line and the tube had to be pulled out. The chemo treatments were doing their job of killing the leukemia cells but the platelet cells that helped clot his blood were being killed, too.

My heart skipped a beat when the oncology resident, Dr. Nami, warned, "Judge, I have to hold down this pressure bandage for awhile to make sure your blood clots and the wound closes."

Fifteen minutes went by filled with small talk about the weather to keep Tim calm when I volunteered, "I can hold it down so you can take a break." I'd noticed her hands were shaking and fingers turning red from the constant pressure on Tim's blanched skin.

Dr. Nami smiled, "I'm okay, just a bit longer."

Fifteen more minutes passed while she pressed harder and asked Tim about his job to keep his mind distracted. I was busy trying to push away my fear of continued bleeding; happily, that didn't happen.

After that frightful experience, Dr. White decided to transfer Tim to the six-bed bone marrow transplant (BMT) unit where the nursing care was one-to-one and they were better equipped to handle emergencies.

I spent all day and every evening with Tim. After tossing and turning on an uncomfortable sleeper sofa in his room the night of Tim's diagnosis, we decided it was best for me to go home at night to rest, feed our cats and attend to whatever was needed there. We were confident that all would be well, especially now that he was in the BMT unit.

On day nine of chemo, I helped Tim shower, wash his hair and get into clean sweat pants and a hospital gown. He was about to begin shaving with his electric shaver — no razors allowed due to his low platelet count — when lunch arrived. Tim walked to his chair to eat a well-done chicken breast and overcooked vegetables. No raw food was allowed that might contain bacteria as that would not be good for a weakened immune system. Amazingly, after enduring almost nonstop chemo, Tim never lost his appetite, was never nauseous, and never lost a single hair.

Sue, our friend and fellow nurse practitioner, showed up and commented on how good Tim looked.

"Tomorrow is day ten of chemo, isn't that great?" I said, repeating the oncologist's words, "Just make it through day ten and all should be fine."

I had no clue why Sue would put a downer on our high, but she worked in oncology and spoke from experience, "You're still not out of the woods."

I glared at her and then quickly glanced at Tim. He was busy eating. I don't think he heard her or at least gave no sign of allowing those words to pierce his heart like they did mine.

Later, when I was getting ready to go home, I grabbed the camera to take his picture. My plan was to start a Caring Bridge website like many families do when a loved one is hospitalized. That way, I could post Tim's status once a day versus spending time answering emails.

"Boo, look at me. Smile."

When our eyes met, I saw my handsome husband looking tanned and healthy, but swallowed hard as I realized his skin color was from the blood transfusion he'd received or possibly the result of a jaundiced hue from all of the chemotherapy overworking his liver.

Tim stopped me and said, "No honey, don't take my picture, I never shaved."

As I lowered the camera, our eyes met again and for a split second my heart skipped a beat. Tim had that "cancer-look," a telltale sign I've seen in many patients, and in his father, my grandmother, and my sister before they died from their cancers. It's hard to describe what I mean, but I can see it in the eyes. It's a glimmer of pain or an inner knowing that time is short. When I see that frightening sign through my personal window, my gut churns with dread.

I walked over to kiss Tim and almost changed my mind about leaving, but his sister, Joey, had just arrived to visit. I pushed away my fears and told myself that leaving would allow them some alone time.

"We'll take the picture tomorrow after you've shaved, my handsome love."

Tim smiled, "I'll call you before I fall asleep. I think I'll watch the Yankees."

When he called around 9:00 and told me he and Joey had left the BMT unit and taken a walk through the oncology floor's long corridors, I was sad I'd not been with him for this first time out of his room. "I hope you didn't get too tired!"

"No, it felt good to stretch my legs but I am tired now. I'm going to watch the game before I go to sleep."

"Okay Precious Pie, g'night. See you tomorrow, I love you."

"Love you too." I had no idea that would be the last time I heard Tim say, "I love you."

BETTER TO HAVE LOVED AND LOST?

2

Do not go gentle into that good night,
old age should burn and rage at the close of the day,
rage, rage at the dying of the light.

— Dylan Thomas

M

y life began with a death.

My father's first wife died from breast cancer at age 42, leaving him and their four children, aged seven to twelve, in shock and despair. Two years later, he married my mother and they had two children: my brother and then me. Our blended family was all I ever knew and as a child, it rarely dawned on me that my father and four half-siblings had had another life before I was born.

My father's grief was never outwardly apparent; however, he often called my mother by his first wife's name so I knew that she was not forgotten. My half-siblings spoke occasionally about their mother but they didn't outwardly grieve, either. And yet as I got older, I began to realize that our lives had been forever changed by this tragedy.

I finally understood the depth of their loss when my husband died before his time. Tim was 69 when complications of chemotherapy took him on November 7, 2009 just eighteen days after his leukemia diagnosis.

Along with the shock of Tim's untimely death came shocked comments about his age. Many people thought he was in his early 50s because he looked so young and fit thanks to daily exercise and a healthy diet. His parents, who had had multiple health problems over their lifetimes, both lived to 86 so we always assumed Tim would live well into his 90s.

Besides an occasional upper respiratory infection, Tim was rarely ill. In his 28 years as a City Court Judge, he took so few sick days, we joked that we could take a very long vacation on his back sick-pay after his mandatory retirement at 70. How were we to know he would never live to enjoy his retirement?

Shock had entered our lives first, in October 2008, when Tim was diagnosed with Parkinson's disease (PD) after we'd noticed a mild hand tremor.

"Where the hell did this come from?" we both asked when the neurologist gave us the unexpected news. No one in his family had had Parkinson's and Tim was so healthy, how could this be?

As he read the *New York Times* that evening, Tim saw that a famous author, whose name escapes me, had died at 93 from complications due to Parkinson's. "Hey, there's still a chance to live past 90," we both said in our usual way of finishing each other's sentences.

Some people were dour when they heard of Tim's PD but one friend joked about it. "Hey, where's 'Shake and Bake'?" Crazy Ed, the Wegmans produce manager, said with a sly chuckle when he didn't see Tim with me at the grocery store one Sunday morning.

"Oh, the Judge is busy stamping out crime in these freaking weekend arraignments he has to do every few months."

Work was the only time Tim and I were apart. We shopped together, went to the gym, rode to and from weekday work together, went to all of each other's doctor appointments, and any place our spur of the moment ideas would take us. People were so accustomed to seeing us as a couple that we would get questioned when one of us was out alone.

But no one came up with funnier ways to ask us where the other was than Crazy Ed, whose characteristic wry smile displayed an active imagination under his somewhat crumpled work cap. You might think Tim would be insulted by the "Shake and Bake" remark but we had long since stopped being surprised by Ed's derogatory, off-color comments and innuendos like, "Hey Anne Marie, I bet you thank your lucky stars for Timmy's hand tremor!"

Ed's sick humor was welcomed and trips to Wegmans gave us some laughs as we pushed our fears of PD to the back of our minds. I never could have imagined that a little over one year later, Crazy Ed, in an uncharacteristic suit and tie — minus the crumpled work cap — would be standing in front of me at Tim's calling hours sobbing as he said, "I'm so sorry for calling Tim 'Shake and Bake.'"

HINDSIGHT

3

It's so difficult, isn't it? To see what's going on when you're in the absolute middle of something? It's only with hindsight we can see things for what they are.

—S.J. Watson

Hindsight can be a comforting friend or cruel enemy. For me, it has been both. Powerful lessons of life and destiny unfolded as I looked back over the two months before Tim died.

The first few days after his October 20th leukemia diagnosis, Parkinson's faded into the background as the reality of cancer blindsided us. Yet, my intuition told me that Tim knew on some level he was not going to be with me much longer. I now realize that there were warning signs that were obvious but ignored because I could not, or did not, want to acknowledge them. They might be called coincidences but I have long since come to a deep knowing that there are NO coincidences.

The first sign came in late August when Tim said, "Hey Boo, tomorrow after work, we're going to meet with John, our estate attorney, about my retirement."

"Okay," I said, somewhat surprised. "But why now? You aren't retiring until next year."

"I just want to discuss our wills and my pension," Tim said matter-of-factly.

Sitting in John's office figuring out the details, Tim made sure his pension distribution was allocated so the majority went to me after he died.

I protested. "Let's just take it all when you retire for both of us to live on. Don't worry about me, I married you for love but I'll marry for money the second time."

John and I chuckled. Tim did not laugh.

Then in early September, Tim ordered four CDs from Amazon. Music has always been a big part of our lives, but when he showed me his purchases, I noticed they weren't what he usually chose. The first CD was called, *Everything You Love will be Taken Away* by Slaid Cleaves. I scowled and said, "Yuck Timmy, that's a morbid title."

Tim shrugged, "But it got good reviews."

The next was Eva Cassidy's *Songbird*, whose music we'd recently heard and fell in love with. How could I have known her music would help soothe Tim during chemotherapy treatments and finally to eternal sleep? I later found out that Eva Cassidy died from melanoma at the age of thirty-three.

Then there was Warren Zevon's *The Wind*, his last recording before he died from a rare form of cancer, peritoneal mesothelioma at fifty-six. We played it the night it arrived and when the song, "Keep Me In Your Heart" came on as I was stirring pasta sauce on the stove, Tim grabbed me and started sobbing.

"Honey, what's wrong?" I cried.

As he choked back tears, he said, "It's this song, I don't know but it's this song."

We held each other tightly as we listened to the end. Tim dried his eyes and said he'd read that Warren knew he was going to die when he recorded the CD. "He wrote that song for his loved ones to remember him after he died."

And so it came to be for us: I played "Keep Me In Your Heart" at Tim's funeral.

The last CD was Barbra Streisand's *Love is the Answer*. I was surprised he bought it because neither of us were fans.

"You got Barbra Streisand?"

"Yes, it's for you."

I searched my mind to try to figure out what he meant. "For me, why?"

"Because I thought you would need it."

I couldn't hide my confusion and asked, "You thought I would need it?" I didn't add my next thought: *Need it for what?*

Tim smiled and walked toward me for a hug, "Yes, I thought you would need it and besides, it got good reviews."

I looked at him with a curious smirk as we embraced and my unspoken words faded away. The realization that Timmy truly did know I would need it came to me when I played that CD's first song, "Here's to Life" for family and friends on the one year anniversary of his death. The lyrics are a perfect description of life, loss, and hope.

I finally knew why he chose those four CDs. He chose them for me.

Another warning sign that we both ignored came from our friend Alexandra, seventeen days prior to Tim's leukemia diagnosis. Alexandra was a medical student from Geneva, Switzerland who came here in early September for a two-month residency at my medical center. She also had degrees in finance and English literature. We became fast friends and I was surprised to learn amongst her many talents that she was an experienced astrologer.

That evening at dinner, when I excitedly told Tim that Alex offered to read our astrological charts, he said, "Sure, but I don't believe in that stuff."

"Honey, you don't believe in anything like that, but it's for fun."

As he swallowed a bite of chicken, he announced for the umpteenth time, "You're right, I don't believe in astrology or God or life after death and..."

"Yeah I know, I know," I interrupted him, not wanting to hear his usual rant but repeating it anyway, "...and when we die, we are dead, and that's it." I raised my glass as if his words were a toast even though these were beliefs I didn't completely share.

"You got it and it's okay with me because when I die, I know I've had the most amazing love and fulfilling life with you, better than I ever could have imagined." Now *that* was something to toast and we both raised glasses and shared a deep kiss.

"I agree with you but don't go making any plans to check out and leave me alone," I said.

"We are all existentially alone, my love," Tim retorted.

"I *HATE* it when you go all philosophical on me, Timmy!"

"Well it's true, we all are alone but I have to die first because I could never live without you, I would *not* survive."

I leaned across the table and pretended to choke him, "And if you keep talking like this, I'm going to kill you so you won't have to worry about living without me."

Three days later, as we sat at lunch after a hike in Sapsucker Woods Bird Sanctuary in Ithaca, Alex started reviewing Tim's astrological chart. "You are about to experience a *huge* event that will be life changing."

Tim looked at her matter-of-factly and said, "I'm retiring from work so that must be it."

"But that's not until next year," I said with a touch of worry in my voice, "you say it's soon, Alex?"

"Yes, it's soon. I'm not sure how soon but it's life changing nonetheless."

Two loudly crying babies at the table next to us drowned out Alex's voice. Tim said, "Let's finish this when you come over to our house in two weeks for your good-bye dinner."

I thought to myself, he does not want to hear this but agreed it was no fun trying to out-shout the babies. I was left with an uneasy feeling and swallowed a large gulp of wine to calm my anxiety.

Something else occurred in October, just four days before Tim's diagnosis. I had an appointment to look at one-level houses with Barb, a realtor friend. I'd called her after Tim and I returned from a friend's Lake Ontario home on our annual Columbus weekend celebration. While there, Tim tripped up the stairs and stubbed his toe hurrying to close a window that had blown open. I was frightened and had visions of him tripping down our three flights of stairs at home since PD often causes walking problems. Tim agreed we should start looking for a new house.

When Barb arrived, I said to Tim, "Are you coming with us?"

"No, why should I go, it'll be your house someday."

My expletive doesn't need repeating, but I was very uneasy as I walked out the door into my unknown future. Yes, he knew.

And I knew. For years, I'd planned how I would face the day when Tim was no longer breathing. I often watched him as he slept. I would wake before him, gaze at his handsome face and imagine what it would look like when he was no longer alive. It didn't feel morbid; I just watched as he took a breath and breathed my own sigh of relief when he opened his eyes and gazed lovingly into mine. Why? Because I knew I would be gazing upon his face one day and he would not gaze back.

It could be said this was because he was almost 15 years older than me. But my father was 18 years older than my mother and they had been married 46 years when he died at age 89. Besides, Tim was supposed to live well into his 90s. We had so much living ahead of us. And yet, I believe my "death watch" was on an intuitive level as I was doing it more frequently of late. In hindsight, I thought it was the PD.

But hindsight is only a brief part of my story. Had I the foresight to know what was going to happen after Tim's first nine days of chemo, I'm not sure I would have believed it.

Your Loving Eyes

4

*In your eyes, I see the
other half of my soul.*

— Author unknown

I hung up the phone with Tim's "Love you, too" ringing in my ears. His words soothed me but then I thought about Tim's eyes.

The tiny hairs on my arms stood up and a chill ran down my spine; fear taking hold from that "cancer look." I talked myself down: *Come on, get a grip, Tim is fine, tomorrow's the final day of his first round of chemo and all will be well.*

For comfort, I grabbed my favorite photo of him relaxing in our backyard: big smile, wine glass in hand, not a care in the world. I closed my eyes and was transported back thirty-one years to the first time I saw Tim's beautiful blue eyes on a warm, late August night in 1978.

As I dressed for my weekend ritual of disco dancing that night so long ago, I was excited to check out a new bar, "The Night Deposit." When I first heard the bar's name that afternoon at lunch with Kate, my disco-hopping Goldie-Hawn look-alike friend, I chuckled, "Hmmm, that's a fun name for a place that used to be a bank, but my naughty brain took me someplace other than a bank deposit!"

"Maybe we'll both get lucky and find guys with big pockets!" Kate said with raised eyebrows and tilted head as she stuffed both hands into the front of her pants. We laughed hysterically imagining the adventures that awaited us.

When I walked in around 10:00pm, I scanned the crowd for always-late Kate and sighed as I took my place in the long line at the bar. I spied a friend who was close to the front and said loudly above the disco beat, "Hey Alan, how're ya doin'?"

Alan turned and smiled; he got my hint, "What are you drinking?"

"A Godfather please, dahling."

I loved my signature drink named after my favorite movie about my possible Sicilian relatives. "Hey, all Sicilians are related somehow," I would say when people asked me why I liked that awful combination of scotch and amaretto.

As Alan passed back my drink, a handsome blond man next to him turned around and our eyes locked. My heart took a leap and my intuition said, *This is the man you will marry.*

"Anne Marie Patti, the beautiful lady with the three first names, this is Tim Higgins," Alan said with great self-assurance, as if he knew this introduction would rank up there with the likes of Romeo and Juliet.

Tim grabbed my hand and said, "Let's dance!"

The electricity we'd felt pulsed through our fingertips as we moved fluidly to the beat of Donna Summer's "Rumor Has It." As I listened to her sing about finding love and fulfilling one's destiny, I thought back to my conversation with Kate and secretly thanked my lucky stars.

Then when the disco mix transitioned to another of Summer's songs, "I Love You" about a man finding the woman of his dreams and thanking *his* stars, the deal with my intuition was cinched.

Our "I love you's" didn't come right away. We fell in lust before we fell in love but it wasn't long until we both knew we'd spend the rest of our lives together.

I thought about how Tim joked that the first time we hit the dance floor, the crowd parted, the sparkling light from the swirling disco ball shined down upon us and we were alone twirling in each other's arms. Then my mind took a trip through the years of us dancing at weddings, nightclubs, and formal events. We'd find a place on a crowded dance floor and make it our own. People often came up to us and asked if we took professional lessons. We'd laugh and say, "Only with each other."

Then my favorite dancing memories came into view — the two of us at home. Music was an essential part of our lives. Our tastes ran the gamut from blues to rock, classical to country, new age to jazz. While preparing dinner, we took turns choosing a CD from our large collection and moved to whatever beat filled the air. This sensual nightly ritual started early in our relationship and never wavered except, of course, when one of us was away, which wasn't very often.

I thought about the longest time we'd been apart — ten days — when I took my mom to Italy to celebrate her 80th birthday and visit my niece, Mea and her family. As wonderful as the trip was, the separation was difficult for Tim and me.

My mind snapped back to the present and I shuddered that tomorrow would make it the second time we'd been separated for a total of ten nights. Not wanting to duplicate that scenario, I packed a bag so I could spend the night at the hospital.

Before I climbed into Tim's side of the bed (my coping mechanism to be close to him) I looked at his photo again and said, "I'm going to sleep there with you from now on Boo, I don't like leaving you at night. I'll get our sweet friend Cheryl to come over and feed Lucca and Vivi; it's such a comfort that our crazy kitties like at least one other person to take care of them besides us."

I drifted off to sleep with high hopes for our future.

BLURRED VISION

5

*Sometimes in our confusion,
we see not the world as it is,
but the world through eyes
blurred by the mind.*

— Author unknown

The insistent ringing of the phone on the bed stand woke me out of a deep sleep. I looked at the clock before answering it. 7am. How did I sleep so late?

"Anne Marie, it's Dr. Nami. Tim is fine," she quickly added as she imagined my horrified reaction at hearing her voice.

"Okay, but…" I said, digging my fingers into the down quilt.

"But he is coughing up some blood. He had a rough night," she said.

"Why didn't anyone call me? You *KNOW* I'm supposed to be called when something happens!" Lucca and Vivi leaped off the bed as my voice grew louder.

"He's okay. It's not a lot of blood and it hasn't been going on very long."

"Is this an emergency?" I asked, not knowing if she was masking the real situation.

"No, it's not an emergency, but come when you can."

"Tell Tim I love him and I'll be there soon." I quickly dressed, made a cup of coffee and downed it as I grabbed some food for the day and my already-packed overnight bag.

As I drove to the hospital, I found myself going 60 in the city's 30 mile per hour zone, passing cars that dared get in my way. Luckily, I'd remembered to put on my hospital ID and wasn't stopped when I raced past the long visitor check-in line.

"Baby!" I cried as I threw my bags on the floor startled by his blood stained hospital gown and the oxygen mask on Tim's ashen face.

"Honey, I feel awful," Tim gasped.

"What *HAPPENED*? She said it wasn't an emergency!" I shrieked at Tim's nurse who was hanging another IV bag of platelets to help clot Tim's blood.

"Tim was coughing most of the night but the blood just started" was the defensive reply of the nurse before he rushed out the door.

I wet a washcloth with cool water and placed it on Tim's forehead. "Ah, that feels good baby, thank you."

In the next moment, the oncology fellow who'd called me entered the room with two physicians I didn't know. When I heard they were from the ICU, my heart started racing and I grabbed Tim's hand, fearing they would take him away. One of the physicians said, "Mr. Higgins, we may need to put in a tube to help you breathe."

Rather than allow myself to fully comprehend what she was saying, I sarcastically corrected her in a ridiculous moment of protocol, "Please call him 'Judge' or 'Tim.' You wouldn't want to be called 'Miss' instead of 'Doctor.'"

She looked at me then continued, unfazed. "*Judge*, we need your permission if we have to proceed."

Tim was coughing and having difficulty breathing. The next moment the oncology attending, Dr. Dorn, walked in the room along with Robin, Tim's day nurse who quickly appeared by my side and whispered in my ear, "This is grim, Anne Marie."

Before her terrifying words sunk in, Dr. Dorn bent down to speak directly into Tim's ear, "Tim, do you understand what they are saying?"

"Yes, but I'm afraid I won't come back." Tim coughed and sputtered as I wiped his brow with the washcloth, sweat from my palms adding to its wetness.

"Tim, it's too soon to give up," Dr. Dorn said as I mentally thanked him for saying words of encouragement. I bent down to be close to Tim's face. My heart was beating out of my chest as I waited for his reply.

"Okay, okay," he said in an exhausted, half-hearted voice.

My lips met his cool forehead. "I love you. We'll get through this together."

In the next instant, I found myself on my cell phone calling Tim's law clerk, "Jack, you need to get here *NOW* with Tim's paperwork."

We had planned a meeting for 10:30am with Jack to sign Tim's retirement and disability papers. My mind was clouded with the words Tim told me in the emergency room just after his diagnosis,

"Honey, if I die and haven't signed my retirement papers, you won't get my pension."

Then I called John, our lawyer, who was also due at the same meeting for Tim to sign new copies of his healthcare proxy and power of attorney.

After that, I found myself leaving words on my brother's voicemail that I never imagined coming from my lips, "Billy, Tim is not doing well, please write *everyone* on my daily email chain and tell them to pray." I had long since given up praying to a God who took our babies away. Now that He was trying to take my husband, my Catholic guilt kicked in as I desperately hoped He would listen this time.

Jack appeared at the door in what seemed like seconds after hanging up. The nurse told me they were transferring Tim to the ICU and we needed to hurry. Jack bent down and gently explained to Tim what he was signing. As Tim struggled to breathe, I held his hand steady while he scribbled his signature.

Immediately after that, several nurses and a respiratory therapist surrounded Tim's bed as he began to lose consciousness. A mask attached to a breathing bag was placed over Tim's mouth and nose. In an instant, Tim's bed was pushed out of the room by the nurses as I held his hand and the respiratory therapist pumped oxygen into his lungs. As we entered the hallway, I saw our lawyer John and told him to follow us.

My eyes were fixed on Tim as faceless, blurred people met my peripheral vision while we raced down the hospital corridors. As they pushed his bed into place in the ICU room, Tim briefly regained consciousness and I told him that John was there with more papers to sign. My hand cradled his as he scrawled, then he began to lose consciousness again.

"Okay, *NOW*," was all I heard from the authoritarian voice of Jim Simon, the ICU chief attending physician as Tim was pulled backward and down by several nurses. While Dr. Simon struggled to place a breathing tube into Tim's throat and trachea, I reflexively grabbed his ankles and watched my husband give up his last ounce of free will as the tube finally found its place against Tim's struggling coughs and gagging.

I watched in horror as blood came gushing into the tube from

Tim's battered lungs. The respiratory therapist started suctioning the blood as the doctor was loudly barking orders for medications to put Tim into an "induced coma" to stop him from struggling against the tube he so feared. The medical orders seemed to go on for several minutes as Tim was hooked up to the respirator, cardiac and respiratory monitors, and several intravenous lines.

I loosened my grip of Tim's ankles and stepped backward to allow the scurrying healthcare professionals do their jobs. I recall running into the back wall of the room and noticing how much smaller it was than the spacious room we'd just left on the BMT unit.

Dr. Simon's yelling finally ended and he breathed a deep sigh as he noticed the last endotracheal tube suction was clear of blood, "Okay, get radiology in here to verify tube placement."

I quickly glanced with disbelief at Tim's face and the endotracheal tube taped around his mouth. I knew I'd have to leave for the X-ray. I kissed his forehead and reluctantly followed all but two nurses and an X-ray technician left behind.

Dr. Simon introduced himself as Jim when we entered the hallway. "Your husband is a very sick man."

I glared at him and said, "But Jim, you'll do all you can."

"Of course, but it's very serious." Then he rushed down the hall to another crisis.

In my daze, I saw our lawyer waiting for me near the nurses' station. "Anne Marie, we could have done without the signatures. As his wife, you would have been granted power of attorney and the old healthcare proxy on file was fine."

"Well, thank you for coming anyway, John." My legal standing intact, I stomped back to Tim's room, a lioness poised to defend my helpless cub.

EYES WIDE OPEN

6

Courage is not in overcoming dangers but in facing them with eyes wide open.

— Jean-Paul Sartre

E ach time a new health care practitioner entered Tim's ICU room, my mantra was the same, "My name is Anne Marie. This is my husband, Tim. Please introduce yourself to him and tell him what you are going to do."

Often I was met with dumbfounded looks, uneasy smiles, muffled laughs, and gratefully, on occasion, respectful seriousness. Interestingly, the people who *got it* were lower on the health care hierarchy. Physicians had the hardest time with my mandatory request but nurses, X-ray technicians, specialized therapists, and even the janitor who had to move Tim's bed to clean up discarded plastic tubing *got it*.

On day two at the evening shift change, I left to wolf down some food and when I returned, Tim's color was ashen. I honestly thought he had died. I shrieked at a nurse I hadn't met before, "Oh my God, he looks horrible, what *HAPPENED?*"

Patricia introduced herself, put her hands on my shoulders and looked me straight in the eye, "Anne Marie, your husband took a rapid turn. He is very ill with an infection we can't get under control. We're doing everything we can. You and I are a team. You must trust me, I will be very busy and I need to you help wherever you can."

I thanked her and started helping the best way I could, I leaned close to Tim's face and pleaded, "My love, you must keeping fighting, we all have to work together, we will get through this."

The next moment, Dr. Sarah Green came in and introduced herself. Dr. Jim had taken the night off to throw a Halloween party and she was covering for him. Looking very grave, Dr. Sarah told me Tim was in septic shock and something drastic had to be done to save his life.

Since he was already hooked up to every machine and medication imaginable, I couldn't fathom what else could be done. Dr. Sarah said an experimental medication might help, but I had to give permission as his health care proxy. I was ready to sign any consent until she explained that one serious side effect could be uncontrolled bleeding. Tim was already getting around the clock platelet transfusions to clot his blood so I asked if bleeding could occur despite the transfusions.

"The transfusions help, but we just don't know what might happen. I really see this as his only hope," she said.

The choice sucked but I felt it was clear. I signed the consent and told myself the worst wouldn't happen as I pushed away intruding images of Tim in a blood soaked hospital gown. The medicine was ordered and I found myself praying again.

I climbed onto Tim's bed, my back against the hard metal footboard. With bent knees, I rubbed my feet alongside his legs willing warmth into his skin. I repeated my plea, "Timmy come on baby, you can do it, come on baby." Patricia encouraged me to keep talking with him as she scurried around the room doing what seemed like a hundred things at once with mind-boggling speed.

Dr. Sarah returned to check Tim around midnight. I pointed to the picture I had pinned on a small bulletin board, "That is us on our wedding day in 1984. Our 25th wedding anniversary is this November 24th. YOU need to get him to that day."

"I'm doing my best, Anne Marie," she said with bowed head.

Around 2:00am, the experimental medication arrived from the hospital pharmacy after a glitch in the paperwork and was finally started. Patricia was still finishing her nurse's notes from the busy evening. I was exhausted but too frightened to leave even though Tim was more stable despite the medication's late arrival.

The new night nurse encouraged me to get some sleep. "Don't

worry, Anne Marie, I'll call you if anything serious happens."

I kissed Tim's forehead, smoothed his hospital gown, looked at his heart and respiratory monitors — my nursing reflexes ever present — and reluctantly walked out his door.

There was no place to sleep in Tim's cramped room, however, one of the benefits of having him treated at the hospital where I worked was the special consideration I received. Instead of the over-crowded ICU waiting room, I was given access to a spare room on the BMT unit that had a broken shower and couldn't be used for patient care.

I don't remember walking down the long ICU corridor, or the elevator ride up to the 10th floor. But when the BMT unit's double doors swung open, a flashback hit me from rushing Tim to the ICU the day before. As his blood-stained gown permeated my muddled brain, I doubled over to catch my breath.

The next thing I was aware of was sunlight streaming in through the window. 7:30? Damn! I leaped off my sleeper couch and quickly changed, not wanting to be late for ICU morning rounds. Once there, I found Jim regaling the residents with his Michael Jackson imitation from the Halloween party. I thought of Jim more as a "bull in a china shop" than a moonwalking Michael Jackson.

"Hey Jim, where's your sequined glove?" I asked with a smile that quickly disappeared when I saw the upturned corners of his mouth pull tense.

"Anne Marie, Tim started bleeding this morning from his intravenous and arterial lines so we stopped the experimental medication."

"So he had the one complication we were worried about?"

"He only had two hours of the medication, not enough to get into his system, so I doubt it was due to that. He's stable now after multiple platelet transfusions and I don't want to take any undue risks."

"But doesn't he *need* the medication?" I could feel myself gearing up for an argument.

"Again, he's stable and I don't think it's worth the risk," Jim said authoritatively, then quickly turned and walked away.

I was left alone with my agonizing thoughts as I second-guessed Sarah's medical judgment, "Damn you Jim, why did you take the night off? Did Sarah do something that hurt him?" But if Jim didn't think the medication caused the bleeding, I had to let it go. That was difficult for me, but I had to learn to do it.

Tim's two sisters, Joey and Nancy, arrived around 9:00am and I explained what had happened the night before. We spent the day talking and watching Tim's heart and breath rate monitors, and his chest moving ever so slightly up and down to the tune of the respirator.

Around 5:00, they decided to go and join their husbands who were home making dinner. As they were leaving, a technician arrived to do a chest X-ray. The nurse called in an aide to help turn Tim and put the bulky film cartridge under his back.

Before leaving, I looked the aide directly in the eye and said, "You take care of him and don't let anything happen while I'm gone." He smiled meekly at my protective mantra.

When I joined Tim's sisters at the elevator, I recalled that I had a plate four floors up in my BMT unit "bedroom" from the meal Joey dropped off yesterday. Just as I retrieved the plate and handed it to my sister-in-law, one of the ICU nurses grabbed my arm from behind, "It's Tim, come quick."

Not waiting for the elevator, the nurse and I raced down the stairs as I frantically repeated to myself, *Hang on baby, hang on!*

The nurse explained that Tim had a heart attack after they moved him for the X-ray. I didn't quite comprehend her words. Last year, after a cardiology evaluation, the doctor said Tim had a strong, healthy heart. They had found a small hole called a patent foramen ovale (PFO) that had been there since birth. But the cardiologist assured me that many people have PFOs, never know it, and live normal, healthy lives.

While running down the ICU hallway, dodging medical carts and white lab coats, the cardiologists final words echoed in my throbbing head, "I could do a minor surgical procedure to close the PFO but it would only be a concern if he had a stroke and Tim is not at risk for a stroke, there is no family history and he is so healthy."

I reached Tim's room filled with several scurrying health care professionals and pushed my way between two nurses. Out of my mouth came my all too frequent cry, "What HAPPENED?" I saw the same ashen face I'd seen the night before. My eyes darted to Tim's cardiac monitor that showed a heart rhythm; it didn't look completely normal but his heart was beating.

One nurse explained that when they turned him, his heart stopped briefly but immediate CPR and a dose of adrenalin restarted his heart. He responded so fast, a second dose was not needed.

"I can't believe it — every time I leave something bad happens!" I shrieked as I grabbed Tim's hand and started stroking his forehead, smoothing his messed up hair.

The head nurse who was standing nearby disappeared and returned pushing a large reclining lounge into the room, "We'll take away one of the smaller chairs and you can sleep here. You don't have to leave again, Anne Marie."

I hugged and thanked her for this rule-breaking decision. Jim appeared and I immediately started my barrage of questions, "Why did his heart stop? Why would turning him stop his heart? He's had many x-rays and has been turned multiple times, what could have happened with this turn? Did they kink his respirator tubing?"

My accusations of possible mishandling were met with calm-in-a-crisis Jim, "Tim has been having heart arrhythmias and irregular beats since he got here so we don't think turning him mattered; we immediately resuscitated him and he responded. We're treating the arrhythmia and hopefully this won't happen again."

Then, when Tim's sisters reentered the room, Jim repeated his words about Tim's persistent abnormal heart rhythm and walked out without further explanation. I climbed into my lounge chair with determination never to leave Tim's room again.

IN THE STILL OF THE NIGHT

7

For it was not into my ear you whispered,
but into my heart.
It was not my lips you kissed,
but my soul.

— Judy Garland

The next two days were uneventful, at least in terms of life threatening situations. I allowed myself brief bathroom breaks and ate my friends-and-family donated meals in Tim's room, another overlooked rule by the empathic nursing staff.

Being treated with compassion by most of my fellow nurses eased my stress level. I was on hyper-alert, ready to pounce at anyone who hurt my Tim. Even though I was a neonatal ICU nurse many years ago and knew a lot about how a hospital is run, Tim's ICU experience was at times confusing and overwhelming. I couldn't imagine what this would be like for a layperson. Although being totally clueless might have been better.

No longer trusting others to do the job carefully, I settled into a routine of helping turn Tim for any procedure. I washed him, did passive exercises of his legs and arms to keep his muscles supple and played music to muffle the sounds of the machines. Eva Cassidy, Alejandro Escovedo, Sarah McLaughlin, Neil Young and a few classical CDs that I'd brought in just after Tim's hospital admission were played over and over. I didn't dare leave to go home for more.

"Hearing is the last thing to go" was one of the fundamental principles of medicine I learned as a nursing student. There are numerous stories of people waking from comas and recounting whole conversations that occurred in their presence while they were supposedly incommunicado. I wanted to make sure Tim's room was filled with his favorite music so that when he awoke, he would remember the songs and my mumblings of love and encouragement into his ear.

The first night in my lounge chair, sleep eluded me. His nurse left for a break and I found myself alone with Tim at 1:00am. I grabbed our wedding picture off the bulletin board, walked to his bedside and held it up for his closed eyes to see. My unrealistic expectation didn't matter; I knew he could see it in his mind's eye.

Lowering the bedrail, I moved in close and nuzzled Tim's ear, "Look how happy we were. What a wonderful wedding day. It took you long enough to get there though! Hey Boo, don't get me wrong, when we met I was not ready for marriage at the ripe young age of 23, even if I knew we were destined to be together. But after six years of enjoying our lust and love relationship, you surprised me with your unique proposal."

"I'll never forget the day: August 12, 1984. After we left your colleague's wedding reception and were driving past abandoned buildings down that dirty stretch of city highway, you said, 'So, how did you like their wedding celebration?'"

"I said something like, 'It was okay' as I stared out the window at a homeless person pushing a rusty grocery cart filled with his life's belongings."

"Then you said, 'Well what do you think if WE did it?'"

"My head snapped around and I said, 'If we did *what*?' not fully comprehending what you were saying."

"When you answered, 'If we got married,' with that sweet, boyish smile on your face, I howled, '*WHAT*? You're asking me to marry you while driving down Erie Boulevard? Are you freaking kidding me? Oh my God, let me roll down the window and puke!' I don't think that was the answer you expected."

"But you made up for it a few weeks later at Corn Hill, our favorite place in the world. After a yummy dinner, we settled into our chairs on the cottage porch with bowls of fresh peaches and glasses of Prosecco. The sun was starting to dip into the inky blue water and a crimson hue lit the Cape Cod Bay sky. You kissed me then gently took my hand and lead me down the wooden staircase to the beach. On bended knee, you said, 'My love, my life, would you please do me the honor of becoming my wife?' Now *THAT* was a proposal I could say yes to!"

I looked at Tim's monitors for a reaction. Nothing. His handsome face was calm and relaxed. I knew he was deeply sedated and hoped recounting our memories took him to a beautiful twilight dream-state where there was no pain, no suffering.

I kissed his ear again, then climbed onto his bed, put my pillow against the footboard, leaned back, entwined my legs with his and continued, "I hope you can drink some champagne when we celebrate our anniversary in a few weeks — or do you prefer Prosecco? We drank a lot of Prosecco on our honeymoon, didn't we?"

"Remember when we went back to our room in Venice after too much Prosecco at lunch and found two giggling Italian maids? The look on one's face was priceless when she pointed to my portable neck traction unit hanging on the bathroom door. She must have thought it was a sexual contraption! Oh, how we laughed!" I again scanned Tim's face and cardiac monitor for a reaction that did not come but continued, knowing he could hear me.

"My neck surgery nine months after our wedding was no fun but at least I didn't need that traction thing any longer! We didn't let my years of neck pain and disability after surgery dampen our life or time away did we?" I looked again at his face. All calm as the machines hummed.

"Boo, we've shared so many wonderful memories in our world travels. I'm so glad you took all of your vacation time every year. I thought it was awful that judges couldn't roll over their days off from year to year but that just made us take every second of your time and we made it count, didn't we? Now that you've signed your retirement papers, we'll be able to travel even more."

I leaned forward and brushed back Tim's hair with my fingers as a memory drifted in. "Why did you make that list of all our vacations and give it to me this August on the 31st anniversary of the day we met? I was shocked that it was three pages long but then again, "Use it or lose it" was the deal with your time off. The list was a bit strange though…did you know this was going to happen and you wanted to get it all down? I know you don't believe in psychic stuff but the timing sure is a coincidence. Okay, you're thinking I'm crazy but you love me that way! I remember your anniversary card said, "The Adventure Continues" and so it will, my love, so it will."

I wiped a wistful tear from my eye and yawned. Tim's nurse interrupted to check his vital signs and draw blood. She had been keeping a watchful eye from the hallway to allow us our alone time. I kissed Tim's forehead, climbed back into my lounge chair and fell asleep, dreaming of our future adventures to unknown places.

The next day was thankfully calm, I woke up after midnight from another fitful lounge chair sleep, grabbed my pillow and climbed onto Tim's bed as a different nurse completed her tasks, then gratefully left us to another night of reminiscing. I knelt over Tim, stroked his hair, kissed his forehead, and then leaned back, wrapping my legs around his.

"Boo, you seemed more relaxed today. So am I. I hope it helps that I'm here with you. You were always there with me for my surgeries and procedures. You were my calm in the storm for my neck surgery, my three fibroid surgeries, and every infertility procedure over those ten long years. How did you do it? How did you sit with me, comfort me when I was in pain or so desperately sad when we lost each baby? You never tried to fix anything; you simply held me and let me cry. I felt so loved and safe in your arms."

My mind drifted back to the hours in grief therapy, with and without Tim, trying to come to terms with the loss of seven babies after five unsuccessful in-vitro fertilization treatments over a ten-year time span, coupled with the death of my life-long dream of being a mother. But I was a mother briefly as each embryo was placed inside of me with a glimmer of hope that each life would be sustained.

"Remember how we started each day, Boo? You would ask, 'How's your beautiful butt today?' after my daily shot of hormones to thicken my uterine lining so that the embryo would implant and grow into the baby we kept tightly locked in our imaginations?"

"I would answer you with, 'My butt is fine, can't wait for you and our babies to kiss it someday!' Then you would kiss me all over after first soothing the injection site."

"I remember how I played music, sang to my belly and meditated on the life inside of me, each baby opening like a gentle flower in spring after the seed was planted in the fertile earth. But when each pregnancy test came back negative after the two-week waiting period, I imagined my uterus as a cold burial ground. And yet, at least they died inside of me; somehow it gave me comfort that our babies would always be a part of me."

Scanning Tim's face again, content that he looked relaxed; I softly landed on a memory that poignantly put an end to our hopes of becoming parents.

"Remember five years ago when I said to you, 'Timmy, we never named our babies; I think we need to do that for us and for them.' Your warm hug and smile spoke volumes as tears welled up in your eyes and you said, 'Tell me what you want me to do, my love.'"

"My imagination took off as I planned our ritual to name each tree you had so carefully planted in our babies' memorial garden. We didn't need to talk about when; we knew it would be on the Summer Solstice, our favorite pagan holiday. Remember how I wrote our babies' names on seven strips of parchment paper, rolled the paper and put each name into the small conch shells we'd found on the beaches at the Cape?"

Hoping for a blip, I checked Tim's heart rate again. Stable. Okay, I'll take it. "Do you remember how I struggled with what to place their names into but that morning, the shell idea came to my mind? A shell contained and sheltered life so they were the perfect vessel for our babies."

"Boo, can you see that special day? As the sun was setting, we read each name and spoke of what we thought each baby would have looked like. I can see myself bending down and putting the shells, one by one next to our dwarf evergreens: the Hinoki cypress, Chinese juniper and the Japanese, Eastern and Canadian hemlocks. You're amazed that I remembered what kind of trees we have, aren't you? I love that we chose different shaped and colored plants to represent each unique baby. Then we walked over to our two tree peonies. The fuchsia one had finished blooming but the white one's petals were late that year; I said it waited for us to bloom that day."

Another hopeful glance, a deep sigh and I continued, "After naming our last baby, we sobbed and spoke of our lost dreams for the future and what would never be. Amelia Marie, Thomas Wentworth III, Rachel Matilda, Marion Grace, Jeremiah Joseph, Livia Anne and Colin Jacob, you remain forever in our hearts, we love you."

As I wiped tears from my face, Tim's nurse came in to give him an IV medication and suggested I get some sleep. "Thank you, I will at some point; I'm enjoying our alone time now."

After a bathroom break, I walked over to Tim and gently touched his face. The nurse got my hint and left. I started our conversation again. "After our baby naming ceremony five years ago, we finally felt on the verge of a more relaxed life when your shoulder started bothering you. I'm so sorry hoisting my too heavy suitcase on our trip to Tuscany led to your torn rotator cuff."

"You used to kid me that when you were old, I would have to pay you back for taking care of me after my neck and fibroid surgeries. Well darlin', you were only 65 so your shoulder repair didn't count as old age payback. Then two years later when you needed hip surgery, that didn't count as payback either. Besides, you recovered so quickly; I didn't have to do much. Washing you in the shower was the fun part though, wasn't it?"

"Then with your Parkinson's diagnosis the next year, do you remember we decided the adage, "bad things come in threes" was true and we were done with the bad stuff? Unfortunately, we had absolutely no idea how bad it could get, did we?"

Exhausted, I again wiped tears from my face, kissed Tim's forehead and said, "Oh Boo, I'm sorry, I don't mean to be a downer; we'll get through this, our love will get us through."

WATCHING
AND
WAITING

8

I am watching your chest rise and fall,
like the tides of my life,
and the rest of it all
and your bones have been my bed frame,
and your flesh has been my pillow
I am waiting for sleep,
to offer up the deep with both hands.

— Ani DiFranco

I was cautiously optimistic on day six when Jim told me Tim was no longer the sickest patient on the unit. "We'll start to wean him off the sedating drugs today and hopefully he'll begin to wake up."

Even though I knew this was the next step for getting him off the respirator, frightful visions of our first few minutes in the ICU filled my brain, "I'm afraid when he comes out of the induced coma, Tim will start fighting the ET tube like he did when you put it in."

"Don't worry, we'll monitor him carefully," Jim said in the first somewhat empathic tone I'd heard him use.

I took a deep breath, "Okay, so how long before he wakes up?"

"Twenty-four to forty-eight hours."

I allowed myself to imagine us talking by the weekend. "We'll get there my love," I said, glancing at our wedding picture.

Day seven began like the others in this new world: I woke from another crappy sleep in the recliner, kissed Tim good morning, checked his heart and respiratory monitors, then rushed to my "bedroom" in the BMT unit. After a quick sponge bath, I grabbed black coffee, my cereal and yogurt from the unit kitchen and rushed back to Tim's room for morning patient rounds.

Jim looked particularly serious when I saw him in the hallway, but he had just come from the room of a patient who wasn't expected to live so I assumed his mood reflected that situation. Unfortunately, his face didn't change when he came into Tim's room.

"Anne Marie, Tim isn't waking up like we expected, so we're

going to do an EEG and brain MRI."

My stomach churned and my quickly downed breakfast came up into the back of my throat. "I — I — I don't understand, you said 24 to 48 hours and it's only been 24 hours since you stopped his sedation. What's the rush?"

"I expected more of a response by now."

Before I could voice my protest, Jim continued, "The EEG will be done this morning, at bedside, then Tim will be taken to the MRI suite later this afternoon."

My heart started to pound and I felt sweat forming on my brow with the thought of moving Tim so far away from the ICU. Simply turning him in bed four days ago sent him into cardiac arrest. Jim assured me that Tim was more stable now. More importantly, we needed to figure out why he wasn't waking up.

I felt that moving Tim outweighed the need to find an answer. "But why can't we wait one more day?"

Jim spoke with God-like authority, "It's best to do it today."

"But isn't the bedside EEG enough information?" I pleaded.

"No, we need to do *BOTH* tests. Don't worry, Tim will be fine," Jim answered as if he knew what the future would hold.

It was just past 10:00am when the neurology tech finished taping what seemed like a hundred wired probes to Tim's head to record his brain waves. I stood next to his bed, holding Tim's hand as I spoke to him telepathically, *I hope the music I've been playing since you were put into your coma has kept your brain supple and active.*

The tech asked me to turn off the music and let go of Tim's hand because he wanted as little external stimuli as possible to get a good recording.

As the EEG began, I silently spoke to Tim again, *Where did you go? For seven days I've stared at you lying motionless but I can still see my handsome you amidst the tubes, wires and machines. I hope your brain has taken a vacation to a beautiful far-away land where pain and suffering don't exist. But now I want your brain to wake up. It's time to come back to me, please.*

After the technician removed the last probe from Tim's head, I asked him if he could tell me anything. Since Tim was admitted, I'd worn my picture ID badge labeled "Nurse Practitioner" to ensure that everyone would speak to me honestly and in medical language.

It didn't help this time. "I'm sorry Mrs. Higgins, you know I can't," he said glancing at my ID.

Disappointed but not surprised, I said, "I know, but please have your attending physician call me when the EEG is read." He smiled and pushed the heavy machine out the door without a word.

Needing some control over the situation, I called radiology and requested that Dr. Jian Chin be available for Tim's brain MRI because we were colleagues and I trusted him implicitly. At 4:00pm, when Tim's nurse announced it was time to leave for the MRI suite, I took a deep breath and kept repeating Jim's words to myself, "Tim is stable now. He'll be fine."

The respiratory therapist got into place, detached Tim's tube from the respirator and began pumping air into his lungs with the breathing bag. Two nurses pushed Tim's bed as I walked alongside holding his hand. My eyes did not leave his face. Luckily, my feet did not betray me but they'd gotten used to maneuvering the hospital corridors while my focus was elsewhere.

The double doors leading into the MRI suite opened and Jian greeted me with a broad smile. He assured me that Tim would be well taken care of and he would see me in thirty minutes. My friend, Sue had called earlier and said she would join me. Rather than go to the waiting room, I stood outside the big doors to meet Sue and see Jian the moment he finished.

After about five minutes, I was startled as the doors swung open and Jian walked toward me with a furrowed brow. As he spoke words my ears did not want to hear, I backed up against the wall and felt the blood rush out of my head and my feet collapse underneath me. My body slowly sunk to the floor. At that moment, Sue arrived and reached down to help Jian pick me up. As I struggled to stand, Jian's alarmed face came back into my view and I asked him to tell me again.

"Anne Marie, it is not good, your husband has had multiple brain hemorrhages."

I wanted to scream and run but felt paralyzed. I closed my eyes and felt Sue's arms struggling to hold me. I yearned for the safety of Tim's strong arms. Instead, I felt my own arms wrap around my waist as I gasped for air. Finally able to speak, with desperate hope that somehow his words would magically change I asked, "What does that mean Jian?"

"It means you should start planning," Jian said in his staccato one-careful-word-at-a-time Chinese accent.

As I mulled his words in my bewildered brain, I found myself asking him the same question, "What does that *MEAN* Jian?"

I don't recall exactly what Jian said but he tried to give me some false hope that hemorrhages could resolve with time, then his voice trailed off as he lowered his head and bid me good-bye.

On the elevator ride back to the ICU, the only noise I heard was the whooshing of the breathing bag as the respiratory therapist pumped oxygen into Tim's unmoving body. *Not your beautiful brain, not your amazingly beautiful brain,* I whispered silently to Tim as I combed his hair with my fingers and kissed his smooth forehead.

Back in Tim's room, Sue sat with me as I tried to make sense of the news. "I keep playing the cardiologist's words over and over in my head that he would have done a procedure to close Tim's PFO if he was at risk for a stroke. Now Tim has had multiple strokes! Why didn't we just do the damn procedure? Did the chest compressions during CPR push blood clots through the hole in his heart to his brain? But how can his blood clot, he has no platelets, this doesn't make sense."

"Anne Marie, there is no way to know why this happened and whether the procedure would have mattered. Tim has been through so much, there are lots of factors to consider here."

"I know Sue, I know." I tried to block images of blood pooling in Tim's brain and the horrifying consequences of multiple strokes. Sometimes having medical knowledge was a curse.

Later that night, my chair lounger felt too far away from Tim as I watched his chest rise and fall in sync with the respirator. Exhausted, I climbed onto his bed and ran my fingers through his hair. After I kissed him, I lay down by his side and carefully placed my head on his chest avoiding all the tubes and wires. My arm caressed his waist as I wrapped my legs around his. "Here I am my love, my life, let's rest now."

The night nurse covered me with a blanket and left us alone to sleep together, once again.

EYES
DISBELIEVING

9

Am I to believe what it is that I see, or is it just my
eyes playing tricks on me.
I thought I saw you sitting there.
Your warming smile, your golden hair.
Your eyes so blue fixed me with a soulful stare.

— Nik S. Navarro

At patient rounds the next morning, Jim arrived at Tim's bedside with a physician I'd not yet met. "I'm Dr. Ravi, neurology fellow," he said.

"Where *were* you last night when I paged neurology to discuss my husband's test results?"

"I'm sorry, we were called to an emergency and couldn't return. Your husband has had multiple cerebral hemorrhages."

I cut him off. "I am aware of that. I was with him in MRI and my colleague, Dr. Jian Chin, gave me the results immediately."

Dr. Ravi looked surprised, "Oh, so you know. Well, this means your husband will need to go to a rehabilitation facility at some point. Most likely he will be paralyzed on one side of his body, possibly both. He may not be able to talk or walk and possibly not able to eat. We won't know exactly how it will impact him."

As dire as this picture sounded, a faint glimmer of hope sparked as I heard talk of the future outside of the ICU. "I'll do whatever it takes. Tim is strong and we'll do this together."

"I understand he is very strong and so are you, Mrs. Higgins. I apologize for last night and I promise I won't let you down again."

I was surprised by his humility, and thanked him for his kind words. "Honey, we'll be okay," I said as I kissed Tim's forehead before leaving for my quick morning routine upstairs in my hospital bedroom.

Around 1:00pm, Tim's sister, Joey, arrived during her lunch break. I explained the recent events. She was upset but tried to be encouraging for my sake. As we discussed rehabilitation facilities in town, Dr. Ravi walked in with another new physician.

"I'm Dr. Verti, neurology attending. Your husband's EEG results were very grave."

I felt my head shaking from side to side as the gut-wrenching news filtered in. "No one mentioned the EEG so I assumed it was normal."

My piercing stare into Dr. Ravi's eyes was met with a nervous glance downward as Dr. Verti continued, "No one brought it to my attention until now, but I believe he may have suffered irreversible brain damage."

As I continued to stare at the neurology fellow, my voice went up a few octaves. "I don't understand. Why was I given the scenario of hospital discharge and rehabilitation?"

Dr. Verti ignored my question and said, "We are going to repeat the EEG and do a Narcan challenge."

As he turned to leave the room, my voice became even more shrill, "You need to explain what that is before you walk out of this room."

He looked at my hospital ID and said, "Narcan is an opiod antagonist," then glanced at Tim's sister and back to me before he continued in common terminology, "it will reverse the effects of any sedation left in your husband's system so we will get an accurate EEG reading and measure of his neurological function. I will write the order and be back as soon as my EEG tech arrives."

After he left, Joey called work to say she would not be back. I was far, far away, stroking Tim's hair and willing his brain to heal.

At approximately 3:30pm, both neurologists, the EEG tech and Jim came in and circled the EEG machine placed near the back wall of Tim's crowded room. Joey was at the foot of Tim's bed and I was by his left side. Long wires and probes were methodically attached to Tim's head by the tech. Tension was in the air.

As the EEG machine was turned on, I was told not to touch or speak to Tim. Tim's stern nurse inserted a large needle into his IV line and waited for directions. I glanced at the doctors huddled around the EEG machine, their eyes fixed to a screen. "Okay, push the Narcan now," Dr. Verti commanded.

My eyes were glued to Tim's face and his head suddenly turned upward. A glimmer of hope sparked in my brain but was immediately pierced by a frightening sight: the corners of his mouth curled and his face contorted into a grimace. That twisted expression was well known to me. As a nurse, I'd seen it in brain damaged newborns and elderly patients who had suffered strokes.

I silently tried to calm myself. You already know Tim has had several strokes, that's all this means.

A male voice broke my concentration and told me to talk to Tim. I leaped onto the bed and straddled Tim's body, leaning my face just above his. "Baby, it's me, come on baby, we need you to wake up. Please wake up now."

I took a deep breath as Tim's beautiful blue eyes slowly opened and met mine. A warm rush of love washed over me as my beloved looked into my soul and carried me away from this dreadful scene.

Our moment of transcendence was interrupted by a voice across the room. "Anne Marie, squeeze Tim's hand."

Tim's deep gaze had given me hope and strength. I grabbed his one IV-free hand and squeezed with all my might. "Come on baby, squeeze my hand, we need you to wake up, please wake up." Tim's limp hand didn't respond, but I kept squeezing and pleading. As his grimace disappeared, his face became calm and his eyes slowly closed. I saw a tear trickle down his cheek. I reached up and wiped his tear with my trembling finger. "Oh baby, I'm so sorry," I said as my mind recalled the tears we'd shed together over so many years. I brought my wet finger to my eye and mingled his tear with mine.

His head slowly turned back to the side and rested on the pillow. I assumed he was tired from the effort, but I wanted to continue to do whatever was needed. I turned to ask for more direction but found only the EEG tech and Joey in the room. She shrugged her shoulders, "Everyone left."

The tech walked behind Tim's bed, detached the wires from his head and said, "I wish you the best with your husband." I thanked him and asked why everyone left without a word. He didn't know. I kissed Tim's forehead, smoothed his ruffled hair, climbed off the bed and walked into the hallway, my lioness armor ready.

I saw Dr. Ravi on the phone and Dr. Verti walking toward the nurses' station. I called his name and he stopped mid-stride. "Why did you leave my husband's room without speaking with me? What do you think about the EEG?"

He said in a condescending tone, "Oh, it was what we expected."

"And what did you expect?" I asked as I felt the urge to slap the smirk off his face.

"There is no hope. In fact, it's worse than yesterday."

I pushed my words through clenched teeth, "I don't understand, my husband opened his eyes and looked into my soul."

"Oh, that was just a reflex."

My angry finger pointed at his face and then Dr. Ravi's, "*YOU* get him off of that phone and both of you get back to my husband's room *NOW.*"

Only the attending returned and I immediately began, "How *dare* you leave my husband's room after you asked me to do something for you. That was the most important event of my life and you leave without a word, then speak to me in a public hallway with this horrendous news?"

Dr. Verti looked down. "I'll keep that in mind for the future."

I could hardly believe my ears, "Don't you be flip with me. How *dare* you speak to me in that tone and manner." He stood silent as I continued. "Tell me why you left this room without giving me the results."

"Well, we were paged," he said.

"Only one of you needed to answer the page. And when exactly were you planning to tell me the results?" I decided his bloated ego was trying to make up for his short stature. To my surprise, he began to sound a bit sheepish, "Well, the chain of command is actually to tell the ICU attending who was also paged out of the room. He ordered the test initially so he should tell you."

"That's *BULLSHIT!* First of all, Jim was in the room but I was so focused on Tim, I didn't know who was there until the end. Secondly, Dr. Ravi told me this morning about my husband going to rehab based upon the results of the brain MRI that *Jim* ordered, so don't tell me you needed to go speak with him to deliver this news. Plus *YOU* ordered this EEG, it's *YOUR* job for Christ's sake."

"Well you know now." I stared with disbelief at his cold, hard manner and decided he was not worth another breath. I turned away and climbed onto Tim's bed.

Dr. Verti lowered his voice and said, "I am sorry, Mrs. Higgins." I stroked Tim's hair and paid no attention as he left.

With head bowed, Dr. Ravi entered the room and walked over to the bedside. I glanced up. "Why did you leave the room without telling me about the EEG?" He immediately apologized and said he wanted to give me time with my husband.

"I've had 31 years with my husband. I needed just five minutes of your time for the most important news of my life and you were gone."

I noticed his bright green eyes had tears in them, "It was difficult for me to face you."

My anger flared, "Well you'd better buck up, because you're a physician and you're going to have to deliver bad news over and over. You were direct with me this morning and now when I needed you most, you were gone."

"I am so sorry, Anne Marie, so sorry."

I continued to stroke Tim's hair then Jim arrived along with an ICU resident and social worker. He said we should talk. I agreed, but not in Tim's room. I didn't want to continue in front of his nurse who'd been no comfort at all plus I wanted to give Tim a rest from the drama. I glanced at his monitors, kissed him on the forehead, and walked out the door with Joey.

Once in the ICU conference room, Sue, my boss and brother-in-law joined us; bad news travels fast. Jim explained the EEG showed no brain activity and there was no hope for recovery. He expressed his deep sorrow and asked me what I wanted to do.

I did not hesitate, "I want to take my husband home."

He looked to the social worker who said Tim had to be admitted into hospice care to go home. She left the room to see what could be done.

Jim was honest with me, "Anne Marie, the ride home will be difficult in the ambulance and honestly, I am not sure Tim will survive."

The weight of his words lay heavily on me. "Why did this happen?" I said, hoping for a logical explanation for this devastating turn of events.

Jim said he did not know and put his hand on my shoulder. I began to cry, head on the table. With visions of Tim alone in his room, I jolted my head up and dried my tears. I had to keep taking care of him so tears would have to wait. I tried to stand but my legs failed me. Tears won out and I lowered my head as they flowed onto the floor.

The social worker returned and said that since it was after 5pm on Friday, hospice wouldn't be available until Monday morning.

"What? Hospice isn't available 24/7? I don't want to wait until Monday; my husband's expressed wish is *not* to be maintained on life support if there is no hope. I don't want to deny his final wish."

Jim looked at me and said, "I'm not sure what else I can do."

The hospice news was upsetting, but it didn't matter. With absolute certainty, I said, "I don't want Tim to die in the ICU, I want him moved back to a private room on the BMT floor to be extubated in peaceful surroundings."

Thankfully, my brother-in-law, Dan, suggested we wait until tomorrow. It was dark and dreary and we all were exhausted. I agreed that now was not the time, waiting until daylight was better, even though "better" totally sucked.

Jim took a deep breath. "I've never been asked this before but I'll put the plan in place for tomorrow morning."

EYES NUMB

10

*I felt very still and empty, the way the eye of
a tornado must feel, moving dully along in
the middle of the surrounding hullabaloo.*

— Sylvia Plath, (from *The Bell Jar*)

My friends and family made sure I got something to eat and bid me a quick good-bye because I was restless and wanted to get back to Tim. I entered his room, checked his monitors and kissed his forehead. Tim's face was pale but relaxed and calm.

His evening nurse greeted me with downturned eyes, "Whenever you are ready Anne Marie."

I could tell that he would give me all the time I wanted. I told him to do what was needed. He checked all the monitors, adjusted a few machine settings and left the room, closing the sliding glass door behind him. I noticed curtains for the first time and pulled them shut.

Like the night before, I climbed onto the bed and lay close to Tim so I could feel his body next to mine. I was careful not to tangle myself in his tubing and wires. I put my head on his chest and started our nightly ritual, "My love, my life, come home with me now."

I took a deep breath then continued, "After walking through the door, you gently turn me toward you. We gaze into each other's eyes and relish our welcome home house hug, a ritual you started when you carried me across the threshold almost 25 years ago. We greet Lucca and Vivi who are meowing their protests that we have left them for so long. As we scoop them into our arms, they purr and forgive us."

I shifted my weight, worried for a moment that I was too heavy on his chest. I told myself it didn't matter, he didn't mind.

"We walk into the kitchen and I pour us each a glass of wine. I start dinner. You pick a CD, Leonard Cohen, cool. We dance around the kitchen; the scent of garlic simmering in olive oil fills our nostrils. I love our laughter as you sweep me into your arms, twirl, then dip me backward for a luscious kiss."

"Dinner is grilled salmon, sautéed spinach with shitake mushrooms, tomato avocado salad and crusty semolina bread. We say, "*That* was a company meal," but we rarely have guests anymore. Most of our friends' lives are filled with kids' sports and activities. We don't know any other couples that have been through our infertility saga but it's okay, we're fine in our own world. Finishing our meal, we sit, hands entwined, and savor last sips of French Rosé as we talk about our upcoming trip to St. Bart's."

I glanced at Tim's face and monitors. No response. Not surprised but I had to look, my desperate hope not yet extinguished.

"After we finish the dishes, we plop on the couch and turn on HBO. You choose *The Sopranos*. I lay back and my legs mingle with yours. We crack up as Tony and Carmella try to salvage their marriage in a session with his psychiatrist, Dr. Melfi. You thank our therapist, Linda, for helping us as we strengthened our bond through our long haul of infertility treatments and their aftermath. Even though we never got to hold our babies, we still have each other and many dreams to fulfill."

"We walk upstairs arm in arm to get ready for bed. Before we go to our separate bathrooms, we kiss and hug again; even this brief separation is marked in ritual."

"After making love and falling into a restful sleep, our arms and legs uncoil and you turn toward me for our full body morning hug. We laugh as Lucca and Vivi jump on top of us, meowing for their breakfast."

As I recalled our daily scenario, my body ached with longing for Tim's touch. I took a deep breath and sighed, "This is our last night, our very last night, how can this possibly be?"

I sat up and gazed at Tim's face and body as memories flooded my mind like a slow motion movie. Exhausted yet somehow peaceful, I lay my head back on Tim's chest and was lulled to sleep by the steady beat of his heart.

EYES RIVETED

11

Lay down your head and I'll sing you a lullaby
Back to the years of loo-li lai-lay
And I'll sing you to sleep and I'll sing you tomorrow
Bless you with love for the road that you go

— Sleep song (Irish lullaby)

The next morning, a few minutes before noon, the nurses gave me the high sign that they were ready to transfer Tim from the ICU to a private room where his endotracheal tube would be removed.

Tim's sister Joey, her husband Dan, my boss, Sue, five other friends, three ICU nurses and one respiratory therapist walked silently with me alongside Tim's bed. All I could hear was the steady pumping of the breathing bag doing the respirator's job.

After a brief ride in the elevator, we gathered in my respite room on the BMT unit. As Tim's bed was placed near the window, a bright ray of sunshine poured across his body, caressing him in warm light.

I climbed onto the right side of the bed and crouched next to Tim's legs, leaning in as close as possible, my eyes riveted on his face. I glanced away briefly as I watched the nurse open the clip on the IV line to give Tim one last dose of morphine to "ease his way." In that split second, the respiratory therapist pulled off the adhesive tape from his face. With a quick yank and slight sucking sound, the endotracheal tube was out. I cringed because the tape had cruelly taken some of Tim's skin from above his upper lip. My reflexive reaction was to touch his face to soothe any burning pain but my mind took over and said, *It doesn't matter, Anne Marie.*

I sighed, turned my head slightly toward my dear friend and said simply, "Sue." She knew what to do as I had carefully reviewed my plan with her just minutes before in the ICU. She turned on the CD player for one last task: soothing Tim to eternal sleep.

As Eva Cassidy's angelic voice poured into the room singing *Fields of Gold,* I joined her in song and watched Tim take one long unlabored breath. *That's it?* I asked myself, willing more breaths into Tim's still body. When the first song ended, Sue fast-forwarded to the last song on the CD. As everyone in the room sang *Somewhere over the Rainbow,* I gazed at Tim's peaceful face and felt a warm rush of deep love connecting us one last time.

An oncology resident, who'd been waiting in the hallway, approached Tim's bed with stethoscope in hand. She bent down and placed it on his chest. I hadn't taken my eyes off of his calm, handsome face but her action prompted me to repeat my usual protective mantra. The horrified look on her face gave away her inner thoughts that I was crazy or in a state of shock.

She apologized and introduced herself to me instead of Tim, "I am sorry, I am Dr. Simi and I, I…"

I interrupted her, "I know why you are here, and I know what has happened to my husband. Please do him this last honor, introduce yourself to *him* and tell him what you are about to do."

Her stunned gaze moved from my eyes to Tim. She reluctantly uttered, "Um, Judge Higgins, I am Dr. Simi and I am here to listen to your chest." Then, after hearing no heartbeat, she noted his time of death as 12:42 pm. She shyly looked back at me and walked out of the room.

Satisfied that I had taken care of Tim's dignity right to the end, I carefully shifted my body to lie next to him. As I held his hand in mine, family and friends kissed me and bid us tearful goodbyes. I hadn't shed any tears; I was on a euphoric high after giving Tim a peaceful death.

Robin, the oncology nurse with the pixie haircut who had warned me this day would come, stayed behind. She did not need to tell me her task. I knew what was next, having been present at many deaths in my nursing career. I told her, "I'm staying; I just don't want to see the gurney." Unfortunately, it was already outside the door and I caught a glimpse of the death cart that would take my beloved husband to the morgue.

I cringed at the sight and swallowed hard as I walked over to the CD player. The choice was easy: to wash my husband and send him on his way to eternity, Alejandro Escovedo would rock the room with his soulful beat and defiant lyrics.

I helped Robin slide the white zippered shroud underneath Tim's lifeless yet still gorgeous body. I carefully removed the handmade neck pillow from underneath his head and whispered, "I will keep this pillow always, stained with your sweat and blood."

Robin handed me a warm, wet cloth and together we washed his body while I sang along with Alejandro's mournful "Sister Lost Soul":

"You had to go without me, you wandered off alone, and all the neon light reflecting off the sidewalk, only reminds me you're not coming home."

When our task was completed, Robin said softly, "Spend whatever time you need." She hugged me and walked out the door.

EYES RESIGNED
12

I promise to love you with my every breath,
Anne Marie.
I promise to love you for eternity.

— Thomas W. Higgins, Jr., a.k.a. Tim
(Marriage Vows — 11/24/84)

I have not taken my eyes off of you and know what I want to see more than anything else. I climb onto the bed, straddle your hips and gaze lovingly at your quiet handsome face. I place my fingers on your eyes and carefully open the lids.

Oh my Love, the whites of your eyes are slightly jaundiced from the ravages of chemo on your liver, but your beautiful blue orbs are unscathed by the trauma of the last 18 days.

I drift back in time to August 25, 1978 when I first looked into your eyes. I become lost in sweet memories of our years of gazing into each other's eyes. Then your eyelids slide closed beneath my hungry fingertips and I sadly resign myself to the present moment.

I know somehow you can read my thoughts and still hear me. "Sleep well, my handsome love, sleep well."

I run my finger down your cheek and touch your lips. Your smile is the most dazzling smile I have ever seen.

How many smiles have we given one another over 31 years of shared joy? How many kisses have our lips enjoyed? How many places on my body has your mouth explored? How many words have we exchanged?

I open and close your mouth, wishing for a comforting word to pass your full, still pink lips one last time. I do not linger disappointed as reality takes over.

I sigh, then comb your hair with my fingers. A glimmer of excitement flashes in my brain and I jump off the bed to look for a pair of scissors. Unable to find one, I climb back on top of you and continue to run my fingers through your hair until I'm satisfied with the amount gathered in my needy, expectant palm. I reach for a plastic bag I'd found in my scissor search and store precious strands of hair, a gift to keep you with me always.

I climb on top of you, lean back and gaze at your gorgeous naked body that has given us both so much pleasure. I breathe in, slowly exhale and lean forward to start my final task. As I kiss your unlined forehead, each eye, your nose, cheeks, mouth, and chin, I inhale deeply to capture your familiar scent before it fades.

I move carefully down your strong, muscular neck and hairless chest that now encases an unfamiliar, silent heart.

How is this possible? Your heart has so many years left, so many memories yet to beat for. It is filled with our love, our life, our fire ignited by our first gaze, our years of me resting on your sweaty chest after love-making, listening to the rapid beat as you cuddle me in our rapture.

I sigh again as I reluctantly speak the truth, "Your heart has ceased to beat my love and I must move on."

As my lips move to each strong, broad shoulder and upper chest, I linger on a small gaping wound from where one of the many tubes, no longer needed, had been pulled out before you left the ICU. "I hope it doesn't hurt you, my love."

Reality check, Anne Marie — okay, okay, I'm back.

My lips slowly move down each arm to your piano hands. "Remember our joke that your fingers are so long and with your broad reach, you could have been an amazing pianist? I got the gift of your gentle touch instead."

After I kiss each fingertip, I feel an urge to be enveloped in your loving arms one last time. I lie on top of you and wrap your arms around my waist but as they fall limply to your side, I am again jarred back to reality. I take the blow and move forward.

As I continue my tender kisses down your stomach, I notice another small wound. Confused, I think for a moment, then recall how swollen your stomach had become when your kidneys failed. "Oh no, your skin pulled apart with the swelling and I hadn't noticed. I'm so sorry. I would have kissed it better for you before now. Thankfully…it feels so odd to be thankful…the swelling has subsided and your body looks almost as it did before this horror began."

My lips continue their quest to your narrow hips and groin where I linger as I deeply inhale the faint musk scent of your pubic hair. I quickly shut off my longing for you as I gather strands of your hair that come loose in my fingers. I add my prize to the stash in the plastic bag. I feel proud of myself for taking more of you with me.

I continue down your legs and finally kiss your feet and toes. "Boo, did you hear the reference to your large feet sticking out of the bed sheets from that dialysis technician, asking if they were in proportion to your unseen body parts? How many times have we heard jokes about your big feet?" I glance at your face waiting for the corners of your mouth to curl and laugh with me. Silence.

I close my eyes, take another deep breath and lie on top of you one last time, holding on tight as I recall so many full body hugs.

"My love, my life," I repeat over and over, paraphrasing Romeo's words to Juliet before his final farewell, "Death that hath sucked the honey of thy breath, hath had no power yet upon thy beauty, thou aren't not conquered, beauty's ensign yet is crimson, in thy lips and in thy cheeks, death's pale flag is not advanced there."

I never utter the words good-bye. It does not occur to me because this is not our end. *You are not really gone. This is just a temporary separation for us. I will see you again. I know I will.*

As these thoughts to you cross my mind, I find myself outside the door, looking back on your lifeless body. I do not know how I got there but I am drawn back into the room for one more look, one more kiss, one more touch.

After a few minutes, I walk out slowly, not knowing how my legs have the ability or strength to move forward as my new life begins, one painful step at a time.

NO END IN SIGHT AS YOUR SIGNS BEGIN

13

All you have to do is to pay attention; lessons always arrive when you are ready, and if you can read the signs, you will learn everything you need to know in order to take the next step.

— Paulo Coelho, The Zahir

October 12, 2009— Rainbow on Lake Ontario

A s I drove home to a Timmy-less house the day he died, I found my thoughts speaking to him again.

When we sang Somewhere Over the Rainbow to you today, I'd forgotten about the strange one we saw at the lake after you'd stubbed your toe. Remember how weird it was that it didn't arc? I said it was a sign for an exciting future ahead but maybe it was a sign of your impending death. Did your spirit travel up into a cloud like the rainbow that ended so abruptly? But you did not end, our love and our life will continue as I live for both of us now.

Soon after, Tim showed me that he indeed did not *end*.

I'd heard of departed loved ones coming back as animals and was thrilled when the wild animals in our backyard started behaving very differently. The first instance was a six-point buck that came through the pergola and watched me the day after Timmy died. He didn't seem afraid of me when I walked out onto the deck and spoke to him. He just watched me then sauntered on after awhile. Then a fawn came through the same way and lingered the morning of Tim's funeral. Deer didn't usually hang around while I was on the deck. I decided they were there to bring me comfort.

The day after Tim's service, I asked Eric, the shy funeral director, to bring me the flowers I hadn't donated to nursing homes to add color to the dull November foliage of the backyard. Our nephew, Tom, and his two sons arrived a few minutes after Eric left. As we pulled apart the tightly woven floral sprays, I said, "At least these flowers will provide food for the wild animals."

Once they were carefully placed along our perennial border, I spoke to Tim in my mind:

We talked about the continuation of consciousness in the form of energy. You told me that energy cannot be created or destroyed; yet you always concluded, 'When we die, we are gone.' Even though you didn't believe in an afterlife, when I see wild animals lingering in our backyard, I have this gut feeling that it's somehow you in animal form. Please help me understand what's going on because I feel like I'm going a little wacky.

My curious thoughts continued unabated so I kept count of the sightings of animals behaving strangely in our backyard. I had no clue why I did this, but it brought me solace despite the confusion and emptiness in my soul.

Three days later, my friend Diane and I were sitting on the back deck sipping wine after a long walk on yet another unseasonably warm November day. I was lost in thought, talking to Tim and staring at trees that had no shape or color. My eyes had ceased to see the world as it was; everything was flat and dull.

November 19, 2009—Buck and fawn nuzzling on Tim's funeral flowers.

Boo, are you keeping me warm? Wherever you are, can you control the climate? Was that you in the buck that slept on top of your funeral flowers we spread in the back yard? Then the buck and fawn were nuzzling on the flowers; how is that possible? Shouldn't he be looking for a mate this time of year? I didn't think a male deer would be so gentle with a fawn but you were so gentle with me.

Reality suddenly hit and I said, "Hey Di, I have an all expense paid trip to St. Bart's in 10 days, wanna go?"

Di smoothed back her wispy blond hair, smiled and said, "I'll have to get coverage for my patients but of course I'll go with you Anne Marie."

As usual, Tim had our one year vacation schedule organized in advance to coincide with his city court calendar; this December in St. Bart's, next March at my niece's villa in Italy, a long weekend in May for another niece's wedding in North Carolina, summer and fall time at Lake Ontario. I decided to go on every trip we had planned and take Tim with me. And so began my plan for the first year of rituals I called my "Circle of Healing" to honor Tim's memory and the places we'd loved together.

The next day, I called the funeral home, "Eric, do you have some kind of "travel urn" so I can take Timmy with me on vacation?"

There was silence for a moment, then he said, "I'll email pictures of what I have and deliver it with Timmy's ashes after the crematorium notifies me he's ready."

I shook my head in disbelief, thinking about getting Timmy "ready" by burning his body sounded so bizarre. I shuddered and tried to block the memory of seeing his closed casket slowly moving into the crematory with the single yellow rose I'd placed on the top. But I wanted to be with Tim as long as I could so I rode along in the hearse and bid him farewell with these words, "Until we meet again, my love."

The day before our 25th wedding anniversary, Eric arrived with an 8x6x4 inch black plastic box. The label on it read, "This Box Is A Temporary Container for the Cremated Remains of Thomas W. Higgins, Jr., No.09-1578, Cremated November 13, 2009. A Permanent Container Should Be Provided For Perpetual Care and Security."

I stared in amazement. All of his 6 foot 3 inch, 180 lb. gorgeous body had been reduced to fit into this? After reading the dire warning, I was relieved that I'd asked a friend and talented artist, Annie, to make a pottery urn for his "perpetual care and security."

Eric, still standing there shuffling his legs, interrupted my thoughts and handed me a small blue velvet box and an envelope, "Anne Marie, the travel urn is inside this box and this is Tim's cremation certificate. You'll need to take the certificate to show airport security if they ask what's in the metal urn."

I thought the box looked like a mini-coffin and said, "This is all very strange, but thank you for everything Eric."

A few minutes later, as my hands cupped the three-inch tall blue cloisonné vessel, decorated with butterflies, I took a deep breath in anticipation of our travels to come.

Somehow, I survived our November 24th wedding anniversary. Concerned phone calls kept me busy all day, then Diane came over to spend the night and talk about our upcoming trip to St. Bart's. We ate pasta with Bolognese sauce (comfort food), and drank a lot of red wine. Around midnight, she followed me into our bedroom after I staggered upstairs in tears.

As I leaned over and reached into the bedside table drawer for my nightly fix, Diane asked, "What's that?"

I showed her the tightly sealed plastic jar that I'd transferred Tim's hair into. "This is my daily dose of Timmy. I gathered his hair at his deathbed and sniff it every night and morning like cocaine. It still holds his scent and comforts me when nothing else works."

She nodded and tucked me into bed like a child. "What's that U-shaped thing around your waist?"

"It's the neck pillow that Timmy had in the ICU. Hospital volunteers made and donated them to patients. His blood and sweat are in its fibers. I wrap it around my waist every night and imagine he's hugging me. I can't fall sleep without it. My comfort comes from what remains."

Two days later, on the way to my brother Bill's house for Thanksgiving dinner, I pulled into the driveway at East Hill Farm, home of the Rochester Folk Art Guild. Annie greeted me at the pottery studio with a gentle hug. Soon, her husband Paul, a musician and David, a master wood-worker joined us. We stood in awe when Annie revealed Tim's urn.

I carried the beautiful blue-green vessel out into the sunshine and set it on a bench. The etchings that swirled in spirals from bottom to top made me think of ocean waves. The urn's brown handle was molded to resemble a tree branch that forked in two — or was it two branches growing together to become one? A tear rolled down my cheek as I decided the two branches were one, and that death would not separate us.

I opened the square black box and pulled out a thick, heavy plastic bag. The contents of fine gray ash were dotted with larger white flecks. David commented it was a "good cremation" because the white flecks that could be particles of Tim's bones were smaller and unrecognizable compared with some other "bad cremations" he had seen.

Not fully able to take in David's words, I silently spoke into the ashes, *How I wish I could magically breathe life back into your bones and body.*

After Annie and I carefully poured Tim into the urn, we embraced in a group hug. I told them my plan to take Tim on all of my travels this coming year. "This is his first stop, with you, my dear friends, who are our family."

I reached into the vessel and took a handful of ashes. Their softness against my skin was soothing. Annie, Paul and David each took a handful and followed me into their vineyard. I placed my portion of Tim's ashes near a grapevine and declared, "I want to taste your wine next year — it will be a great vintage."

Three days later, after another ash spreading ceremony with my family and Thanksgiving under my belt, I walked down the steps of a small commuter plane in St. Bart's with steadfast Diane, not knowing how I was going to survive my first vacation without Tim.

The week at the villa went by fast as we swam and tanned, ate and drank (too much), laughed a lot and cried even more. The day Diane had to leave, the sun was beating down through a cloudless sky. Just after finishing lunch, we walked solemnly to the edge of the deck. I opened Tim's travel urn and sobbed as I poured handfuls of his ashes into our palms.

When we let him go into the air, huge raindrops showered down on us. We stared at our wet hair and clothes in disbelief. Then, we looked up into the infinite blue and said in unison, "Where the hell did that rain come from?"

I burst into laughter and jumped up and down, "It's Timmy! He's here! He's crying along with us!" Diane laughed and hugged me in agreement as we declared this to be a true sign from above.

An hour later, I dropped Diane at the airport. As her flight left, I waved and sobbed. Kind bystanders consoled me. Somehow, I drove myself back to the villa, past beautiful beaches where happy vacationers enjoyed the day. I rushed out onto the deck, looked skyward and yelled, "Timmy, you have to come back now. I have another week here alone. *I CAN'T STAND IT!*"

When no new Timmy signs appeared, I began to hyperventilate. My heart was beating out of my chest like a captive bird fluttering its wings, trapped, trying to escape with nowhere to go. I jumped into the pool thinking it would calm me but after swallowing water and choking, I climbed out for fear of drowning.

I yelled up to the cloudless sky again, "Diane, please come back, you're a doctor, I need you here NOW to save me; you saved me all week with your care. I felt alive and now I want to die."

I walked in circles, and tried to breathe deeply, but began to cough and choke on my own tears. I tried talking myself down, "You've got to get a grip, Timmy would kill you if you die."

Somehow, I found my way to the phone and dialed my yoga friend, Callie in the United States. When she answered, I crumbled to the kitchen floor sobbing, "I'm all alone, I can't do this, I can't breathe."

She began a soothing mantra, "You're fine, I'm here, you're not alone, center yourself and breathe."

The next morning, after a fitful night's sleep, I walked into Diane's empty bedroom, tears spilling onto my cheeks. "Everyone leaves you, Anne Marie, everyone."

My mind drifted back to the evening after Tim's funeral when I found myself without cat food. I had a refrigerator filled with food from well-meaning friends and family but how could I not have food for our babies? I started to feel my pulse rise as I raced to the phone and called my neighbor, "Ellen, do you have any cat food?"

I took deep breaths to squelch impending panic as the bell rang in what seemed like a split second after I hung up. I opened the door and Ellen was standing there, both arms filled with cans of cat food. She shrieked, "Why are you ALONE?"

Her question brought me back to reality; my brain engaging in another activity averted my panic. My lame answer, "I don't know," was followed by thoughts of defense for my family and friends who'd been in attendance almost continually since Tim died. But in the next instant, I felt abandoned and wished I were Jewish like Ellen so someone would be sitting Shiva with me for seven days.

My next panic attack occurred in the late afternoon, three days after Tim's funeral. I was walking around the house looking for him. I kept asking the air, "Where are you, where are you, where *ARE* you?" My voice reached a crescendo pitch and I began to hyperventilate. I somehow found my way to the phone and called Tim's sister.

"Joey, I can't breathe, I can't do this, I can't do this!"

"Take deep breaths, I'll be there soon."

It seemed like only a minute later and she was there, but she lives several miles away so time somehow fast-forwarded in my muddled, oxygen-deprived brain. When the bell rang, I found myself on the floor. I got up, opened the door and grabbed Joey almost pulling her down, "I can't stand it, I can't stand it, where is he, *WHERE IS HE?*"

Joey held me tightly as we slid to the floor wrapped in each other's arms not caring about the cold, hard tile beneath our crumpled frames. After what seemed like an hour of non-stop sobbing, I pulled my weary head off Joey's shoulder and apologized for getting her shirt wet. She didn't care; her tears were mixed with mine.

I heard a noise that snapped my mind back to the present. I rushed out of Diane's bedroom onto the pool deck and saw a ceramic potted plant had blown off the table and shattered, its stem and blossoms were buried beneath the weight of the pot and the dirt. "Great, just great, even this damn plant left me."

As I swept up the pieces, I thought my life was like the shattered pot. What was once beautiful and whole was now broken. What was filled with life lay dead at my feet. All I wanted to do was join the plant and Tim.

"Anne Marie, *YOU* are still alive, you must breathe and go on." I heard the words Callie used to calm me down yesterday. I stood up and repeated them over and over until I began screaming, "But when will this pain *END*, please Timmy tell me when will this *END!?*"

The next few days went by with my question unanswered. I realized my grief had its own life now. As I sat on the deck and watched the last sliver of sun dip below the horizon, I grabbed my journal, a glass of wine and wrote a letter to Tim.

Precious Mine,

My grief has grown into a sapling that began from the seed of your seemingly insignificant toe injury. Every moment of your suffering, each loss you endured through chemotherapy and invasive treatments filtered through me as I grew roots into the deep mud of the pain I pushed away to stay focused on you. After you drew your last breath, my roots grew deeper and my journey upward out of the mud began as I emerged from the dark to seek nourishment and light.

As my young grief branches grow, I'm learning her intricacies. I nurture and tend her, giving the time she needs to flower. During this first month of my grief's early growth spurt, my initial shock and numbness was a gentle bud that unfolded slowly then burst unexpectedly into full flower panic attacks; like time-lapse photography where a closed bud turns into an amazing blossom in an instant. It's frightening but at least I'm not numb anymore. I feel my rapid heart beat, catch my breath and know I am painfully alive.

Thank you for your cleansing shower when I sent your ashes into the wind. It was a sign of your love raining down on me, soothing my pain and urging me to keep breathing, keep living, keep growing. Help me please; I'm not sure I can do this on my own.

Yours Forever

On my last day of vacation, getting ready to drive to the airport bound for home, I looked at the glass vase in the window where I'd put a small stem of the broken plant. White spindly roots hung below the water line and a tiny purple flower had sprouted out of the top.

Signs You Are Still "Hear"

14

Lose your mind and come to your senses.

— Fritz Perls

Whon I walked in the door from St. Bart's, I was thrilled to see Lucca and Vivi but crushed to return to a Timmy-less house. Our cats are our children but they couldn't fill the cavernous void.

Timmy where is my welcome home house hug? How am I supposed to go on without it, without you?

Feeling the enormous weight of my empty arms, I climbed into bed and finally fell asleep, exhausted after sobbing on Tim's pillow.

The next day, after a two-month absence, I returned to work. Supportive co-workers were helpful for a time and my boss had become a lifeline for me. I called my boss "Oz" because of his keen intellect. But it was his unwavering support that sustained me; he was with me every day in the hospital and at Tim's deathbed, he called or emailed every day after Tim died, even in St. Bart's. I knew I could count on him.

What I didn't know, was that in the not-so-distant future, some people would either desert me, betray me, or simply get tired of being there to support me. A friend, whose husband died the year before Tim, told me to take advantage of the attention now because it wouldn't last. So I allowed friends and family to take care of me with check-in phone calls, frequent visits and dropped off meals.

When I was alone at home, I talked to Tim, hugged our kitties and pushed thoughts of the future without him far into the back of my muddled mind because it was too painful to bear. Yet I needed my brain to function. I had to work and figure out how the hell to do everything Tim had always done for us.

In the past, I joked, "I have a wonderful wife." Tim was an avid gardener and fabulous cook. (I enjoy cooking but he was better at it.) He often did the dishes and cleaned. He shopped for groceries and clothes with me. He gave me daily approval of my fashion choices so he was also my best girlfriend. He did the traditional "male" tasks — from snow shoveling to taking care of our cars and finances. The only household chore I was fully in charge of was the laundry; he would somehow shrink everything. Now, my grief-clouded brain had to figure out how to do everything — alone.

The most difficult thing was the money part. As sole-beneficiary of his estate, I had to mail several important documents to the New York State Retirement Office to transfer his IRA and get the distribution of his pension going before the year ended. The problem? I didn't know where any of the papers were. I found myself walking around the house talking to him in my mind, *Timmy, where the hell did you put this stuff?*

It's all in the safe in the basement. Tim's voice spoke in my left ear as clear as if he were standing next to me.

It was weird to hear his voice, but rather than think about it, I stayed on task. Racing down the stairs, I walked into the dark wine cellar, lifted the metal top off the cement safe and stopped cold.

Damn, I don't know the combination! Timmy, I remember you wrote it on a piece of paper and hid it but where is it?

Sweat formed on my forehead and my heart raced. I walked out of the wine cellar and opened the window to clear my head. The rush of cold air jolted me. Feeling a tug on my right pant leg, I reached down to pet Lucca coming to my rescue as he always did under stress, but he wasn't there. My pant leg tugged again so hard they were pulled off of my waist. I yanked them up, looked down, no Lucca.

Are you trying to get into my pants, Timmy? I laughed out loud then chided myself, "Quit your wishful thinking Anne Marie."

Look in the record album of Verdi's opera, La Forza del Destino, Tim's voice whispered in my left ear.

"Right! You told me you hid the combination in a record album but I only half-listened because I had YOU to do everything for me!" I yelled in frustration at not having my "wife" by my side, but maybe he was, after all, he just told me what to do! Or was this how a widow loses it and goes crazy? I didn't care.

I walked into the storage room with a six-foot long shelf of hundreds of old, non-alphabetized record albums and promptly put my hand on the correct album. I opened it with shaky hands and found a folded paper with numbers in Tim's handwriting tucked inside the cover.

A few minutes later I got all of the needed certificates out of the safe, as tears trickled down my cheek. *Boo, please keep talking to me. I need you. I can't do this without you.*

Timmy's voice said, *I am right here. I will never leave you.*

As I caressed my left ear and sighed with desire for Tim's lips, I put back the album and thought of the tragic opera title translation, *The Force of Destiny.* How appropriate — this is surely true for me. I feel forced by fate but I must keep moving forward, uncertain of what my future will bring.

The next morning when I awoke to my unrelenting bitter reality, I looked at Lucca and Vivi nuzzled in the quilt on top of me and announced to Tim, "Well, at least I have our babies between my legs!" When his usual chuckle was not forthcoming, I started my rant.

"Okay, so what the hell was that yesterday when you told me where the safe combination was? Are you a freaking ghost? How can you talk if you have no voice box? I granted your request and burned you. You are here in this beautiful urn staring at me when I sleep — well, I guess you can't stare because you have no eyes either but you are ashes for Christ's sake, how did you TALK to me?"

I waited for an answer in my left ear. Nothing came.

"I don't believe in this, whatever the hell this hearing your voice thing is! I WANT to believe because it gives me hope you aren't gone but damn Timmy, YOU don't believe in this! You were an atheist and a judge! Logic was your guide. This defies logic and sanity and yep, I'm definitely going insane!"

Silence.

"I'm a nurse, a believer in science and research and concrete proof of FACTS! How the hell am I supposed to understand what happened yesterday?"

Lucca and Vivi were now fully awake, huddled at the end of the bed, staring at the madwoman who had taken over their Mommy. I leaned forward and scooped them into my arms. Perhaps he would listen to our cats who, like all animals, are much more perceptive than humans, "You tell your Daddy he's got a lot of convincing to do before we believe he's here talking with us. And if he is here, then tell him I want *HIM* to join you between my legs!"

SEARCHING FOR SOMETHING TO BELIEVE IN

15

*Those whom we love and lose are no longer
where they were before.
They are now, wherever we are.*

— St. John Chrysostom

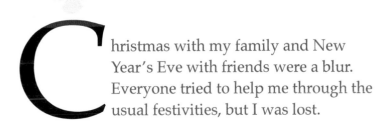

Christmas with my family and New Year's Eve with friends were a blur. Everyone tried to help me through the usual festivities, but I was lost.

I thought of one of Timmy's favorite quotes from Woody Allen, "Tradition is the illusion of permanence." I imagined Timmy saying this to me as I was going through my tradition-filled holiday illusions with tears streaming down my face.

On New Year's morning, I woke and stared at Timmy's urn and picture. *My Love, how do I go on? My body, heart and soul ache for you. I want to believe the surprise rain shower when we spread your ashes in St. Bart's and the voice in my ear were signs from you, but who do I ask? I've asked you and you haven't answered. Besides, you're as much of a skeptic as I am.*

I scooped Lucca and Vivi, my go-to "creature comforts," into my arms. And in the next moment, I was surprised to get an answer to my question.

Alex's face just appeared in my mind — did you put her there, Boo? I remember her predicting a "life-changing" event in your astrological chart before your diagnosis. Of course, she's the one to answer my questions! I'm emailing her.

A few days later at our agreed upon time, as I stared at her crystal blue eyes on Skype, I blurted "Alex, why didn't you tell me Timmy was going to die?"

It was late evening in Geneva, Switzerland and Alex's eyes still sparkled despite being tired from her daily medical school grind.

"Anne Marie, I didn't know he was going to die. I knew something life-changing was about to happen but his chart goes on, his spirit and soul continues somewhere in the cosmos."

"So he's not really gone? His soul is floating around somewhere?" This sounded pretty nutty to me, but I felt that way most of the time in my wacky widowed world.

"Yes Anne Marie, he is an old, wise soul. His vibration is very strong and he is high energy. If you see or hear things out of the ordinary, that's Timmy."

I stared at her lips forming words that made me feel less crazy. "Alex, I do see, feel, and hear things and I want it to be him, but I don't understand what's happening."

Alex adjusted herself in her chair as if she knew she was in for a long conversation. "He is no longer in this realm. He is on a different journey. In fact, when I first met him, I thought he was not fully connected here; he was already, unconsciously, belonging to another place. Tim was living in this world, but *you* were all that mattered to him as if he knew his time would be over soon."

"You sensed that in your first introduction from the back seat of our car before we dropped you at your sublet apartment?"

As Alex emphatically shook her head yes, I was surprised she never mentioned this during her two-month medical residency and the hours she spent with us. I liked hearing that I was all that mattered to Tim, but not that she sensed his time was ending.

"In hindsight, there were signs I ignored because I had no idea what they meant. Had I known they were predicting his death, I'd have tied him to the bed so he couldn't leave! Why did he leave me?" I saw my small Skype image on the lower corner of the screen. My face was red and blotchy with tears streaming down my cheeks. The all-too-familiar face of intense grief looked back at me.

"Anne Marie, your sorrow is mixed with anger. You must accept this trial. This intense emotional energy is not allowing you to see beyond all the losses you have been through."

"Alex, this is one horrific loss too many."

"You must understand that Tim is going through a major awakening, an adventure you are not on."

"Oh, great!" I threw my hands into the air. "He leaves me desolate and grief stricken while he is off on some grand adventure?"

Alex smiled, "He's not completely gone. He's learning something new and it's time for you to learn new things, too."

"I don't want to, I want my old life back." I'd turned into a child having a temper tantrum with a loony demand, as if Alex had the power to bring Tim back to life.

She sighed and said, "You're still connected to Tim. Your bond will get stronger as time goes on. He will continue to influence you, more so in a year from now. Your sorrow will slowly get better, but now there is an imbalance."

Finally I heard some words I could relate to. "I feel totally out of balance, Alex. Half of me is gone. It's so incredibly painful, like I'm physically split in two, open, raw and bleeding."

She tried to reassure me. "It's horrible but you must face this emptiness and know you will have your own awakening. In time, you *will* get something positive out of this awful experience."

"I can't imagine anything positive coming from this."

"Anne Marie, please know that Tim is happy. He is an enlightened, charismatic soul. His chart goes forward in an extraordinary way. He has intense energy and much knowledge to share with the universe."

Hearing Tim sharing his afterlife with others just pissed me off. "But I want him back here to share more with *ME!*"

Alex bowed her head and took a deep breath. "He is partly here but you have your own path now."

"I have no freaking clue what to do with my own path! We were on the same path and now I'm alone!" I buried my head in my hands, a temporary, unsuccessful escape from reality.

Alex waited patiently. "Your love was deeply intense and your loss is as well. Tim did not want to leave you. He had to have a physical struggle and be shocked in a powerful way to finally go. But even though his body is no more, he is not completely gone."

"But his physical absence is the *WORST* part!" My head ached and stomach churned as we kept going in circles.

Alex disappeared for a moment and returned with her astrological guidebook in her hands. After a few minutes of studying, she said, "You have three parts to your life Anne Marie: before, with and after Timmy. I see in your chart that your destiny takes a new direction, but it will be awhile before you have a major change in your life."

"I couldn't stand another major change."

"Wait another year and you will be able to start anew. I see a fresh direction and you will have the energy to move on. Between now and then, you need to make sense of what you are going through."

"Nothing makes sense right now. Nothing." My fingers rubbed my temples to soothe the pounding pain of reality.

Alex persisted and said, "Timmy will help you make sense of your loss and the direction your future will take you."

Suddenly Lucca and Vivi appeared and climbed on my lap as if to say *they* were my future or at least part of it. I cuddled them and asked, "Did your Daddy send you here? Of course you are my future, you are the main reason I keep living."

Alex chided me, "Anne Marie, you must live for you as well."

I ignored her. "Alex, I know they see Tim and feel him."

"Of course they do. Animals intuition is on a different level than humans. They are in tune with spirits and their magnetic vibrations. Your cats can feel Tim's presence."

"Yes they do; they've gone to his chair and stared at it as if he was sitting there. They sniff the air and meow like something is present I can't see." I then told Alex about all of the strange signs I had experienced since Tim died.

"Those are signs to pay attention to, Anne Marie. Tim is trying to explain things through other means."

"Can't he call or write? Why can't I see him?" I felt like a child again, wishing for the impossible.

Alex laughed, then got serious. "You'll know when it is Timmy. Your sight will improve through intuition. I don't mean you will actually *see* him but you'll feel harmony when you allow yourself to be attuned to Tim's soul."

"Alex, I have no clue how to attune to him. But if he's already come to me then I guess I do know how."

"It's your love that connects you, it always will. Don't worry; you'll have rich times together. Tim will continue to stay in touch."

"Great, and I'll need to stay in touch with *you* so I know what the hell is happening."

"Anne Marie, you know more than you realize. Trust in your process."

ONE MORE THING TO BELIEVE IN

16

Something very beautiful happens to people when their world has fallen apart: a humility, a nobility, a higher intelligence emerges at just the point when our knees hit the floor.

— Marianne Williamson

I felt better after speaking with Alex but despite her reassurances about Tim and my future, I was in despair a few days after our Skype call. I'd heard from another widow that "the only way out is through." The truth of those words was becoming increasingly apparent.

I felt trapped in a dark, tunnel with no escape from the waves of suffering that came crashing in. Like the ebb and flow of the sea, there were moments where the waves subsided only to come back and pound me with their weight and depth. I had no choice but to surrender to the tears, the longing, the pain and the overwhelming presence of Tim's physical absence.

I found myself walking in circles asking, "Where are you? I need another sign. Please give me another sign!" I was becoming a junkie who needed another fix to ease my misery. I thought of Alex's words and told myself more signs would come.

Two weeks later, my 55th birthday arrived. I took the day off from work and tried to fill every moment not to feel the crushing agony of my first birthday in 31 years without Tim.

Ironically, the County Bar Association was having their annual memorial service to honor judges and attorneys who had died the previous year. On my way there, I wondered, *My love, did you make sure this was scheduled on my birthday? Is this a sign from you?*

As I received hugs from Tim's colleagues and family at the ceremony, I decided Tim knew I would need human touch today so I accepted it as his gift. As crazy as that sounded, I'd take anything to bring some comfort.

That afternoon, I decided to buy myself a birthday present and went to our favorite jeweler to look at lockets. When I told the salesperson what I wanted it for, to my surprise, she walked over to a case, pulled out a velvet-lined tray and said, "We have just what you are looking for."

An hour later, I left with a silver heart-shaped locket engraved with my chosen words, "Two Souls, One Heart."

When I got home, I played Warren Zevon's song, "Keep Me In Your Heart" for the first time since the funeral. As tears streamed down my face, I carefully poured some of Tim's ashes into the new locket for his perpetual care.

As I fastened the chain around my neck, I thought, *Boo, did you give me this idea so I could literally keep you in my heart?*

Days blurred together, but each one started the same way. After I unwrapped Tim's stained neck pillow from my waist, I walked to his urn and photo on the shelf across from our bed. I kissed the urn, then ran my finger down his face and said, "Good morning my love. I adore you." Next, I opened the sealed plastic jar with his hair inside and took a big sniff for my daily fix of Tim.

Even though the agony of Tim's loss was a constant companion, there was also numbness beneath the surface of my consciousness. It was a feeling of disconnection from the world and from myself because I didn't know who I was without my other half.

One morning after working out, I found myself sobbing in the shower. Lost in time, I felt as if something had taken control of my body. I tried to move but was frozen with my head glued against the tile wall. I suddenly became loose and the hard porcelain met my knees as they buckled underneath me. Dazed, I slid open the shower door and crawled onto the bathroom rug.

Lucca and Vivi came in to greet me but ran out as more sobs began. I rolled into a ball and a deep guttural howl escaped my throat. The primitive sound frightened me and I screamed, "I can't stand the pain, help me someone, I can't move, I can't breathe!"

I have no idea how I found my therapist's number and dialed it — I was still in a crumpled position on the floor. "I can see you in one hour," Linda said.

My therapist, a slender woman who possessed keen intellect and deep compassion, began by saying, "Anne Marie, may I say that you and Tim were by far the most accomplished couple I have ever worked with in terms of your commitment to one another and dedication to your mutual growth. I admire you deeply."

Her compliment gave me some clarity. "Thank you Linda, that means a lot to me, but how am I supposed to go on without him? We worked so hard to get through our infertility and the stress of that ten-year battle that pummeled us. You saw it all."

"Yes, I did. You and Tim were remarkable supports for one another. Unlike many couples with such a strain on their marriage, your bond was strengthened by it."

"Five years ago when I last saw you after we ended our baby quest, I said I'd be fine as long as I had my Tim. Now he's gone and I'm lost. How do I go on?" I felt like that catatonic woman on the bathroom floor and my unrelenting sobs started again.

Linda waited until I was able to raise my head. When her wise eyes met mine, she said, "Anne Marie, you go on one moment at a time and I will be here for you. Your devastating loss is a clean cut to your heart and psyche. Because of your deep love and mutual respect, there are no jagged edges to resolve. Your grief will heal well because the wound is so clean."

I took a deep breath and knew I would somehow survive. Thus began my weekly lifeline that proved to be the support needed when — as predicted — true and false friends fell away, never to return.

YOUR PROTECTIVE EYES

17

Hold fast to dreams,
For if dreams die
Life is a broken-winged bird,
That cannot fly.

— Langston Hughes

Confused, I asked Dr. Haller, "How did I get this narrow-angle glaucoma? You said it's an eye disorder that requires surgery? Did I get it from crying a million tears since Tim died?" I thought, just my luck, my yearly routine eye exam and I get bad news without Tim by my side.

Waiting for me to finish my barrage of questions, he finally said, "Anne Marie, I've been watching this develop for awhile and decided not to tell you until it was time to do surgery. There was no need to worry you about it before now."

I looked at Dr. Haller, the ophthalmologist I had trusted for years who expertly cared for my mother-in-law's macular degeneration and diagnosed Tim's detached retina. But instead of trust, today I felt anger. "Why did you keep this from me? I could have talked with Tim about it and at least anticipated this time would come. Now he is gone and I have to deal with it alone."

"I'm sorry. I thought my decision was in your best interest, but perhaps not. The surgery is outpatient. You'll need to take the day off and get someone to drive you. You may have blurred vision for a few days so we'll plan for the end of the week and you'll have the weekend to recuperate."

Tears welled as I thought about my upcoming Circle of Healing ritual. "I'm leaving for Europe in two weeks to spread Tim's ashes at a friend's house in France and my niece's villa in Italy. I need to have the surgery and enough time to fully recover before the trip."

Dr. Haller's usual calm face cringed as he scanned his schedule. "I have an opening next week at 8:30am on April 1st; you'll have several days to heal before your trip."

"And when I arrive the morning of surgery, please tell me these last five months have been an April Fool's joke so I can go home with eyesight intact and Tim by my side."

My sarcastic reply was met with uneasy silence as Dr. Haller walked out the door. As I tried to focus my dilated eyes in the exam room mirror, I said, "I can't believe I'm having eye surgery on April Friggin' Fool's Day! Damn you Timmy, where are you now that I need you?"

The day after my unexpected news, I concentrated on pre-vacation errands, needing to accomplish some things that were in my control. As I drove mindlessly down a picturesque stretch of country road on the way to the tailor, I was startled by a shadow in my left peripheral vision. I turned my head and saw a gorgeous hawk flying next to my driver's side window. Our eyes locked for a moment and my heart took a leap. *"TIMMY?!"* I shrieked as the hawk flew forward in slow motion then disappeared in the sky without a trace.

Small stones hit the windshield as I swerved back from skimming gravel on the unpaved side of the road. I righted the car and found my way to the tailor a bit shaken. As I waited in a nearby coffee shop, I pushed the hawk sighting to the back of my mind and amended my to-do list: Jacket sleeve fixed for trip — check.

On the ride home, as rolling hills came into view, another huge shadow appeared. I caught my breath as what looked like the same hawk flew directly across my windshield. His eyes met mine in a slow motion, time warp lock-down stare. A feeling of exhilaration rippled down my spine, and then the hawk was gone.

I shrieked, "Timmy, it IS you! You ARE here! You know I'm scared about the eye surgery and you're here to help me through it!"

My mind traveled back years ago to when Tim and I visited the local zoo's birds of prey exhibit. I leaned on a wire fence to pull a small pebble out of my shoe and in a split second, a hawk flew down and his talon grazed my finger. I was shocked but I wasn't hurt. I remember feeling oddly intrigued by it.

After making sure I was okay, Tim said, "The term hawk-eyed certainly applies here! He was perched way on the other side of this huge cage a second ago!" Then Tim explained, with his encyclopedic brain, how hawks' eyes are designed for high visual acuity and can make fine discriminations eight times the distance of the sharpest human vision.

"Well, I guess his eyes didn't notice until the last second that my finger wasn't his prey!" I said with relief.

Even after I was attacked, hawks remained our favorite bird. I thought about how, whenever we went to Sapsucker Woods Bird Sanctuary in Ithaca, we were always thrilled when we saw a hawk. And today's close-up sighting totally blew my mind!

When I got home, I raced to the computer and found my fingers typing, "hawk animal symbolism" into Google. As hundreds of websites on animal symbolism appeared on the screen, I thought, *Why didn't I think of this before?*

I read the first site, http://www.whats-your-sign.com: "Hawk is considered to be a messenger between the physical and spiritual worlds. It is about visionary power and guardianship. The hawk is very protective of the young in its nest. It teaches us about providing for family and self. The hawk has keen eyesight, it is about opening our eyes and seeing that which is there to guide us."

I glanced at our framed wedding photo and stared into Timmy's eyes, *Boo, what a perfect symbolic bird for us, especially with my upcoming eye surgery. Your hawk eyes will watch over and protect me. Thank you for this beautiful sign.*

I looked back on my calendar for the past four months where I'd noted animals acting unusual in my backyard and googled the symbolism for each one.

A deer meant "gentleness and unconditional love." That certainly explained the gentleness of the six-point buck and fawn nuzzling each other on Tim's funeral flowers. And I thought a male deer in November would only be interested in females that could reproduce!

The morning after the deer appearance, a red fox was sleeping on Tim's funeral flowers. A fox symbolized "finding your way around obstacles and being able to camouflage the self." The fox came out in the open and walked over to me as I watched it from the deck so he certainly wasn't camouflaged.

Boo, I love that you're not hiding yourself from me. Like Alex said, you are communicating with me through animals but I wonder, other than this relentless grief, what other obstacles do I have to find my way around?

I'd also noticed that crows, blue jays, robins and cardinals seemed to just hang around while I was outside. I'd assumed they liked my bird food but then again, they often just sat nearby and watched me without feeding.

Desperate to preserve these new ideas, I made a list of the animals, their symbolism and the dates of their sightings. Then I added the other signs of hearing and feeling Tim in our home and on St. Bart's. I labeled my list "Positive Coincidences" and felt a sense of accomplishment having documented the signs and their meanings. I'd found a new source of comfort.

As my uncharted life unfolded, I added any unusual experiences to the list as they happened. I would come to know intimately that these were a key part of my "Awakening" that Alex had foretold.

MY FIRST YEAR CIRCLE INTO THE UNKNOWN

18

Life is what happens to you while you're busy making other plans.

— Allen Saunders

My eye surgery went well as I envisioned my protective Timmy hawk watching over me. I was ready to continue my Circle of Healing tour and was watchful for new signs.

The trip to Europe started with a detour that wouldn't have happened had Tim not died. My destination was Bagneres-de-Bigorre, a small village in the French Pyrenees to visit the couple who own the villa we rented in St. Bart's. Even though I had never met them, Henry and Anne-Marie invited me because they felt a connection to Tim: they lost their four-year old granddaughter to leukemia a year earlier. Shared grief, especially when it's due to the same devastating disease, bonds people in a special way. Plus, Henry told me I must be a kindred spirit since his wife and I have the same name.

After three days of wonderful meals, sharing memories of our departed loves and bittersweet laughter, we scattered Tim's ashes among the tulips in their garden. I felt peaceful imagining a part of his afterlife continuing in the French countryside.

Despite travel warnings west of France, I wasn't worried about leaving for Italy. The sky was deep blue without hint of a cloud. Henry and Anne-Marie drove me to the airport and waited to make sure I was safely on my way.

While going through security, I was stopped. Henry came to my rescue and asked the guard in French why I'd been detained. He explained I had a metal box they needed to examine. Even though the guard spoke English to me, Henry stood by just in case. When asked what was in the metal container, I said, "That is my husband."

After shocked guffaws, the guard cleared his throat and asked, "Your husband is in a round metal container madam?"

I chuckled to myself, then said, "Oh no, that is not my husband, *that* is paté."

Henry cracked up but the guards maintained their professionalism and asked to examine my purse. When the round metal tin of French paté was pulled out instead of the square box containing Tim, Henry and I breathed a sigh of relief.

The unfazed security guard announced, "Madam, you may keep your husband but you may not keep your paté!"

I was taken aback that a tin of French paté could transform me into a terrorist, but relieved to have been granted the privilege of keeping part of Tim. With double-cheeked kisses, Henry left, paté in hand. (I was not about to give that culinary delight to the security guard, even if he did let me keep my husband.)

About an hour later, just as I was about to board the plane, the loudspeaker announced all flights were canceled because a volcanic dust cloud was approaching from Iceland. When we learned that the cloud might persist for days — halting all air traffic in Western Europe — Henry and Anne-Marie returned to the Toulouse airport to drive me to Rome to meet my niece, Mea. Those kinds of friends come once in a lifetime, if you are lucky.

When I got into their car, Anne-Marie silently handed me a beautifully wrapped package. "Oh, how lovely, how did you have time to get me a gift?" I unwrapped it like a child at Christmas and found my almost confiscated French paté!

"Now pack that 'tin-that-is-not-your-husband' inside your suitcase," Henry advised with a wry smile.

We crossed the Italian border just after midnight and found a lovely hotel by the sea. With a restful sleep and quick breakfast under our belts, we were off again. The roads were especially busy with all air travel suspended. After a few hours of harried driving on the Italian Autostrada, we stopped at a crowded café for lunch. Another quick meal was downed then back to the car where we rolled with laughter at the sight. All of Henry's car windows were covered with white dust. We'd seen a cloud cover eerily following us since the beginning of the trip but didn't realize it was from the volcano.

Henry washed off the front windows and added his own flair to the back one: "Volcano Dust, Roma or Bust" was etched into the white powder and we zoomed away on the last leg of our two-day road trip. Thumbs up gestures and waves from other drivers looking at our back window added to our fun on the ride.

Several hours later, we met Mea and spent two days enjoying Rome's treasures before she and I left for her home in Southern Italy. When we bid Henry and Anne-Marie goodbye, I felt blessed by our new friendship, borne of shared tragedy and a lust for the adventure of life.

It was bittersweet to be in Puglia nine months after Timmy and I had visited there the previous July. This trip was supposed to have been a romantic get-away for us to tour the last three of Italy's twenty regions we'd visited since our honeymoon in 1984. Instead, Mea and I decided our time would be dedicated to cooking, reminiscing and honoring Tim.

Fortunately, the volcano cloud dispersed by the time I had to go home. As Mea and I spread Tim's ashes under a majestic carob tree overlooking her vineyard, I felt a warm sensation in my left ear and whispered, *My Love, someday I'll take you to Molise, Basilicata and Calabria but for now, you'll stay in Puglia and enrich this fertile soil.*

My travels continued in May to Raleigh and Bald Head Island, North Carolina for a family wedding. It was wonderful to be with my family but Tim's absence was keenly felt all weekend. Nothing was more painful than during the ceremony when I almost doubled over in tears at hearing the words, "Until death do us part."

Back in Raleigh after the wedding, I said to my niece, Courtney, "Isn't that hummingbird acting strangely?" We had just walked inside after scattering Tim's ashes over a yellow rose bush in her garden.

"Annie, that's the first one I've seen this year. Why is it hovering at the window like it's watching you?"

"It must be Timmy!" I said as I touched my finger to the glass while it fluttered in front of me for several minutes.

"It isn't behaving like any hummingbird I've ever seen before!" Courtney declared with eyebrows raised. "I hope Timmy isn't hungry because I don't have my feeder set up yet."

The Googled symbolism of this special sighting left me perplexed: "Hummingbird brings joy and lightness of being. With its ability to fly forward and backward, it is about adaptability and resiliency" (http://www.spiritanimal.info). I wasn't feeling much joy in my life but I was adapting as best I as I could, one step forward and a million steps backward.

In July, when I scattered more ashes in a pond near the Lake Ontario rental cottage, a muskrat suddenly appeared in the same spot where Tim had photographed one last summer. As the ashes hit the water along with my tears, the muskrat surfaced, looked up at me and lingered for several minutes just below where I was standing on a wooden dock. I was shocked because muskrats are skittish and usually swim away from us.

Muskrats build their dens the same way beavers do against the flow of water. I later read on my most frequented website www.whats-your-sign.com, that the symbolic message of the muskrat is to "change the course of your life flow by structuring your dreams into your physical reality."

Oh Tim, since my life course has been irreversibly changed, I have no clue what my dreams are now that your physical reality is gone. I guess I've got my work cut out for me, as long as it doesn't require building a new den. I'm happy staying in our home where I feel your presence most.

In late September, another niece, Kathleen, invited me to her vacation home in Brewster on Cape Cod. It was a spur of the moment idea when her husband had to leave on a business trip. "Kiki, this is so perfect. I wanted to visit all of our favorite places to spread Tim's ashes during this first year and now you are making that happen."

The morning after I arrived, a red-tail hawk swooped down and perched on a nearby telephone wire as Kathleen and I ate breakfast on her deck. "I've never seen a hawk here, especially one that's just sitting there like it's staring at us."

"That's Timmy watching over me. I guess he picks a specific animal, inhabits it to give me a sign, then goes back to his realm. I'll have to find someone who knows how spirits do that, won't I?"

Little did I know when I went down that road, it would take my life into an entirely new direction.

Later that evening, after our drive to Truro, six of our friends from the Cape joined Kathleen and me at Corn Hill. With ashes in one hand and champagne in the other, we stood on the cottage deck where Tim and I had watched countless sunsets over 25 years of cherished vacations.

As I read one of Tim's favorite poems, "The Layers" from *The Wild Braid* by Stanley Kunitz, I lingered on the last stanza:

"Live in the layers,
not on the litter.
Though I lack the art
to decipher it,
no doubt the next chapter
in my book of transformations
is already written.
I am not done with my changes."

As the sun hit the inky blue water and the champagne toast cooled my parched throat, I threw some of Tim into the gentle wind, wondering how many more layers of changes I had yet to endure.

FULL CIRCLE?

19

When our eyes see our hands doing the work of our hearts, the circle of Creation is completed inside us, the doors of our souls fly open and love steps forth to heal everything in sight.

— Michael Bridge

Karen, my dearest college friend, flew from Chicago to be with me at Lake Ontario so I wouldn't be alone on the anniversary of where our horror began. "Wow, I was expecting a small cottage but this house is huge and beautiful! Look at all the flowers! No wonder you and Timmy loved to come here," she said.

I silently shook my head as I unlocked the door and walked into my past. "Karen, stand here with me so I can catch my breath." I kissed my fingertips, leaned forward on the staircase and gently touched the wood, as if my kisses would heal the wound in my heart.

After I honored the step where Timmy stubbed his toe, I was ready to move forward with hope for a fun time. The bittersweet weekend held beach walks, beautiful sunsets and lots of good food and wine — much like the weekend Tim and I had had one year ago.

On Monday afternoon after the car was packed, it was time for the ceremony. The culmination of my circle of healing of firsts felt unreal and overwhelming. My body was shaking as I cupped some of Tim's smooth grey ashes in my palms. We walked to the flower gardens facing the lake and Karen held me as I tried to contain my sobs.

I turned my face to the sky and said, "My love, my life, how could this year have gone by without you by my side? I am devastated. I miss you so much."

We bent forward with outstretched hands just above a delicate pink rose. The instant Tim's ashes left our palms, five geese flew directly over our heads, honking mournful cries; then they disappeared. I shrieked and ran forward to watch them fly over the lake but they were nowhere in sight.

A visibly shocked Karen ran in back of me and breathlessly said, "Where did they come from? There's a forest in back of the house and no open land for them to fly through. How could they have flown over that huge house and swooped down so close to us? And where did they go?"

I was not surprised by her reaction. I had gotten used to unusual animal behavior, but this was new for her. "Sweet Karen, they are gone. Timmy was leading them with two pairs of geese guiding his way. Did you know geese mate for life? Whenever you see a lone goose, it has lost its mate. That was my precious husband on his own journey, but he was telling me he watches over me always."

Karen was wide-eyed. "I've never felt anything so powerful and amazing!" She stretched out her arms and showed me goose bumps.

"Someone told me those are called 'confirmatory goose bumps,' when you experience something out of the ordinary. And they were caused by geese, how cool is that?" I said.

As we chuckled, Karen said, "Annie, I never would have believed this had I not experienced it. I truly felt Timmy was with us."

On the ride to the airport, Karen admitted she had delved in metaphysical stuff like Angel and Tarot cards and had even been to a psychic. "Annie, why don't you go see a psychic? That way you could talk to Timmy."

"He talks to me. I have conversations with him in my mind and sometimes I speak out loud, *REAL LOUD,* when needed! But I'm not ready to do the psychic thing. I've thought about it, but it has to be the right person. Timmy will tell me if and when it's right."

When I entered the airport exit ramp, a huge red-tail hawk flew over my car. We squealed with delight and said in unison, "Thank you Timmy!"

As we hugged good-bye and tears ran down my cheeks, I felt a horrible pang of loneliness. "Karen, it's wonderful how we picked up from where we left off without seeing each other for years."

"That's what good friends do, sweetie, especially in times of need."

"Oh this was so needed and so appreciated, more than my words can express."

After our last wave, I got back into my car and my eye caught something shiny on the floor mat. I reached down and picked up a penny. I remembered when a widowed friend told me her departed husband left her pennies where she was sure to find them. It was only a few days after Timmy had died and as much as I wanted to believe her, I was in too much shock to comprehend it. I filed her story away in my brain drawer labeled, "Crazy Stuff to Figure Out Later." I was ready to pull open that drawer now.

When I pushed through the airport rotating doors, I saw Karen in the passenger line. "Honey, look what I found on the floor where you were sitting, did you see it there?"

Karen stared at the penny. "No it wasn't there. I'm sure because I bent down and picked up an emery board just before I got out and asked if you dropped it."

"Oh, right, I forgot you asked. Could the penny have dropped out of your purse?"

"No sweetie, my purse was on the back seat and besides, I don't keep pennies."

"I don't keep pennies, either. Whenever we were given pennies in change, Timmy and I had contests to see who could fling them the farthest. Of course, he always won. And when we saw one on the ground, we'd never pick it up and risk wrenching our backs. A quarter maybe, but never pennies!"

We examined the coin carefully. "It feels very light, like it's not real. And it's dated 2009, the year Timmy died, how amazing is that?"

"Completely amazing, Annie! Oops, there they go again! " Karen said as she showed me the tiny bumps on her outstretched arms.

"Look on the back, the figure looks like a lawyer — duh — Lincoln was a lawyer and so was Tim! Karen, this is freaky."

We hugged a final teary farewell but these were tears of joy. As I drove home, I felt protected and less lonely with a new Timmy sign carefully stashed in my car change tray.

I'll keep your penny there always and feel safe knowing you are riding along with me.

COUNTDOWN TO D-DAY

20

When an angel misses you,
they toss a penny down.

— Charles L. Mashburn

The year anniversary of Tim's diagnosis was approaching and I was filled with angst. It was five days before D-day and the Ronald McDonald House was holding a semi-formal fund raising dinner. Many of the long-distance patients and families that we saw at our medical center stayed there, so I wanted to extend my gratitude.

Since it was a special occasion, I chose Timmy's favorite "little black dress" and imagined him telling me how beautiful I looked. I hadn't lost my enjoyment of adorning myself on the outside, despite feeling awful inside. When given a compliment I would say, "It is better to look good than to feel good," channeling Billy Crystal as I did my best to look "Mahvelous, Dahling!"

As I was about to leave, Timmy told me to pick a different purse. His messages had changed from the first time he spoke into my left ear, to a voice in my mind like a flash of intuition, a kind of knowing. I always listened, especially if he told me to do something different than what I was about to do.

Okay, Boo, I'll change my purse if you say so. How do you like my dress? I asked, as I spun around in front of the mirror. I put away my silver bag, grabbed my patent leather clutch, packed it with lipstick, credit card and hankie then was out the door.

When I arrived, several colleagues greeted me with warm hugs, then were quickly off to join the partying crowd. It was difficult being with a bunch of seemingly happy people, especially when I felt so alone inside. Because I never knew what would trigger my tears, Tim's handkerchief was my constant companion. This one had its fair share of use that night.

I got home around 11pm and reached into my clutch to grab Tim's hankie for the laundry, when a shiny 2010-D penny fell to the floor. I stared in disbelief, knowing I'd been in and out of my purse all evening with no penny in sight. In fact, the last time I'd used this bag was on my European trip. As always, I'd emptied its contents, cleaned it out and stored it for the next event. This new sign was indeed its own event. I slept well with Timmy's penny tucked safely under my pillow.

The next morning was Saturday so I decided to sleep in but was awakened by the insistent ringing of the phone. I groggily answered and heard our massage therapist, Amy crying, "Annie, I'm so happy and sad."

"What's wrong?"

"Yesterday was the year anniversary of the last time I gave Timmy a massage."

"I know sweetie, it was hard for you, huh?"

"Yes, but when I went into my office to look at Timmy's memorial card, I found a 2010-D penny on the floor."

I gulped then continued, "It's a good thing I went to the bathroom in the middle of the night, because I'd be peeing my pants right now. I found a 2010-D penny last night in a purse I hadn't used for six months. This is so freaking cool! That's a symbolic full year from the 2009 penny he gave me Columbus weekend to our 2010-D pennies."

"Yeah Annie, he must be keeping track of all the anniversary dates."

"Do ya think he has a calendar wherever he is?"

When we both stopped laughing, we began to cry, missing Timmy and wanting his physical presence instead of his pennies.

Sunday afternoon I took a long walk near our home. Two blocks away is the cemetery where Tim's parents are buried. After stopping at their grave and thanking them for the millionth time for giving me their son, I turned away and breathed a sigh of relief.

My love, I'm glad you aren't here but home with me where I can kiss and touch you every day.

I continued my walk on trails that connect a flat section of the cemetery with a hilly one. Tim and I often walked to the hilltop because we loved the long-range eastern view of forest and sky in contrast to the short-range view of headstones: life juxtaposed with death.

Today, as I walked amongst the dense vegetation, a fabulous red-tail hawk swooped down over my head.

Did you hear me talking to you? What are you doing in here? I usually see you perched on a wire or soaring in the sky.

He landed on a low branch nearby and I walked over to continue the conversation.

Since you flew by my car last March, I've been thrilled with all of your visits. You've never been this close, so in case you haven't heard me, thank you for appearing whenever I was at the airport or on a car trip. I've felt so protected.

I had stopped being amazed each time I saw a hawk because it happened so often. Recently, a skeptical friend said to me that hawks are always around and I was only more aware of them because Timmy died.

Since skepticism is a companion I visit with each new sign, I might have agreed with her. Instead, I said, "The sightings are too frequent and besides, hawks are our favorite bird so we always paid attention when we saw them. No, this is my Timmy and you can go right ahead and think I'm crazy, I'm getting used to people thinking I'm crazy."

As I continued my hike, the hawk flew from branch to branch until we reached the top of the hill. I gazed at the colorful fall foliage in the distance and touched my heart locket in gratitude for Tim's visit. When he emerged from the woods and soared into the open sky, I waved good-bye. To my delight, he turned mid-air and tilted one wing up as if he were waving back.

A FREAKING FEATHER?

21

Hope is the thing with feathers
That perches in the soul
And sings the tune without the words
And never stops at all.

— Emily Dickinson

T im's pennies and hawk visit helped me survive the weekend. My countdown to D-Day continued, two more days to go.

On Monday, I had lunch with Sue. She was there every day of Tim's hospitalization until his death, and had been a continual support since. "Did you get my invitation for Tim's one-year anniversary luncheon? I plan to honor his memory and all of the extraordinary people who helped me through this awful year."

"I'm really bummed, I have a conference in Denver but I'll be with you in spirit, just like Timmy. Well, not exactly like Timmy," she chuckled.

"I'd welcome being with Timmy in spirit, if not for Lucca and Vivi," I sighed with eyes far away, staring out the window.

Sue reached over and gently squeezed my arm. "I know you love your kitties but you have to live for you."

"I am Sue, kind of, I just don't know why I'm alive and he's not. It's so bizarre." I pushed my salad around the plate.

"I can't begin to imagine. How are you going to get through the upcoming anniversaries?"

"Other than dinner with Tim's family on Diagnosis Day and the luncheon on Death Day…oh my God, two D-days, how awful…I'm planning to let time unfold and take it as it comes."

"Sounds like the best plan to me."

Sue dropped me back at work. We hugged good-bye and as I got into the elevator, sharp stomach pain jolted me. By the time I reached my fifth floor office, I was doubled over and could hardly breathe. I called my internist and was told to come in immediately.

The irony of being in the same exam room so close to the year anniversary of Tim's diagnosis did not escape me, nor did it our doctor as he kindly spoke of missing him. After a quick physical, Sean said I had food poisoning. He gave me several prescriptions and told me to go home and rest.

My boss dropped me off and then went to fill the prescriptions. I literally crawled up the stairs and lay on the bathroom floor writhing in pain. I stripped off my clothes and grabbed a comfy velour outfit. When I pulled the pants on, I shrieked; they were anything but comfortable. I looked down at what felt like a needle prick in my thigh and found a white feather sticking out of my leg.

"What the hell?" I pulled it out and examined the plume carefully. It was pure white and about an inch long. My leg wasn't injured, and to my surprise, my stomach pain was completely gone.

Suddenly, Tim spoke into my left ear, *Did my feather help you feel better, my love?*

Startled, I looked around the room, *Is that you, Boo? Are you freaking kidding me, how can a feather make me feel better? But I do!*

My boss returned with my prescriptions and I feigned continued pain knowing he wouldn't believe my feather story. I assured him I'd be fine and he went back to work.

Feeling absolutely cured, with no trace of pain, I Googled, "pennies from heaven" for a second time. I remembered when I'd looked up last week's pennies events, one website also mentioned feathers (http://www.selfgrowth.com/articles/pennies-from-heaven). I'd only read a few lines before and now as I read the rest of the site, I had to keep my skeptical side in-check to absorb the words: "Spirit has many interesting ways to communicate with us, and always on a very personal level. Your spiritual signs and signals can range from the truly spectacular to the very mundane. And sometimes they can be found in the most unusual places, or when they are least expected. Two of the most commonly sighted phenomena are coins or pennies, as well as feathers."

So Boo, now that you've done the so-called "common signs," can you move into the truly spectacular ones?

I continued to explore Google. My usual go-to, www.whats-your-sign.com said that a feather is "a link between those who have crossed over and birds who bring messages." That made sense to me with all of my hawk sightings, but I didn't think they had pure white feathers.

Boo, what kind of bird did you get this white feather from?

No answer came so I continued my search, "White feathers bring hope in times of despair, provide protection from the angels and the peace and blessings of a fresh start" (http://www.ask-angels.com).

I was happy about hope and the fresh start of being relieved of my stomach pain. But this was my first encounter — other than my Catholic upbringing — with the concept of angels.

Timmy, I'll take pennies and a feather from you but I'm not sure about this angel thing. Does this mean you're an angel? Now THAT is hard for me to believe. I can't see you flying around the cosmos like Michael, the irreverent angel in that movie starring John Travolta. But you were always a great disco dancer so maybe being an angel is a natural evolution for you.

TIME ALONE DOES NOT HEAL

22

Time does not heal,
It makes a half stitched scar
That can be broken and again you feel
Grief as total as in its first hour.

— Elizabeth Jennings

The day before Diagnosis Day, I was scheduled for a teeth cleaning and check-up. I thought of canceling but our dentist and the rest of his staff loved Tim, so being with supportive people seemed like a good idea. My clean bill of health and hugs from all boosted my spirits.

As I got into my car, I noticed something shiny on the floor mat. Two coins were in the exact place where I'd found the 2009 penny last week. I picked up the coins and stared at them. My skeptical self started looking for a rational explanation, while my intuitive self argued with her. They definitely weren't there before. I didn't bring a purse but I don't keep pennies, anyway, plus, my car door was locked. Although if it was Tim, I guess that doesn't matter, spirits can go through solid stuff, right?

I looked more closely at the 1999 penny and realized the other coin was a 2001-P copper-colored dime. Why the hell is this dime copper-colored? Both of my selves had no clue copper dimes existed. I thought back to something I'd read on the web about spirits being attracted to copper and that they often leave pennies and other copper-colored objects.

When I got home, I Googled "copper-colored dime." The US Mint website said that dimes are minted with a copper core and the silver color is added last. If a dime falls out of the minting tray on the way to the final color coat, it stays copper. These minting facts didn't matter to me except when I read that copper dimes are relatively rare.

Okay Timmy, where the hell did you find a copper dime? Do you have a private stash?

I compared the two new coins with my 2009 and 2010-D pennies. I'd also read that the D meant it was minted in Denver. But to me, it symbolized those two devastating "D-Days," Diagnosis and Death.

So Boo, I get the 2009 to 2010 full year symbolism but what do these mean? 2001 was the year of your re-election but the other date doesn't make sense to me. And what does that "P" symbolize, other than it was minted in Philadelphia?

My Timmy answer came quickly: *P is for plus, add them together.*

Okay, what do I add 1999 to? That year doesn't mean anything to me but a dime is ten cents so do you mean the tenth month of the year? My rational mind started taking over and nothing was making sense. I took a deep breath and asked, *Tim, please just tell me what you mean.*

My answer came, *Add 19 plus one, the penny is one cent.*

Okay, that equals twenty, and OMG, the twentieth of October was the date of your diagnosis! Boo, since last week, you've given me four coins that represent this full year of hell.

I was ecstatic about this new sign, confusing as it was. But I figured Tim came as close as he could to getting his message across with these particular coins.

My ecstasy was short-lived. *Okay Boo, now you have to get me through tomorrow, and then the next eighteen days.*

D-Day number one arrived and I found myself in a better frame of mind than I thought I would. I'd realized that the time leading up to an anniversary date was often worse than the day itself. But I took a personal day so I didn't have to deal with any office crap and meaningless platitudes. No one there could possibly understand what I was going through.

After kitty cuddling to warm my aching-for-Tim arms, I sat down and started typing everything I could remember about that terrifying day.

I was no stranger to writing. I'd kept a daily grief diary starting on our 25th wedding anniversary, 17 days after Tim died. Tucked in a drawer, I'd pulled out a beautifully bound journal of hand-made paper we'd bought in Venice on our honeymoon. Tim used to tease me that I'd never used it. Now I knew why — it had been waiting for this purpose, all of these years. Getting down the day-to-day cascade of thoughts and emotions that overwhelmed my existence helped as I tried to make sense of my life without Tim.

But today's D-day writing felt different, I felt compelled to go *back* in time and get every detail documented from diagnosis on so it would not be forgotten. I planned to recall one day at a time to chronicle the horrendous events of last year.

Tim always teased me that I had the memory of an elephant. Traumatic events tended to stay with me. I surprised even myself as the minute details came forth. This heart-wrenching record became my tribute to Tim, to honor all that he (and I) had endured during his last 18 days in this physical realm.

STRANGE
HAPPENINGS

23

Some people feel the rain…
and others just get wet.

— Bob Dylan

As I relived and wrote about those first nine days of Tim's hospitalization, visits from friends and check-in phone calls kept my emotions on a somewhat even keel. Then something strange happened.

I didn't want to be alone on the eve of Day Ten so Sandi came for dinner. Over the past year, she'd dropped off a meal almost every week. This time, I wanted to take care of her and cooking was therapeutic for me. We ate well and had way too much wine as we listened to music, laughed and cried.

I told her about my daily chronicle and how I was dreading tomorrow. "Writing has been difficult and healing at the same time. But remembering the day when Timmy coughed up blood and was rushed to the ICU will be a slice of hell."

"I'm amazed by your strength and willingness to face it again."

"This feels like something I have to do for him *and* for me. 'The only way out is through' as they say, whoever *they* are!" I felt something buzz in my ear. "Oh my God, what is *THAT*?"

Startled, Sandi yelped, "Yikes! Something just flew by my head!"

I heard another buzz and then a fly landed on the tablecloth. "Well, Mr. Fly, you weren't invited so make your exit or I'll do it for you."

The bug ignored my threat and stayed still, like it was watching us. "Gee, Sand, he doesn't look like a typical house fly. He's almost clear and kinda' thin."

"Yeah, it's weird Annie."

"Maybe he's young, like a little kid pestering us."

Sandi laughed then noticed it was past midnight. "Speaking of kids, I've got to get home to mine. Are you going to be okay?"

I waved off the annoying bug as it buzzed around my head, "I'll be fine as long as Mr. Fly doesn't carry some dreaded tropical illness."

In unison, we said, "If its Timmy, he's free of germs!"

We laughed at our shared words but weren't surprised. We were often on the same wavelength and she was in tune with me about Tim's signs. At least Sandi didn't think I was crazy!

The next day, I awoke at my usual hour, made coffee, then settled in front of the keyboard waiting for the horrible memories to come pouring out of my fingers.

A buzz came by my left ear. *I thought you left with Sandi.*

What looked like the same translucent fly landed on the nearby lampshade. I glanced at him and began to type. As my fingers hit the keys, he flew to my right hand and crawled onto Tim's wedding ring on my middle finger.

His band had been there since I put it on one year ago today, when the ICU nurse told me to take it off in case his fingers swelled. It was too big for me, but I kept it in place below my father's wedding band that Mom gave me after he died. I had Dad's sized down to fit because I wanted a jeweled middle finger to flip off anyone who annoyed me. Now I had rings of the two men I loved most to help me for that purpose as needed.

Fascinated, I watched the fly crawl all over Tim's band then he flew to my left hand and did the same on mine. Normally, I would've been grossed out, but I closed my eyes and allowed myself to *feel* what was happening. My arms tingled and a chill ran down my spine as he repeated the back and forth ring dance for several minutes and then flew to the lampshade.

Are you Timmy? Are you here to help me write about this horrible day? I got back to my task and started to type.

Defiantly, my skeptical self started in, "You're freaking crazy. You're talking to a fly and letting it walk all over you! How gross!" My other side argued, "So what? You don't understand what the hell is happening. Just go with the flow."

I gave in to the intuitive part of my brain, typed a few sentences, and then began to cry as memories flooded in. When I could no longer see the keyboard, my eyes overflowing with tears, I reached up to the fly. He repeated his dance from one hand to the other moving slowly over the gold as if he was savoring every millimeter.

With my unoccupied hand, I Googled "fly symbolism" and was shocked when I read the first website: "The fly shows how to be quick to act and respond to achieve results. Although flies are known for carrying diseases in unfavorable surroundings, the lesson of the fly is in the value of carrying your emotions, thoughts and feelings in order to act quickly in unfavorable or uncomfortable conditions. It takes about two weeks from hatching for new eggs to be laid, likewise, two weeks is significant in one's personal development. Are you ready for quick and abrupt changes? Fly will show how to make quick changes for rapid growth"(www.starstuffs.com/dictionary_of_insects).

OMG! I yelped as I counted the days. The time I was beginning to write about — from the day when Tim was admitted to the ICU to his funeral on November 13th — was exactly two weeks in length. The fly's message perfectly described those fourteen days when each horrendous moment unfolded into the next abrupt change.

Skeptical me re-emerged to blend with my other half and I was both confused and ecstatic. *Timmy, how do you do this symbolism thing? How do you know to send a specific animal and now a freaking insect that fits the situation? And how did you get so small to be inside a fly? What next, Spiderman? Oh please, forget I said that.*

Later that afternoon, my niece, Julie drove almost two hours to spend the day with me. Eleven years ago, her mother — my sister — Camille died from bleeding complications due to leukemia treatments so Julie was especially empathic about Tim.

I hadn't seen "Timmy Fly" since early morning so I assumed he was done with his task of enlightenment. I was still trying to absorb the synchronicity of its symbolism and the simultaneous events one year ago.

As soon as we settled on the couch with wine glasses in hand, he landed on my left hand and crawled onto my ring. I mentally spoke to him, *Welcome back, Boo!*

Julie leaned forward. He then buzzed by her ear and landed on her pant leg. "What the hell is that Annie, a freaking fly?"

"It's Timmy. He's been here for two days."

Julie's eyebrows raised, then she gave a knowing smile. She was open to believing it was Tim; it gave credence to her mother's visits, mostly in dreams. She'd also felt her mom's presence, especially during difficult times. "I guess our departed loved ones know when we need them."

We talked for several hours as he flew back and forth between us. When Julie left, I thought I saw him whiz out the door and was content with what he'd given us.

The next day, I needed retail therapy to get me out of the house and soothe my emotional exhaustion of intense writing. I returned home in the late afternoon with several new outfits. After dinner, I turned off the outside lights and closed the blinds. It was Halloween and I was not in the mood for cheery trick-or-treaters.

I settled at the computer and began my work. After two hours of remembering and writing about how Tim almost died Halloween night, I wandered into my dark living room and collapsed on the couch.

Lucca jumped up to give me his cat comfort. Over his purring, I heard Timmy Fly whiz by my ear. I sat up and turned on the light. He landed on my right hand, then the other, repeating his ring dance. *Hello there, I thought you'd left with Julie.*

When he flew to my pant leg, Lucca pounced. "Hey, that's Daddy, leave him alone!" A playful game of cat trying to catch insect in midair ensued. Then Timmy Fly disappeared. I went to bed relieved Lucca hadn't caught his prey.

Monday morning arrived and I went about my usual routine of early gym class and then off to work. When I got home and started to make dinner, Timmy Fly appeared on the kitchen cabinet.

Hey love, what'cha been doin' all day?

He flew to an empty yogurt container I'd washed and put in the sink to dry that morning. *Sorry sweetie, I finished the last of it.* He didn't seem to mind as he crawled around the rim.

Boo, am I nuts to believe you're inside a fly? This unending grief is making me crazy, so I guess I'll accept anything to stay connected to you. Your signs help, but I'd prefer you come back as my human Timmy with your gorgeous bod intact. Is that possible?

That night was his last visit. I blamed myself for asking the impossible. And yet, the improbable happened one year later when another Timmy Fly appeared and stayed with me those same four anniversary days. By then, I'd gotten used to strange happenings.

A HINT OF
SPIRITUAL
AWAKENING

24

When the heart weeps for what it has lost, the
spirit laughs for what it has found.

—Sufi Proverb

Agorgeous red-tail hawk appeared and hovered above my car two days before the anniversary of Tim's death. I'd just bought a case of wine for my luncheon to honor his memory.

When the hawk flew forward, as if beckoning me, I got out of the car and followed it. I lost sight as it disappeared behind a building. My eyes turned to a sign by the entrance that read, "The Spring." In my frequent visits to the wine store, I'd never noticed it. *Go inside,* my intuitive self told me — or was it Timmy?

When I opened the door, I saw several cases of jewelry, art objects, greeting cards and shelves full of books. A woman walked toward me with an aqua pashmina draped around her shoulders. It made her look taller than her five-foot frame. Or maybe it was her warm smile.

"Hello, I'm Sandy, how may I help you?"

"What *is* this place?" I asked, and then wanted to kick myself for sounding like a befuddled Dorothy entering the Land of Oz.

Sandy smiled, "This is The Emporium, a gift shop for The Spring. We're a non-profit organization for the Healing Arts and Center for Spiritual and Cultural Unity."

"That's a mouthful!"

I looked beyond The Emporium and saw several doors. Sandy took me on a tour of the Center starting with a large light-filled room where non-denominational Sunday gatherings took place. An ornately carved wooden screen graced the front and original artwork hung on the walls. I felt very peaceful as I looked around the beautiful space.

"Yoga classes are also held in this room a few evenings a week." Sandy explained.

"It's perfect for yoga, so soothing to the body and soul," I said as I imagined myself in a relaxed *savasana* pose.

Then she showed me three smaller rooms used for meditation, Reiki and various healing practices. The first had a circle of cushy floor pillows and the other two had massage tables covered with colorful blankets. Candles and art objects graced each room. She handed me a brochure that explained all of The Spring's programs.

"Sandy, thank you for showing me this beautiful place. I must run," I said, distracted by my list of errands, but intrigued by the feeling of calm induced by the surroundings.

Just before I walked out, I accepted Sandy's invitation to add my email address to their guest book. I would soon come to find out that that was the best decision I could have made.

THE END OF THE BEGINNING

25

When you gaze at the sky at night,
I'll be living on one of those stars
I'll be laughing on one of those stars,
And you'll feel as if all the stars are laughing.

— Antoine De Saint-Exupery
(The Little Prince)

As I carried Tim's perpetual resting vessel from our bedroom to the living room, I'd forgotten how heavy it was. But it didn't matter. I would have lifted anything for Tim that day. At 12:42pm, on November 7th, 2010, I lit a 24-hour candle next to his urn and handsome picture to mark the time of my beloved's death one year ago.

Forty-two close friends and family gathered for the occasion. Through tears, I thanked everyone for their extraordinary gifts of food, time, shoulders and ears that sustained me through the year.

I told the story of the four unusual CDs Tim had purchased two months before his death. I recounted our conversation when I saw the Barbra Streisand CD, *Love is the Answer*.

"You got Barbra Streisand?" (A few friends chuckled knowing Timmy's musical tastes and why I'd be surprised.)

"Yes, it's for you."

"For me, why?"

"Because I thought you would need it."

"You thought I would need it?"

"Yes, I thought you would need it, and besides, it got good reviews." (More laughter came from friends who knew Tim's habit of carefully researching all of his purchases.)

I took a deep breath and continued. "For some reason, I was thinking about that conversation yesterday. I finally listened to the first song, "Here's to Life" and realized that Timmy indeed knew I would need it. It was for today."

As the song about life and loss played, not a dry eye was left in the room. With the last verse, "Here's to life, here's to love, here's to you," we all raised a glass of champagne in celebration of Tim's life and our love.

Just as the song ended, a startled friend noticed movement outside our large picture window and yelled, "Look at that!" We ran to see a six-point buck followed by a fawn jump over the backyard fence, run through the yard and disappear through the pergola surrounded by the arborvitae hedge.

I smiled and said, "Something similar happened last year with two deer after Tim died." It didn't matter to me if people thought I was crazy when I declared, "Tim is with us today. Maybe the fawn is one of our babies." No one in the room seemed to care — all of them wanted to believe.

We ate a delicious catered lunch of roasted pork tenderloin, baked salmon, orzo with lemon, grilled asparagus and eggplant, and fruit cobbler with raspberry sauce. The bittersweet afternoon was filled with shared stories and memories of Tim. I'd also made a pot of Tim's favorite Provençal fish soup from a recipe we'd gotten in France and several friends stayed on for dinner.

As the evening progressed and much wine was consumed, the conversation turned to politics and TV shows. I was not interested, and my mind drifted to be with Tim. *Boo, these people have no clue about life. Who gives a crap about politicians and actors? You died for Christ's sake and this is what they talk about?*

I couldn't stomach their drunken babbling so I walked down the hallway into our library. Enveloped in quiet solitude, I felt relief and comfort. Grief had taught me the importance of turning inward to listen and to heal. Being with others didn't allow for that. Over the past year, many people, thinking they were being helpful, told me to get on with my life and be social. Nothing could have been further from the truth of what I needed, especially right now.

Sandi noticed I'd left and came to find me, "Hey, you okay?"

"Now that I'm in here away from the fucking mundane conversation, I'm fine."

"Yeah, it is pretty lame. Anything you need?"

"Timmy."

"Oh sweetie, I know you do." She hugged me and then had the good sense to let me be.

A few minutes later, all remaining guests decided to leave after their offers to help me clean were turned down. I explained, "My after-party ritual is washing dishes while listening to opera. Timmy and I will be fine doing what we always do. Thank you all for being here for us today."

Having honored Tim's anniversary and my intuitive self, I had a sense of deep satisfaction as I climbed into bed late that night. I drifted to sleep tightly hugging his neck pillow around my lonely waist.

SECONDARY LOSSES

26

Grief is in two parts. The first is loss.
The second is the remaking of life.

— Anne Roiphe

I

slept well, but woke up in despair.

Timmy, it's been one year and I did all the things I was supposed to do. I lived through each "first" without you and now you have to come back.

Each day he did not materialize, I grew more despondent. Then I berated myself for my insane, preposterous expectation. (Did I mention grief makes you crazy?)

Over the next two weeks, I found two more pennies, a 2009-D in a small purse I hadn't used in years and another 2010-D in a black patent leather purse I'd emptied, as always, after the last use. I was happy with each new sign but kept asking for more, *Darlin' if you want to make me feel better, you should start leaving silver dollars.*

Just after Thanksgiving, I went to St. Bart's with my friend, Diane again. I needed a break after reliving so many horrible events that happened during the month of November. We enjoyed our vacation — drinking, eating and tanning — but I returned home to a depth of grief I'd never known.

I remembered just after Tim died, a widowed acquaintance told me the second year was worse than the first. Unable to hear it then, I'd pushed the incomprehensible idea into the back of my brain. Now, three weeks into year number two, I felt devastated as I realized the truth of her words.

When I went to see Linda, my wise and steadfast therapist, she explained that now that I'd survived all of the "firsts," I was beginning to live through the "secondary losses" that come with the realization of a future without Timmy. All of our dreams and plans would never happen: our Summer Solstice trip to Finland to meet Tim's relatives on his mother's side, our retirement cross-country "I Love America" tour, downsizing to a one-level house near a lake, the dream of growing old together, celebrating our 50th wedding anniversary when Tim reached his anticipated nineties.

I somehow had to plan a different life but was clueless how to begin. My weekly sessions and a few in-between frantic phone calls with Linda had been helpful, but now I needed more.

Six months ago, I'd tried a local bereavement support group but it wasn't helpful. Some widows had been there for ten years and spoke as if the loss was yesterday. That scared the crap out of me and I thought, am I going to feel this way forever? Plus, I realized I was putting on my therapist hat when I spoke with one widow who hadn't been able to work for five years. At the coffee break, I ran out the door thinking, what the hell am I doing here if I feel like I have to play shrink to the others?

Reading several grief websites about secondary losses brought reassurance that I wasn't losing what was left of my mind. But the knowledge didn't matter. I felt exhausted, empty and bereft. Every cell of my body ached with physical and emotional pain. I was bound in a straight jacket of unending grief.

Something different was needed to reach the deep pain. Traditional grief therapy and journaling were helpful as was retail and wine therapy, but they had their limits. My intuition told me to seek some kind of mind-body healing. But then basic daily survival would use up the energy needed to search for something more. I was really stuck.

A week before Christmas, an email I didn't recognize appeared in my inbox. The subject line read, "Come to the Burning Bowl, White Stone Ceremony to Celebrate the New Year." I was intrigued and read further, "Spend the morning in celebration of the New Year observing these Sacred Traditions: a Burning Bowl Ceremony in which we release all ideas and thoughts from our past that no longer serve us. We then take away what we want for our future, a new way of being through a White Stone Ritual."

When I noticed that the information came from The Spring, I remembered my hurried but pleasant tour of the Center with Sandy.

I'd never taken the time to look at their brochure but their website was listed on the email so I clicked on it. Along with their Sunday Gatherings, they offered healing practices, many I'd never heard of like vibrational healing and Qigong. After reading about the "laying on of hands to heal one's life force energy," I decided Reiki was what I needed. I so desperately missed Tim's gentle hands; my body ached for touch, even if it wasn't sexual.

I dialed and the Center's Director and Reiki Master, Patsy Scala answered in a comforting voice; I immediately felt a connection to her. "Is it possible to schedule a Reiki session to get me through the holidays? I'm a widow and this time of year is not easy."

"I just had a cancellation for Wednesday, December 22 at 4pm. Will that work for you?"

Feeling a glimmer of hope, I said, "I'll make it work. See you then." I counted the days.

When Patsy greeted me at the door, her heart-shaped face glowed with an empathy that was palpable. I could feel calm envelope me in a way it hadn't in a long time. After a warm hug, she invited me to tell her what I needed. As I described my grief process, rituals and what I'd done to get me through the first year, I showed her Tim's laminated memorial card. His face and dates of birth and death had traces of lipstick from my kiss, my ritual whenever I handed his card to someone.

Patsy smiled, "I knew your Tim. He was the judge who married good friends of ours a few years ago in a garden wedding ceremony. It was a lovely day and he is a lovely man."

"How wonderful you met him. He *is* a lovely man. I noticed you used present tense."

"Of course, he *is* with us. His body left this realm but his spirit is here and is eternal. He will guide you always."

She turned the card over and saw our favorite picture of Lake Ontario with a picnic table on the beach and our wine glasses glimmering in the setting sun. She smiled as she read aloud the inscription, "*Ring the bells that still can ring, forget your perfect offering, there is a crack in everything, that's how the light gets in.* I love that Leonard Cohen verse."

"I somehow have to find those bells, I'm lost without my Tim."

Patsy smiled and assured me. "But he's here. I'm inviting him into your healing session and I know he will help us."

We entered a dimly lit room and I lay down on the massage bed. Patsy covered me with a blanket and lit several candles. She explained Reiki is a Japanese term that means the universal life energy that flows through seven major lines in the center of our bodies. These energy lines, called chakras, correspond to our organs and nervous system. When these energy lines are blocked, our bodily functions and emotional wellbeing become impaired.

After holding a pendulum above the seven energy lines from the middle of my lower abdomen up to my head, she explained that each chakra's energy force was low. I was mostly blocked in my root chakra located at the base of the spine that relates to primal survival needs, a sense of belonging and security as well as my sacral chakra, just below the navel that relates to intimacy and sexuality. Tim was the grounding root of my life and sexual soul mate so that made sense.

Patsy asked permission to touch my body. When she gently placed her hands on my lower abdomen, I began to cry. I closed my eyes, took a deep breath and relaxed. I went into a deeply meditative state unlike I'd ever experienced. After the session, I felt like a huge weight had been lifted.

"Patsy, thank you. That was amazing. I feel lighter, like I'm emerging out of a dark place."

"The healing will continue and stay with you. I could feel Tim's presence and immense love for you. You are grieving in just the right way with all of your rituals. You're using every aspect of your being, your right-brain and left-brain to move forward. Your Tim is guiding you and making things happen to help ease your way."

"How do you know this?"

"Other than what you told me about your healing process, I could intuitively feel what Tim is doing for you. For one thing, he brought us together; I never answer the phone at The Spring but something told me to pick up the line even though our receptionist was sitting right there."

"You feel like a *lifeline* right now. I believe the light I need to let in is starting to come through the cracks. Thank you Leonard

Cohen, Timmy and *you* Patsy!" We hugged and promised to connect after I got back from the Christmas holidays with my family.

As I walked to my car, cold winter air and fluffy snowflakes circled my body but I still felt warm all over. When I opened the door, I was delighted too see Tim soaring just overhead.

You are such a magnificent hawk, Timmy. Thank you for the gift of Patsy and always watching over me.

WHAT THE HELL IS AN ORB?

27

Why, sometimes I've believed as many as six impossible things before breakfast.

— Lewis Carroll, Alice in Wonderland

Oh my freaking God, it's the second New Year's I'm waking up without you. How have I survived and when will this nightmare end?

Lucca and Vivi looked up from their spot between my legs as I reached over to touch Timmy's empty side of the bed, smoothing the creaseless sheets where his body should be. I reflected on the last month and how I drifted aimlessly through holiday traditions without him. The hole left by his absence was too big to fill. My family and friends were supportive, but no matter how hard they tried to make me feel better, death is not fixable.

I'd turned down New Year's party invitations and spent a quiet day looking through vacation photo albums with a glass of wine in one hand and both cats cuddled in my lap. At least I had my first Sunday Gathering at The Spring the next day to motivate me out of the house.

The next morning, as I was about to leave for The Spring, I noticed the backyard bird feeder was empty. I opened the sliding door and saw movement along our arborvitae hedge. Snowy days had not materialized that Christmas or New Year's, so whatever was moving blended in with the brown earth. It stirred again and I realized from a flash of white on its tail, that it was a fox.

I grabbed my camera and took several pictures because he kept going in circles trying to find a comfortable spot. He finally settled in. I took one more shot and asked, *Are you Timmy or do I keep watching for hawks?*

I looked at the clock and realized I had to leave now or I'd be late for the 10:30am gathering. Timmy wouldn't have been surprised because I'm always at least five minutes late for everything.

Look at the pictures when you get home, Timmy's voice announced in my head.

Okay will do, now I'm off to see what this Spring thing is all about!

When I walked into the large room, decorated with evergreen boughs and soft white lights, Patsy hugged me. She then introduced me to a group of about thirty smiling people, aged nine to sixty-nine, seated in a circle around a multicolored-cloth skirted table. Candles were burning around the room and soft new-age music was playing. I took it all in as I sat down next to Patsy.

The service began with welcome remarks from Reverend James Stacey who was dressed in a dark blue suit, Hermes silk tie, French cuffed shirt with garnet cufflinks showing just below his coat sleeve. (I would notice these details because that's how Tim dressed.) He read Rudolf Steiner's "The Foundation Stone Meditation" and discussed the message of the "Spirit-light of the world entering into our daily lives of earthly existence."

I realized I wasn't in Kansas anymore — or the practice of religion I was brought up with. Tim and I had been "fallen Catholics" for years so this was fine with me. I was hungry for something new and found myself both fascinated and confused by his references to the human soul and returning to our spirit recollections. Is this what Timmy is doing now? I thought.

Sandy, who greeted me the first day I walked into The Spring, read from Isaiah. But it wasn't like any Gospel reading I'd ever heard, it was written in modern understandable language. Then Reverend James talked about the "Christmas of Selfhood" and the complex, often conflicting feelings we all have but may not voice about holiday traditions and family rituals. I couldn't have agreed more.

A silent meditation followed, broken after several minutes by soothing instrumental music. When I opened my eyes, a smiling young girl was standing before me with a wicker basket. I took a blank piece of paper and pen and waited for instructions as my nostrils took in a faint scent of jasmine from the nearby burning candles. I closed my eyes again until we were told to write down what we did not want to bring into this New Year from our past. I wrote one word: *Despair.*

Reverend James explained that we would burn these pieces of paper as a symbolic ritual of extinguishing what no longer served us, followed by taking away a white stone for our future intention. He walked to the table in the center of the room and lit an oil-burning candle that was surrounded by a circle of white stones.

I followed Patsy's lead, held my paper over the flame and watched my *Despair* of this horrendous past year smolder and disappear into the fire. Then I took away a white stone and touched it to my lips. I named my heart-felt intention for the New Year "*Hope."* As I returned to my seat and looked around the room, I felt a rush of that exact feeling wash over me. I breathed a deep sigh knowing I'd found my much-needed "spiritual family."

After the ceremony concluded, the Gathering continued with refreshments and light snacks. I was filled with gratitude after talking with my newfound community members for almost two hours. We discussed topics I could never talk about with my colleagues, family or friends who didn't "get it." Hell, I didn't get it until Timmy died. Oops, I can't use that word anymore; the proper term — according to Patsy and other members of The Spring — is "transition." His body died, but his spirit transitioned to another realm.

When I got back home, I excitedly called out, "Lucca, Vivi, I found new friends who don't think I'm crazy that I believe Daddy is here and comes to me!" My kitties greeted me with tilted heads and meows as I happily scooped them into my arms.

"Come sit with Mommy while I get all of this down in my journal."

Look at the pictures, Timmy's voice insisted before I got myself settled into his reading chair.

Oh right, sorry Boo, I forgot.

I found our digital camera on the kitchen counter and clicked on the picture review button. My eyes transfixed on something I'd never seen in my life. *What the hell is THAT?*

Along my backyard arborvitae tree line was a small blurred object in front of the trees. It didn't look like a fox. I squinted and tried to focus on the object that was obscured by a green-orange colored haze in the foreground. I clicked through the six consecutive pictures and the haze became progressively larger then round white circles appeared amidst the haze. The circles had small dots inside them, or depth, something I couldn't figure out. They reminded me of pictures our infertility doctor gave us of the live embryos transferred into my uterus with our in-vitro fertilization procedures.

January 2, 2011—These auras and two large white orbs— right of center and upper right — obscure the fox in the background.

Boo, is that what you look like without a body? I was shocked by my words because that concept was so foreign to me. Where did that idea come from? This is too freaking weird! I closed the camera and poured a glass of wine.

Timmy, please explain what the hell this is because now I know I'm crazy and may need to check into the loony bin.

The next morning, after no Timmy voice had come through, I knew who to call. "Patsy, I took pictures of a fox in our backyard yesterday and there are these weird circles and colors all over the pictures!"

She said in a calm, soothing voice. "It sounds like Timmy sent you a definite sign yesterday. Can you come in at two o'clock and show me?"

"I'm counting the hours!"

"Oh, what lovely auras and orbs!" Patsy exclaimed.

"Pardon me, auras and orbs? I don't know what you mean." I refrained from my usual profanity in her presence.

"An aura is energy surrounding all objects, both living and spirit. This energy is made up of different vibrations and also colors. It's like when you see a heat haze above the road on a hot summer day, and the air is a different density within the haze."

"But it's January and it's cold."

"Oh it doesn't have to be warm for an aura to appear, it's pure energy. Orbs are beings of light conserving their energy by remaining in a concentrated mass of spiritual energy. Orbs are all around us, but they can be difficult to see and sense. When your soul leaves your body it has no way of containing and protecting itself so the soul concentrates into a round mass that you see in this picture as an orb."

"Uh-huh, so are you saying this orb is Timmy?" My skeptical mind was in full flower.

"Oh yes. There is more than one, so other spirits accompanied him to visit you. They are giving you a clear sign that they are here with you to guide you. This New Year is starting out very well for you, Anne Marie."

I closed my eyes and swallowed hard trying to make sense of what I'd heard. "Okay, so I actually *love* that you say it is Timmy, but now what?"

"Now you accept his gift and pay attention to the animal that was sent to you."

"Oh, I completely forgot about the fox."

"This is your power animal for the New Year."

"My *power animal*?

"Yes, power animals protect us from harm, like guardian spirits. They also lend their wisdom as they protect you."

I leaned forward in my seat, excited to hear something that linked to what I'd already been experiencing. "Each time I see an animal doing something out of the ordinary, I look up its symbolism and the description always seems to fit for what I'm feeling at the time."

"You've told me about your hawk and I believe hawk is truly a lifetime power animal for you but this fox will help you with what you need specifically for this year."

"Okay so what is he helping me with?"

"Your grief process, your work, friends and family. Pay attention to his lessons for this next year. Let's see what he has to say."

Patsy pulled out a deck of Medicine Cards. She explained they help answer life's questions, drawing on the wisdom and healing medicine of animals. She looked through the deck, found the fox card and read the description: "The fox represents the feminine magic of camouflage, shape-shifting and invisibility. When a fox shows up in your life, the process of creation is beginning. New beneficial patterns will emerge as you move into new dimensions in your life but you must learn the art of camouflage and use it to your benefit" (*Medicine Cards: The Discovery of Power Through the Ways of Animals* by Jamie Sams and David Carson).

I thought about work and how I didn't feel like I fit in with the women in my office suite, especially since Timmy died. My life was always different from theirs and now even more so. I kept pretty much to myself anyway but perhaps the card was right that I needed to pull back even more. I had a gut feeling I shouldn't trust them. I also wondered what "new dimensions" were coming.

She continued, "Practice blending into your surroundings. Learn to control the aura energy field around your body so you harmonize with others to protect yourself. The fox has excellent hearing and it is tied with the ability to hear spirit. Fox also has the ability to see spirit, this will happen if fox has come to you."

I was speechless but felt an urge to scream with excitement. I squelched it and instead said, "So my Tim is with me and I hear him speak to me, but is he the fox or the orb?"

"He's the orb in this picture but he sends messages through animals and can inhabit them when needed to share their wisdom with you. Spirit Guides use animals or animal imagery and symbolism to communicate their purpose and to help you continue in your life without them."

"So he's my Spirit Guide now?"

"He certainly is and you have others as well but he is your main Spirit Guide. He loves you and wants to help ease your way."

"It would help me most if he came back in human form."

Patsy smiled and ignored my impossible wish. We agreed to get together again after I absorbed all she had told me.

IT'S A WHOLE NEW WORLD

28

*The real voyage of discovery consists
not in seeking new landscapes,
but in having new eyes.*

— Marcel Proust

I drove home pondering Patsy's revelations. As soon as I walked into my house, Timmy told me to look at the rest of the pictures in our camera.

Since he transitioned, I hadn't downloaded one picture because I didn't know how. He was the camera guru. Whenever I took pictures, I just snapped away and forgot about them. I knew I'd eventually look at them, but it wasn't a priority. Grieving was my primary activity.

I found the camera directions and figured out how to put them on my computer. After looking at the photos I'd taken since Tim's transition on my various trips and at home, I was completely blown away and out of my mind ecstatic! *Timmy, you are everywhere!*

I spent the next several hours looking at thousands of pictures Tim had taken over the years. Once I finished reviewing all he'd downloaded onto the computer, I pulled out our old photo albums. The skeptical me, despite the proof before my eyes, had to make sure the pictures I'd taken were different from his. Not one orb or aura was found in any of his photos.

At my next Reiki session, I brought my newly discovered orb and aura pictures to show Patsy. She smiled, "Timmy speaks with you so beautifully. He will always be with you; you must see that now."

"I'm still trying to believe my eyes. It's so new and strange but these *cannot* be denied."

Now whenever I take pictures, I always check for orbs and auras to assure me of Tim's presence.

On March 21, 2010, I took a picture while hiking at Wehle State Park, Lake Ontario with friends. On the rocky-cliffed shoreline, at the base of a birch tree where we'd spread some of Tim's ashes, a large creamy blue orb appeared.

Near Bagneres-de-Bigorre, France, on April 15, 2010, I took several pictures at the pig farm where I got my infamous paté. There were multiple white orbs on seven nursing piglets.

Boo, I think they symbolize the seven babies we lost. Is that what you were trying to say to me? Well, it's my story and I'm sticking to it!

While at Tim's memorial ceremony on September 18, 2010 at Corn Hill Cottages, Cape Cod, our niece, Kathleen, took a picture of friends gathering to spread Tim's ashes. There was an orb and red-orange streak aura on the photo. I was thrilled to see that Tim showed up on a camera other than mine. (These three photos and more are on my website, www.dancingintworealms.com.)

For this memoir, I decided to include my favorite, most impressive photos. I'm sharing these photos to give others hope that our loved ones are still with us.

July 23, 2010—Timmy's dwarf blue globe spruce in our babies' memorial evergreen garden. This was taken immediately after Tim's memorial shrub was planted. Note the multiple orbs and large white aura.

October 12, 2010— A fawn was born in our backyard that summer and I named him Timmy. When he got bigger, he tried to jump over our fence but was too small and injured his leg. After speaking with the department of animal conservation, I was told to take pictures to see if he needed their assistance. The fawn never stood still long enough, so I never sent the pictures. But he was fine and now I know why: "Timmy Hawk's" wing transposed over the fawn and traveling orbs and auras were there to heal him. These are the most amazing pictures I've ever seen. I showed them to a professional photographer and he agreed they defied explanation.

CONTINUED
AWAKENING
29

Wisdom begins in wonder.

— Socrates

So Tim returned, as my astrologer friend Alex had foretold last January when she said, "By this time next year, your balances will be in tune; you'll reconnect in a new way and have rich times together." Appearing in animals, auras, orbs, and ways I never could've imagined certainly felt rich. While my skeptical self still popped up and questioned each new sign, my intuitive self just sat back and smiled.

Alex's prediction of my personal awakening also began to flourish at The Spring. Besides Reiki sessions, I attended a meditation hour before each Sunday Gathering. I delved into some of their other therapies such as vibrational healing, energy restoration with essential oils and qi-gong. Each modality was different but they shared similar philosophies of healing through connection to spirit. What mattered most was some comfort for my physical and emotional pain.

In addition to helpful books I'd read about grief and widowhood, I explored topics about metaphysics, the paranormal, psychic phenomenon and spiritualism. I needed to understand Timmy's signs and convince my ever-skeptical self that he was communicating from another realm.

I was amazed at the body of written material about concepts I previously knew nothing about or wrote off as incomprehensible: the after-life, reincarnation, psychic communication with the dead, spirit guides, power animals, angels, other realms. All of these held essentially the same belief — that there is something else beyond physical death. Even if "energy cannot be created or destroyed," the soul's transition from the body into an orb had been too *out there* for me initially. But I had a growing curiosity about things I couldn't explain because they brought me closer to Tim.

January 19th arrived and I needed something special to get through my second birthday without Tim. I scheduled an intuitive reading along with my usual Reiki session. Even though she is not a psychic, Patsy often received messages from spirit during her healings and shared what she received. She explained the addition of an intuitive reading included a deeper connection to spirit through meditation and focused assessment of my chakras and individual energies.

"All energy is intuitive Anne Marie. I will tap into different dimensions of consciousness in your mental, emotional and physical energy bodies. I'll use my hands as usual but the session will be longer."

"Okay Patsy, I'm all yours."

Even though I was confused, rather than ask questions, I went with the flow and kept my skeptical brain quiet. I'd always felt sensation during our Reiki sessions but this one was particularly powerful. With the lingering of Patsy's hands on each chakra, my body felt as if it had traveled to another place. Once I grounded myself, I moved from the Reiki table to a nearby couch, anxious to hear Patsy's wisdom.

She extinguished the candles, turned on soft lights and joined me. "Tim spoke with me. He said he is with you always. I saw him and many floating orbs in the room."

I looked down at Tim's ever-present memorial card and ran my finger across his face. "But I want more than an orb and a voice in my head. Life is incredibly hard and painful despite his signs."

"Of course you miss him terribly. Try to understand, he completed his soul's path and purpose in this life which was to find divine love with you."

"Oh *great,* he gets to leave and I'm stuck here. What the hell do I have left to do for my soul's purpose?"

"We all have different life lessons. Tim will help you find yours and assist in your journey until you meet again. It'll be awhile though; you'll be old when you die. I see a part of your soul's path is to find joy and love again. You'll also help women in the future. This new relationship and healing work will come to you. It is your path. You do not need to seek."

Her predictions met with my closed mind. I was not ready for another love or changing careers. "But what if I don't want that?"

"You will come to both in your own time. The work with women will be through your grief. You will help yourself by being of service to others in mourning. You've had so much sorrow in your life."

"Yeah, I must've killed someone in a previous life."

Patsy chuckled, "Of course you didn't, but you and Timmy planned your life this way before you were born."

"We planned for me to lose seven babies and for him to die young? What were we smoking when we did that?"

Patsy laughed again. "I saw your unborn children. They are with Tim. Whenever souls come and go so fast, they are highly evolved and their message is quick. Your children's message in their short energy lives was to bring you and Tim closer. You, Tim and your children are all in the same soul group and will be reunited."

I had no clue what she meant by "soul group" or how we could have planned this life. My sarcasm and skeptical brain were in full flower. "Hey, what a great idea, losing our babies was to bring us closer through suffering."

"You and Tim developed a strong bond in your relationship through love and shared loss. Your soul mate path was to find divine, death transcending love and you both have done that. Your bond continues still, it is eternal."

As tears streamed down my face, I twirled Tim's wedding band on my middle finger, "It's true. Our losses could have divided us but brought us closer for sure."

"Oh, I almost forgot, I saw a wedding band and a bee or some sort of insect on the band but it didn't make sense to me." Shocked, I told her the wedding band/Timmy fly story from last October.

"Timmy certainly communicates well and finds unique ways to come to you!"

"Yes, he's quite creative isn't he?"

I put away my skeptical brain and allowed myself to accept Patsy's words. I looked up and said to Tim, *Make sure you keep those messages coming, my love!*

Patsy said she was late to meet her husband. She hugged me and rushed out the door before I had a chance to ask her anything else. I made a mental note to Google "soul group" and "before birth planning." They both sounded hokey to me.

SALVATION

30

At every crisis in one's life, it is absolute salvation to have some sympathetic friend to whom you can think aloud without restraint or misgiving.

— Woodrow Wilson

I n late February, I returned home after honoring Tim's birthday for the second time with my nursing school classmate, Judy at her vacation home on Useppa Island, Florida. I was somber but content having repeated our first year's ritual of releasing Tim's ashes and rose petals into the ocean at sunset.

As I was catching up on emails, I opened my hospital's newsletter to see what I'd missed while I was away. My eyes caught the word "widow" and I opened the link to "Community News" and a review of Syracuse University alumnus, Joyce Carol Oates' new memoir, *A Widow's Story*. At the end of the article, there was a recommended website: www.sslf.org. I clicked it and realized I hadn't found every possible Google link to grief and widowhood known to cyberspace.

This is really cool, I thought, as I read the home page: "Soaring Spirits Loss Foundation is a 501(c)3 non-profit organization that provides peer-based grief support programs worldwide. SSLF is an inclusive, non-denominational organization focused on hope and healing through the grieving process. We are positive, and forward thinking, while focusing on offering our members the tools and resources they need to rebuild their lives in the aftermath of the death of a loved one."

This is what I've been searching for, Boo!

The SSLF home page was organized by various links along the info bar at the top. What intrigued me initially were pictures of widows and widowers smiling and having a good time. Where the hell are these fun people? They look so young to be widowed.

Timmy's voice interrupted my thoughts, *News flash, Anne Marie!* *YOU are young.*

Oh right, thanks Babe!

I clicked on their online blog called "Widows Voice" where an author for SSLF writes their innermost feelings on an assigned day of the week. When I clicked on today's link, a lovely, careworn face stared back at me. The title of the blog post was "Tired." Yep, I know that face; I see it every time I look in the mirror.

As I read Kim Hamer's post describing all of the things she'd gotten tired of since her husband, Art died in April 2009, I thought to myself, I could have written this. I feel everything she is feeling! When I read the last words of her blog, "I'm tired, I am so, so, so fucking tired. So, honey? When are you coming back? 'Cause I'm tired of this shit!" I was thrilled to have found a kindred widow who uses my language to describe this hell we are living!

My next click was on their program called Widowed Village: "We offer live 24/7 chat, forums for deeper discussion, ways to find others close to your age, date of loss and geographical location…The village is a place for widowed people from all walks of life to find people who 'get' them."

Timmy, look at all of the different chat groups listed here! You choose groups based on what you have in common, like the year your love died, parent groups and look — widowed without children — so I'm not the only one, YEAH!

I continued exploring. What's this, a dating service? "SSLF's Widow Match Program will match you with another widowed person for one-on-one supportive e-mail correspondence. We will connect you with three other widowed people (widows are connected with widows, and widowers with widowers) who are within ten years of yourself in age, have lost their spouse or partner within six months of your loss, and who have the same parenting status as you do.

Wow Timmy, this is so cool. I'm gonna do it!

The last program cracked me up. *What the hell is "Camp Widow?" Do we go into the wilderness and cry around campfires?*

I read the description: "Camp Widow is a weekend-long gathering of widowed people from across the country, and around the world. We come together to create a community that understands the life altering experience of widowhood. Camp Widow provides practical tools, valuable resources, and peer-based encouragement for rebuilding your life in the aftermath of the death of a spouse or partner...all in a fun, uplifting, laughter filled atmosphere. Take a look at the photos, those smiles are real..."

So that's where those fun people's pictures came from! Count me IN! After I made my reservations and booked my flight for the first weekend in August, I embraced my urge to tackle something new. Here I come, San Diego! Can't wait to dive in head first to finally be with others who get me.

From that point forward, I started each day with the Widow's Voice blog, joined Widowed Village and their chat group, "widowed without children" and was connected with my perfect Widow Match.

In response to their match query, I'd been given three emails of widows; one never wrote back, another wrote once and said her life was very busy and she'd not be able to write that often. But my third match, Roseann, was the charm. We progressed quickly from emails to long phone calls and made plans to meet during the summer while I was at a medical conference near her hometown in New Jersey.

Boo, I found someone who really gets me. Did you send her? Don't worry; you're still my best girlfriend!

BEYOND ANY
REASONABLE DOUBT
31

*Be patient toward all that is unsolved in your heart
and try to love the questions themselves.*

—Rainer Maria Rilke

After Timmy communicated through Patsy, I felt the need to speak with him directly — even though I was still hearing him in my mind — but I shied away from having a psychic reading despite friends' encouragement. I trusted my gut along with my healthy dose of skepticism and speaking to a psychic didn't feel right.

Since this horror began, I'd spent countless hours Googling topics on grief and loss. Each search brought different resources that helped me better understand my feelings of craziness. One evening at the beginning of March, I found a blog called, "The Alchemy of Loss" by Abigail Carter, a widow who'd lost her husband in the September 11, 2001 terrorist attacks on the World Trade Center. Abby's wit and depth drew me in. I found myself reading her blogs past midnight.

When I was about to go to bed, I saw the word "psychic" and decided, okay, one more post. Abby told the story of a woman who came up to her in a restaurant and asked "Did your boyfriend or husband die recently?" The woman, named Lisa, explained she was a psychic and had a message from Abby's husband, Arron. This caught my attention.

Lisa accurately spoke about their life together and Arron's continuing love for Abby and their two children. A later blog described the ongoing relationship Abby had developed with Lisa where she delved into Arron's afterlife messages.

Intrigued, I Googled the psychic's name. When I saw Lisa Fox's smiling face framed by short auburn hair, I felt the now familiar, "confirmatory goose-bumps" sprout on my arms that told me I was on the right track.

This is cool Timmy! The auras, orbs and fox in our backyard were a message: YOU brought me to Lisa Fox. She is the one you will communicate through! And she is lovely and normal looking, not all freaky and spaced out like some other psychics photos I've seen on the Internet.

After several emails, Lisa and I confirmed a reading for March 10th on Skype. The skeptical me raised questions about not communicating in person but Lisa assured me the majority of her readings were done this way, "Spirit is everywhere, so distance and my mode of communication don't matter, Spirit will find us."

When I read that, I said to myself, it damn well better be Timmy's spirit who finds us because I'm not interested in talking to anybody else.

Our time finally arrived, but Lisa's Skype video feed wasn't working. She messaged me that sometimes the Internet on Vashon Island in Puget Sound was spotty so we'd use the telephone. Other than my first name and email, Lisa knew nothing about me.

She'd encouraged me to make a quiet space where we wouldn't be interrupted. I decorated the dining room table with several of my favorite pictures of Timmy, our wedding picture, all of the orb and aura pictures, his ashes, and the pennies and feathers he'd given me. I donned Tim's favorite multi-colored linen shirt and tied his well-worn green sweater around my shoulders. Satisfied I'd created an inviting atmosphere, with shaky fingers, I dialed the phone.

"Hi Lisa! I have you on speakerphone. Let me hit the start button on my digital recorder." I didn't say anything more. My skeptical self kept me silent, not wanting to give any leading information.

After a warm hello, I could hear Lisa take a deep breath. "A spirit has come through, a woman who is very important to you, she has a lot of mother energy, but she is your sister. She passed from cancer and there is another woman with her who passed from a female cancer."

I was blown away, "Yes, that's Camille, my half-sister, who was like a second mother to me. She died of leukemia and her mother died from breast cancer." (I'd made a deal with myself that if Lisa was correct, I would confirm, but I was reluctant to give any clues.)

"They are together saying hello. Often one spirit comes to bring another. I see male energy with them, your husband."

I had to squelch a sob. *My love, I'm so lost without you.*

Lisa laughed, "He is handing me a box of tissues for you and says, *Dry your eyes honey because I have a lot to say.*"

My sobs burst forth as I struggled to speak. Hearing Tim's words coming through another person felt strange. When Lisa spoke, I imagined his voice in my mind and responded with my thoughts first, like I usually do, before I replied aloud. *I miss you so much baby.*

Then Lisa continued as Timmy, speaking directly to me. *I'm here. Oh sweetie, I'm so sorry for your grief and your pain but I'm always with you.*

Baby, I know you are here at times but it's so horrible not to be able to see you and be with you.

Lisa commented, "What a lovely man. I can see he's a real sweetheart, very humble and self-effacing. He has a genuine heart, a heart of gold." It didn't dawn on me to ask if she could see him or how she knew that about him, but her description was accurate. "He wants you to know he has been around you, he comes to you and speaks to you on your left side."

Again I was shocked. *Yes Boo, I hear you in my left ear.*

"He passed of a multiple system breakdown. He is showing me that when he was in the hospital you were always there." Then Lisa went back to speaking as Tim, *Thank you for all you did to care for me and especially for the kisses on my forehead, they meant the world to me.*

Oh my God, you felt my kisses? My fingers traced my lips, yearning for more kisses.

Of course, and I heard every word and felt you holding my hand and touching my skin. You were amazing the way you took care of me. You must not be angry anymore about what happened with that doctor at the end.

My mind was jolted to the formal complaint I'd written about the neurologist who was so unprofessional, but I never filed it. I couldn't imagine appearing at a disciplinary hearing and keeping myself composed. Instead, I kept the anger bottled inside of me. *You know about that?*

Of course, I was there. I could hear every word. I loved the way you stood up for me but I was already past the point of no return. He was such an asshole to you and so fucking arrogant but it was my time. Please don't waste any more energy on him. Let go of your anger. You need to gather all of your energy for your own healing now.

This sounded so much like my Timmy that my skeptical self went out the window. *Baby, I'm doing all I can to heal but it's so incredibly hard, I miss you so much.* I began to sob again.

I miss you so much too, our hugs, our love, our friendship but we will be together again. Now you have to go on and be a part of life, your life.

I don't know how, it doesn't feel like a life, it feels like a half-life without you.

You are stronger than you know. You have many things left to do. I can't return. Our babies are with me and we will wait for you.

Our babies? I recalled what Patsy told me and now I was hearing it again.

Lisa added, "He is showing me that your pregnancies were very short but their souls are with him."

She went back to speaking as Tim. *Honey, they are beautiful. They helped me cross over. We'll be there to meet you when it's your time. But you won't be coming for a while. You'll be well into your 80s. Now you must live.*

I was shocked by another confirmation of what Patsy said about my old age. *It's hard to imagine living so many more years without you by my side.*

But I am by your side. I'll continue to speak to you and send messages. Trust your intuition.

So you are speaking in my brain and do you come to me in animals and orbs and leave me feathers and pennies?

Lisa took over, "Yes, Anne Marie, all of those signs are from Timmy and he can send other signs."

"Really, like what?"

Lisa explained, "Spirits can play with electrical devices."

How cool! Okay Boo, I want as many signs as possible, every day, all the time. Was that you who played the song "My Immortal" *on my computer?* I thought back to when I was sitting in his reading chair and that mournful song played spontaneously from my computer down the hall in our library.

"Yes, that was Tim; he often gives you messages through music, especially on the radio."

Boo, are you the Sirius Satellite radio DJ? When I'm driving, the perfect song often plays to fit my mood. It's really amazing, like you are singing those words to me!

Lisa said, "Music is one way spirits communicate. And he can do more. Do you want him to flicker the lights?"

Yes, please flicker away!

Lisa stopped for a moment, then said, "He's showing me around your house."

Boo, I'm trying so hard to keep up. The house is such a responsibility. I had you to do almost everything. You were like having a wife!

Lisa chuckled and said, "He's sorry you have so much to do and is pleased with what you are doing without him. But he's worried about a potential water leak problem."

"What do you mean?"

"I see a large snow and ice pack outside your front door and he is showing me gutters and a drainpipe."

Timmy started speaking again. *There's a potential leak in a cement wall in the basement, a leak in a basement pipe and a fluid line problem with your car.*

I was almost speechless. *Okay Timmy, I'll look in the basement but the water pipes to the outside are turned off and the ground is covered in snow. It's been a severe winter. I guess you know that. What do you mean by a problem with my car? It's a new car. I bought it last fall. Actually YOU bought it for me with some of your life insurance money. Thank you very much!*

I'm here to protect you and keep you safe. Maybe you ought to get a dog.

You were supposed to raise a dog when you retired but you died! I don't want to raise a dog alone and Lucca and Vivi would freak. Besides, how can a dog help me with all these potential leaks? My sarcasm felt good, like I was really talking to my Tim.

Then Lisa asked an odd question, "Who's Deanna?"

Confused, I said, "I don't know anyone named Deanna."

Lisa said, "You'll know in time," then continued, "I see your husband's heart is full of love for you. He knows you keep him in your heart."

"Does he see my heart locket with his ashes inside?" Tears streamed down my cheeks as I yearned for his physical presence rather than his ashes.

As I clutched my locket and wiped my face with Tim's handkerchief, Lisa said, "Yes, he loves the design and engraving."

Thank you for the wonderful memorial service, the music, your beautiful words and bringing David to town to read my favorite poem. Thank Joanie for the poem she wrote, it touched my heart.

If my eyebrows could have risen any higher, they would have been off my forehead. *You heard all of that? Oh yeah, you were right there in the coffin. I hadn't burned you yet.*

And sweetie, thank you for the gorgeous yellow roses and the red roses last year and white roses this year. Judy is a good friend.

I was practically wetting my pants as I explained to Lisa, "His funeral spray was yellow roses, and twice on Useppa Island, Florida my friend, Judy and I put rose petals into the Gulf of Mexico on his birthday; last year's were red and this year's were white."

Lisa chuckled and said, "He has another warning about a road trip. Be sure to take a friend because you can't drive with your hurt back."

You know I hurt my back again?

How am I supposed to protect you if you do things you're not supposed to do? I tried to tell you!

Oh right Timmy, I heard you telling me not to shovel the snow but I did it anyway. I should have listened. Thank you for trying.

Pas du tout, not at all. I laughed at him speaking French to me, then I realized why. *So when you go to Montreal, bring someone with you.*

Don't worry, Boo, I'm not going to drive. I can't believe you know about my trip to Canada. I'll be sure to tell Alex we talked. It'll be interesting to hear what she has to say reading my astrological chart again.

Trust your good friends and be careful of co-workers who pretend they are friends. Be watchful and at some point, you won't have to worry anymore about the annoying people at work. You're the bigger person. Just do your job and ignore those who don't understand.

I thought of the fox symbolism about staying in the background and detaching from my surroundings while observing with my senses. *Yes, the sympathy about your death has ended. The women at work think I should move on. I thought I'd get at least a year, but their patience waned at about six months. Thanks Boo, I'll heed your advice.*

Lisa continued, "You have so many gifts to share with other women, someday you'll work with grieving women and it will help you heal. You'll not be alone the rest of your life. You'll find love again, but not now, you're not ready."

I grabbed Tim's photo and held it directly in front of me, shaking it for emphasis as I spoke. *I am so NOT ready! I love YOU! I can't betray you, Timmy.*

It's not a betrayal. It's in your soul's journey to find joy and love again. I can't come back and you are in the physical world. You need to grieve and heal then come out of the dark into the light. Don't worry, I will always be with you.

I grabbed Tim's photo and held it directly in front of me, shaking it for emphasis as I spoke. *I am so NOT ready! I love YOU! I can't betray you, Timmy.*

Lisa continued describing the life we shared and how much Tim misses our dancing, music, cooking and our physical bond. He told her about a black cocktail dress he loved on me. *Don't ever forget how hot you are, baby!*

I laughed through my tears. Then my heart sank. *Oh no, do you have to leave?* I pressed his picture to my heart as if that would somehow keep him here.

"Yes, it's time for him to go but here's a bit more from him," Lisa said as she returned to speaking as Tim, *Trust your intuition baby. Listen and know it's me when you feel chills on your left side. Be alert for signs, especially birds. I'll continue to watch over you as a hawk. When you see an orb, know it's me, and other spirits who will help guide your way. Remember, I am always with you.*

My skeptical self, still hanging around, was astonished. I hadn't specifically mentioned hawks so Lisa could not have known. She and I spoke a little longer, and then she thanked me for the privilege of reading for us. She said I could email if I had questions but suggested I let everything sink in first.

I sat frozen then looked down to Lucca and Vivi who'd climbed onto my lap halfway through, "Daddy was here and I am blown away."

That night, as I relished a long hot shower with water pulsing onto my hungry-for-Timmy skin, the bathroom lights flickered continually. *Thank you, Boo. Your spirit light shines through my soul.*

I felt content with all I'd been told until Tim's disastrous news bulletins started to break.

REVELATIONS

32

The events in our lives happen in a sequence in time, but in their significance to ourselves they find their own order, it is the continuous thread of revelation.

— Eudora Welty

Two weeks later, I arrived in Montreal to see my astrologer friend, Alex, who was there for part of her medical school residency. After dinner, I recounted my mind-boggling psychic reading.

Alex was unfazed. "Lisa confirmed some of what I'd read in your chart and added what Timmy wants you to know. He's protecting you. But you must live your own life now."

"I AM living my own life, what choice do I have? I'm working and traveling and living, sort of. Most of the time, I just feel empty."

"I know it's hard. Let's see what else I can tell you." With furrowed brow and taut lips, Alex studied her thick, worn astrology handbook.

Noticing her expression, I nervously asked, "Oh no, Alex, is it that bad?"

She lifted her head, pushed her blonde locks away from her face, and smiled, "No, Anne Marie, but you have challenges ahead. You'll leave your job and your boss will leave as well — he'll retire."

"What? You must be wrong. I have to work. I'm only 56. I can't stand the cliquey women in my office suite, but I love my job, my patients and my boss. And you're wrong about his retiring. Other than his family, healthcare practice is his life. He won't stop working until he dies. Oops, he's not gonna die is he?"

"No, but he's definitely going to retire."

"But how is his life in *my* chart?"

"It's not. You told me his birthday when I was working with you and so I read his chart. I wasn't sure how your charts would mesh but they do. You'll continue to work together, but each of you will do something different as your paths move in other directions. I see pain in your workplace until you leave. Those women don't understand you. After you're free, you'll be in service to women in grief who'll help you on your journey as well."

I was confused. Leaving my job, even though it was inviting, was frightening. And helping other people in grief seemed impossible because I felt so mired in my own.

"I can't seem to get away from grief. Patsy, Lisa and now *you* are telling me this is my path."

"You'll have joy again too. For now, you've got a few more struggles."

"Well isn't that just freaking great? Pour me some more wine — I may as well stay drunk if I've got more hell to deal with."

After I returned home, I contemplated the last three months with almost identical predictions from my Reiki master, psychic and astrologer. I was bewildered with all of this news about where my life was headed. It seemed so bleak without Tim.

I tried to put everything in perspective as my skeptical self wrestled with my intuitive self. I had to keep my day-to-day reality in the forefront. Grief, work and basic survival were so exhausting; I couldn't allow anticipation about an unknown future to overwhelm me.

NOW YOU
SEE IT
33

*Sometimes you never know
the value of something, until it becomes a
memory.*

— Dr. Seuss

Spring began slowly in Syracuse and the snowmelt turned into drizzly ice with cold, unrelenting April rain. Easter was cool but finally brought some sun.

I always dressed up for Sunday Gatherings at The Spring — a habit of my Catholic upbringing — and Easter traditionally called for a new outfit. I donned a stylish pale-red seersucker suit that I'd grabbed off a designer rack at my favorite outlet store.

Getting ready to leave, Timmy's voice said, *choose a tie*. I wasn't in the habit of the Annie Hall look but decided to go with it. After searching through his rack of hundreds of silk ties we'd carefully chosen over the years, I decided on his Hermes "lovebird tie" with kissing birds and red hearts suspended over their heads. Uh-oh, problem, how do I do the knot? Frustrated after a few clumsy attempts, I threw it back and ran out, afraid of being more than my usual five minutes late.

In the car, I apologized. *Hope you're not pissed at me Boo, you shoulda' taught me how to tie the damn thing before you DIED on me!* I still couldn't wrap my skeptical brain around the concept that he'd "transitioned."

Two days later, as I was about to get into the shower, Timmy told me to go look at his lovebird tie. I walked into our dressing room and searched the rack to no avail. I panicked. *Help Boo, I can't find it!* In the next second, I found it buried in back of several others. This was certainly not where I'd left it.

I grabbed it and held it to my pounding heart, happy to be found. Why did it mean so much?

What now, Boo?

Silence.

I carefully studied its colors and pattern, remembering how he always wore it when he performed weddings. I thought maybe he wanted me to look up 'tie symbolism,' if there was such a thing.

Then I remembered, just before we hung up Lisa said Tim told her we were real lovebirds. Maybe that was why he was showing me the tie.

Thank you, Boo. You will always be my lovebird. I kissed it and carefully placed it front and center on the rack.

As usual, I was running late. I hurried into the shower and quickly washed my hair. When I opened my eyes after rinsing, I noticed an image on the shower door. Looking more closely, I saw a heart through the hot water mist. I rubbed the glass with my finger but the image didn't go away, it was on the opposite side of the door.

I got out of the shower and stared at what looked vaguely familiar. It dawned on me that this heart was a replica of the one on Tim's lovebird tie. *Oh my freaking God, Timmy, you drew me a heart!* I shrieked at the top of my lungs as Lucca and Vivi jumped off their perch on the toilet seat and dashed past their crazed mother!

April 26, 2011... Timmy's Shower Door Heart...how did he draw it without fingers? Only Spirit knows for sure ☺!

I grabbed my camera and took several pictures. Ah-duh, Anne Marie, you can't take a picture of glass without the flash going off! I found a blue piece of paper, put it behind the door, and snapped a decent photo.

The heart only appeared when hot water steamed up the bathroom. Needing credible witnesses, my ever-skeptical self invited my Reiki Master Patsy, Qi Gong Healer and Yogini Katrin, chiropractor Sandi and massage therapist Amy to see the heart "miracle." They all were amazed.

I also showed our house cleaner, Joanie, and asked her to never wash that corner of the shower door again. It remained intact for three months, until Joanie came to me in tears.

"Anne Marie, I'm so sorry, I was cleaning the bathtub and absent-mindedly wiped the shower door. I think the heart is gone."

After the steamed up bathroom revealed our fears, I said, "It's okay Joanie, everything in life is impermanent." I had to learn to let go yet again.

The evening of the shower door transgression, I was making dinner and couldn't open a jar. *Damn you, Timmy, where are you when I need you?*

I looked for our rubber jar grip and remembered I'd left it at the lake cottage. Do I have to hire a freaking handy man to open my jars?

Keep looking, Timmy said.

Looking for what, Boo?

I rifled through our utensil drawer and found a red rubber jar grip in the back. Odd, I'd never seen it before and I'd stocked this drawer sixteen years ago when we moved here. (See how often I clean out my drawers?) I stepped back and looked at the grip more carefully.

OMG Timmy, this thing is red and heart shaped! Did you put it there for me so I had another heart after Joanie destroyed yours today? This is too freaking weird. I'm ready for the loony bin but until someone hauls me away, I'm sticking with my story.

I placed Timmy's newest "sign" near his picture on the kitchen counter, never to be used again.

WATER, WATER EVERYWHERE

34

Heavy rains remind us of challenges in life.
Never ask for a lighter rain.
Instead pray for a better umbrella.

— Sebastiano Serafini

The harsh winter was followed by weeks of dreary cool rain. Finally, the unrelenting spring showers stopped on May 10th with 75-degree temperatures and bright sunshine.

In the last month, I'd noticed rainwater sheeting straight down from the roof instead of flowing through the gutters. I assumed the heavy snow and hanging icicles had pulled the gutters away from the roof edge. I called my handyman to inspect the eaves troughs, but it was too dangerous to climb onto the wet, slippery roof. Now with this break in the weather, he said he'd be there at 10:00am.

My mother and brother, Bill were visiting for a few days to celebrate my mom's birthday. While they finished breakfast, I did my stretching routine in our basement workout area. I heard the doorbell ring; the handyman had arrived. On my way upstairs to greet him, I noticed a brown smudge on the carpet near the wall where the cat-run is suspended.

"Lucca, Vivi, did one you have an accident when you were chasing each other up and down the wall?"

I grabbed a cloth and knelt down to wipe up the spot. When I stood up, my knees were wet. I leaned over and touched the carpet; it was soaked. My face became ashen as I thought back to Timmy's prediction about the gutters and potential leak in a concrete wall in the basement.

Holy freaking hell, Timmy! This basement wall is a concrete retaining wall and the gutters are on this side of the house. It's been raining almost non-stop and on top of the ice and snowmelt, the soil is saturated. Ground water seeped into the basement through the wall. I spoke out loud in anger, "So why the hell didn't you STOP it for Christ's sake if you knew it was going to happen! I thought you were going to protect me!"

"Who are you taking to?" my brother yelled down the stairs.

"Just cursing my crappy luck!" I said as I started sopping up the water with towels. (I hadn't yet revealed my psychic reading to anyone in my family.) *Damn Timmy, do these walls have ears?*

An hour later, after my brother helped me set up floor fans to dry the carpet, I asked, "Hey bro, as long as you're down here, can you turn on the water to the outside faucet? It's hard for me to reach in the ceiling. Timmy always did it. Now that it's warm, I want to set up the birdbaths."

Bill reached up through an open space in a ceiling tile and turned the valve in the pipe. "Geesh Annie, this pipe is leaking water all over. Did it leak last year?"

I swallowed hard as I remembered Timmy's other warning about a pipe leak in the basement.

Okay Boo, this is freaking me out, what else did you say? I've got to listen to the recording again to make sure the house isn't going to fall down!

Two weeks and a few thousand dollars later, after the basement waterproofing project was done and the gutters were repaired, I asked Timmy, *If you can predict the future, would you please tell me the next winning lottery numbers?*

DO YOU BELIEVE IN MIRACLES?

35

*There are only two ways
to live your life. One is as though
nothing is a miracle.
The other is as though
everything is a miracle.*

— Albert Einstein

Four days after an enjoyable time with my mom and brother, I attended a much-anticipated event with my "other family" from The Spring. *Journey Through the Seasons of the Soul*, a woman's retreat was held at Patsy's beautiful contemporary home in the middle of the woods.

We started with a reading from *Women Who Run With The Wolves* by Clarissa Pinkola Estes, then a guided meditation followed by journaling. Unfortunately, the weather reverted to cool showers so our nature walk was postponed.

After a lunch of vegetarian chili, cornbread and fruit, the rain stopped. All fifteen brave souls ventured outside to continue our journaling. My rain poncho nearby, I sat at a picnic table with a view of a cascading waterfall. As I was writing a passionate note to Timmy, a bright ray of sunshine broke through the clouds and shone directly on his ever-present memorial card that I'd placed on the table. I thanked him for the sunshine and allowed the rays to warm my face.

Look at the sun on the card, Timmy told me.

Okay Boo, whatever you say.

His handsome face was beaming at me from the front of the card and when I turned it over to the sunset picture and Leonard Cohen poem, I noticed a small dark spot inside the setting sun. I brushed the laminated card with my fingers, thinking something from the waterlogged picnic table had adhered to the surface. The spot was still there. I picked at it with my fingernail but the dark image remained.

My intuitive mind sprung into action. *It's Timmy! He's showing me he's in the sun, he's in the light!*

I let out a whoo-hoo shriek and retreat members gathered around me. "Look, this spot was not there before the sun's rays just shone down on it."

A close up of the two cards: "A spot of Tim" in the sun on bottom and not on the top.

I got my purse and pulled out another laminated memorial card. (I have about 20 cards displayed all over our house and keep one in my car, one in my purse, and one always with me.) I compared the two cards.

"Look everyone, there's no spot on the other card. This sunspot is Timmy!" I didn't hold back, I was in a safe place with like-minded people.

Each of the women looked at the card and tried to brush off the spot. Patsy came forth with her wisdom, "Timmy is definitely showing you he is now in the sun. He lights the way for you and all of us to shine our own light in this life until we meet in spirit."

I felt great comfort in her words. "Another miracle, Patsy."

She nodded, having seen the shower door heart and now this impossible image imbedded within a laminated card with no opening except for Tim's sign of love and light to guide us.

With each new sign and "miracle," I longed for more. They were like crystal meth to a junkie. Every hit left me hungry for my next fix. Alex warned me Timmy's signs would diminish over time as his spirit had things to do on his own path, but I selfishly implored him to stay with me awhile longer.

Timmy, you've got eternity to do whatever the hell your spirit has to do but I need you to keep coming until I get a few more human years of grieving and healing under my belt. Is that so much to ask?

He didn't disappoint. Hawk sightings, pennies in purses and coat pockets continued into the summer along with a new bird that kept appearing day after day, flying low over my backyard. When I looked up its symbolism, I felt hopeful: "According to North American Native tradition, the Great Blue Heron brings messages of self-determination and self-reliance. It represents an ability to progress and evolve and reflects your need to follow your own unique wisdom and path. You know what is best and need to follow your heart rather than the promptings of others. When you choose to follow the promptings of your heart, you soar with magnificence" (www.blueheronenv.com/meaning).

After our next Reiki session, I asked Patsy, "With this new bird sighting, is the fox no longer my power animal for this year?"

"Stay with the wisdom of the fox to use your instincts for observation and add the heron, each one comes when needed, both can help you. Of course, your hawk is always with you."

And for what I was about to encounter, I needed all the power animals I could get.

SURREAL SUMMER SOLSTICE

36

Sunset in the ethereal waves:
I cannot tell if the day
is ending, or the world, or if the secret of
secrets is inside me again.

—Anna Akhmatova

A strange noise emanated from the back of my ten-month-old car. I tried to ignore it, but after two weeks, I relented and took the car to the dealer. When I was told I needed a new fuel pump, I sighed — yet another prediction had come true.

Okay Timmy, is this the last of it or do I need to call Lisa to find out what else is going to go wrong?

I cringed when I heard that the part had to be ordered. I hated to leave my beloved, sleek black Volkswagen Tiguan overnight because I felt safe in Timmy's afterlife gift.

As I climbed into the dealer's loaner Jeep, I had a deep sense of unease. I tried to calm myself, "It must be that you're not used to driving this kind of car." Still, all the way home, my gut was churning. To add to my apprehension, that evening I planned to attend a Summer Solstice celebration with Dave, my friend from The Spring and now I'd have to drive this clunky car.

The Summer Solstice was Tim's and my favorite pagan holiday. We watched the longest day of the year's sunrise and sunset from wherever we were in the world. But this year, the cherished ritual was not to be; thunderstorms rolled in just before sunrise and then again as I was leaving for the event that evening. I waited for a break in the rain and pulled out of the driveway.

Boo, I hate this damn car and these freaking storms and why the hell am I going out tonight? Since my eye surgery, my night vision sucks! Will you be my eyes?

Driving down the hill a block away from home, I noticed a small dog near a mailbox at the side of the road. I'd never seen a dog at that house before and wondered what it was doing there. I heard a thump and the car jolted. *NO!* I shrieked as I looked in my rearview mirror at the crumpled body of the dog in the middle of the road. I pulled over, jumped out and screamed, *NO, NO, NO! I hate this car! Timmy, HELP me!*

A man ran from a house across the street and scooped the limp dog in his arms. "I'm so sorry, Diego. I shouldn't have let you out."

I ran up the hill, crying hysterically. "I'm so sorry. He was by a mailbox and then he disappeared. He must have run under the car. I'm never out at this hour and didn't want to leave, I *knew* something bad was going to happen with this loaner car. I'm so, so sorry!" I was making no sense as the man tried to calm me.

"It's my fault. He doesn't go out but I let him this one time because he was scratching at the door and begging to go."

"My name is Anne Marie. I live on the street up the hill. Please, let me help you in some way."

"I'm Carlos. It's okay, really. It must have been his time. My sister died a year ago today and Diego was her dog. I think she must have needed him in heaven with her."

My head was reeling. "Oh my God, I'm so sorry for your loss and now this sweet dog. I know about loss; my husband died 19 months ago."

"Oh how terrible for you. But Anne Marie, it's okay; Deanna is happy now that Diego is with her."

My heart skipped a beat when I heard his sister's name, remembering my psychic reading when Lisa asked, "Who's Deanna?"

The rain began again. Carlos and I hugged then I kissed sweet Diego good-bye and reluctantly drove to the Solstice event. I knew if I went home, I wouldn't be able to function.

Still shaken when I arrived, I told Dave what happened and he said, "Let's talk with my wise friend and Reiki master, Ellen before the ceremony starts. She's in her office finishing a Reiki session. She'll help you."

After I described the events with tears streaming down my face, Ellen gently placed her hands on my shoulders. "Anne Marie, Native American folk lore tells that when an animal is needed in the spirit world, it chooses a human to help it on its way. It's a high honor to be chosen. Deanna had no way to get her dog without your help. You've been given a gift. You must be very close to the animal world."

Her words were soothing but I still felt traumatized. She gave me a Reiki healing that calmed me somewhat. I pushed away visions of Diego in the road and tried to steady myself as we walked into a large, candle lit room where about twenty people were sitting cross-legged in a circle. I found an empty floor pillow and joined them.

The Solstice ceremony began with music and chanting. A woman in a long flowing robe read tributes to the sun and summer season. She introduced herself as a Shamanic Priestess and stood before each person to give a blessing. When she placed her hands on my head she said, "You have a powerful spirit standing behind you. You are very well protected. You are a light bearer who will give to this world. Do not resist. This is a change point in your life. Let it come."

I was totally taken aback and thought, yeah, I'm protected but poor Diego wasn't.

After the ceremony, Ellen stopped me on the way out and said, "Anne Marie, you must believe you were chosen and the dog is where he needs to be. Accept your gift and know all is well; you have much to do."

As I got into that dreaded car I said to myself, *What the hell is a light-bearer? I don't feel light; I feel dark and sad.*

I arrived home, poured a glass of wine and wrote a note to Carlos explaining what I'd been told by Ellen. Despite their reassurances, I apologized to him again for taking Diego's life. I cried myself to sleep as thunder and lightning cut through the night.

The next morning, I put on my raincoat for another impending storm and walked to Carlos' house to put my note and some flowers in his mailbox. As I turned the corner and began walking up the hill with another flower to mark the spot where Diego was hit, I could see something in the road. I gasped when I saw a small white and brown feather. It was curved slightly and looked like an underbelly feather. The road was wet from the all-night storm but the feather was fluffy and dry.

I knelt down, examined it more carefully and exclaimed, *Timmy, it looks like a hawk feather!*

Timmy's voice was as clear as if he was standing next to me, *Yes, my love, thank you. Deanna is happy and I get to play with her dog!*

I picked up the feather and smiled. *Okay Timmy, just don't get any ideas that you need to play with our cats!*

A few months later, when I showed this feather to a wild bird handler, she confirmed it was an underbelly feather from a hawk.

HOPE AND HEALING

37

Compassion is not a relationship between the healer and the wounded.
It is a relationship between equals.
Only when we know our own darkness well can we be present to the darkness of others.
Compassion becomes real when we recognize our shared humanity.

— Pema Chodron

On Friday, August 5th, I stepped onto my hotel balcony in San Diego and breathed deeply to center myself for my first Camp Widow experience. I hoped this wouldn't be a recreation of the other bereavement bust where I'd become the group shrink.

Unpacking, I turned on the TV and saw a funeral in progress. I hurriedly switched channels to where two children were talking. That looked tame. I continued hanging clothes, then heard one of the children say, "You're in your personal heaven, Susie."

WTF is this? I asked myself as I watched the happy children twirling around in a surreal otherworldly scene. I clicked on the TV info bar. It was *The Lovely Bones*, a movie about a child who'd been murdered.

Timmy, this is freaking me out! Why the hell am I being reminded of death? I do NOT need this!

I shut off the TV, grabbed my purse and found myself crying at the elevator. My practical self talked my Sicilian superstitious self down. You need to get a grip. You'll be okay. This is not a bad omen. Maybe it's a metaphor. I relied on my fallback coping mechanism and channeled Scarlet O'Hara, "I can't think about that right now. If I do, I'll go crazy. I'll think about that tomorrow."

I walked to the Camp registration desk with trepidation. I'm not sure what I was afraid of but those feelings melted when I saw Dan Cano's face, just as he appeared on the website, with a long brush cut and dark, expressive eyes. "Dan, you're real! I love reading your blogs on Widows Voice!"

Dan laughed and patted his 'Death Sucks' T-shirt. "Yeah, I think I'm real. Last time I checked I was, anyway!"

"It's wonderful to meet someone I spend so much time with, so to speak. I'm Anne Marie."

"It's good to meet you, Anne Marie, even though we belong to a club we never wanted to join."

"You got that right, Dano!"

I thought back to the first time I read Dan's post about the devastation of losing his husband. I was impressed that Widow's Voice had a gay man writing about his experience as well as an African American woman married to a Caucasian man. This is certainly an inclusive, non-discriminatory group...my kind of peeps!

Then Michele Neff-Hernandez, founder and director of Soaring Spirits Loss Foundation (SSLF) walked by, deep in conversation with a hotel manager. I got my registration packet, nametag and goody bag, then followed her and waited until she ended the conversation.

While waiting, I carefully added a "One Year" ribbon to the bottom of my nametag. I was amazed to see a box of colorful ribbons with various time spans representing how long we'd been widowed. One year was yellow, two years was blue and so on up to ten years; they even had a 0-6 months and 6 months-one year.

Wow, they think of everything, don't they, Boo? Even though it's closer to two years, I'm in no hurry to claim that label until it's official in three months. And then I'll be wishfully thinking backwards about ten years. Oh well, time waits for no one.

I thought back to when Michele and I had spoken last month. I was amazed that she answered her phone, was available to answer questions about Camp, and listen to my story. I recently learned that after three years as a non-profit organization, Michele became the only paid staffer of Soaring Spirits. All the other people involved with Widow's Voice, Widowed Village and Camp Widow were volunteers.

"Hi Michele, I'm Anne Marie..."

"Oh you're Timmy's Anne Marie. It's wonderful to meet you!"

With raised eyebrows, I asked, "How could you possibly remember me?"

"Because I enjoyed our conversation and I *love* your tribute tile; we all cried when we read it."

"Oh I didn't check my bag for Timmy's tile. I saw you and wanted to thank you."

Michele's shoulder-length auburn hair framed her oval face, which was lit up by a bright smile. Her eyes transfixed me as if her words were coming directly through them from a place of compassion and intelligence. We hugged then with a smile and wave, Michele was whisked away by another staffer.

I glanced back at the registration area that had become filled with hundreds of people. OMG! Everyone here is widowed, how is that possible? How can so many people be in one place grieving the loss of their loves? And many are much younger than me.

I spied a sign for Widowed Village. Curious about my online support community, I crossed the lobby to see what "Widville" offered. I leaned over the booth and a tall spectacled woman jumped up, hands filled with brochures. "Whoops, I didn't see you there. Did I startle you?"

"No, I'm okay. Are you Supa?" Her intense brown eyes took me in. (If you haven't figured it out yet, I'm an "eye" person.)

"Yes it is I, Supa Dupa. And who are you, lovely lady?"

"I'm Anne Marie…"

"Oh you're the funny lady who calls herself *Vedova* (*Vay-do-va*). I couldn't stop chuckling after we spoke about setting up your online chat page."

"Yes Supa, thanks again. I'm good at screwing up things on the computer."

She smiled, "I've told many friends about your preference for the Italian word for widow. Did I pronounce it correctly?"

"Yes you did. Vedova sounds sexier and believe me, anything that has to do with sex is something I could use right now!"

Robin Moore Lasky, aka "Supa Dupa" and founder of Widowed Village, laughed and said, "That's a subject we *all* agree on!"

She was busy with the pre-conference set-up, but before she turned away, Supa pointed to her right and said, "There's the tribute tile wall, Anne Marie. I know you have a handsome husband to show the world."

I walked over to the six-foot tall, rectangular wood-framed display board with several photos already in place. It was double-sided and joined in the center, like an open book. I sighed and thought, "There are so many stories are in these faces." The perfect header, "Well Loved" stretched across the top of the display.

As I carefully took off the bubble wrap from Tim's 4x4 inch square laminated tile, I thought about when I took his picture in our backyard. He'd just sat down after manning the grill, pleased with the progress of his tenderloin roast. I held the tile in my hands and stared at his smiling face gazing back, wine glass in hand, a bright future yet to be revealed, or so we thought.

The fourteen allotted words I chose in his honor came easily when I wrote up the tile order. But when I read them printed on his picture, I was taken aback: *My Love, My Heart, My Soul, My Spirit, My Inspiration, My Beauty, My All.*

That's it? That's all that remains? It's as if this tile makes your death real. It's been 20 months and 29 days since you died. I've lived day in and out with your death but somehow this solidifies that reality.

Hands shaking, I reached up to place his tile amongst the others on the memorial wall and broke into deep sobs. Supa rushed to my side and held me tight. As I melted into another widowed person's chest, it was the first time since Tim's death I felt truly understood.

My initial workshop was called, "Write It Out." I'd long been interested in writing something more than a daily journal but never took the time with my nursing career and fulfilling marriage.

Our first exercise was to write a Six Word Memoir. The instructor, a thin, attractive blond widow of ten years, said that according to literary legend, when Ernest Hemingway was challenged to write a story in six words, he responded: "For sale: baby shoes, never worn."

The words jolted my heart and ripped open another wound from the past. Why do I need to be reminded of our babies here, isn't it enough to grieve my husband? I looked at the fourteen other widows and one widower in the silent room; most were also visibly shaken. I thought, every one of us has a unique story of loss; there is so much pain here. And yet, we were there to share our sorrow and, hopefully, add to our healing.

With tears streaming down my face, six words emerged from my pen, "Red Shoes, Well Worn, for Keeping."

I thought back to ten years ago when Tim, after admiring red leather loafers of an Italian friend, ordered a pair from Lee-Kee shoemakers in Hong Kong because Tim's size 14AAA feet were difficult to fit. When told to trace his foot on a piece of paper for sizing, we joked that the Chinese would think Tim was the jolly green giant because his foot took up the entire length of a yellow legal pad.

We cracked up at the name of the company but his red shoes arrived intact, fit perfectly and were quite elegant. Tim put them on and played a disco CD while we danced around the house. These became Tim's official dancing shoes and got a lot of use at home, at weddings, out to nightclubs, and wherever our dancing tootsies took us.

My mind fast-forwarded to the last time Tim wore his red dancing shoes in his full-body casket at his funeral before I took them off for safe-keeping from the oblivion of cremation. I always hated seeing half a body sticking out from beneath a partially opened casket covered in flowers. Eric, the funeral director told me full body caskets were common in the South but he'd never seen one. No matter, Eric filled my "tall order" and Tim's beautiful 6 foot, 3 inch body was fully shown in his dark blue linen blazer; yellow, green, red and blue swirled silk tie; mustard-colored silk slacks and red dancing shoes. The colors were a rich blend that behooved my Tim's eclectic fashion style.

When my mind returned to reality, I sighed, *God how I miss dancing with you Boo. My body feels so deprived from your touch and our fluid motion. This just really sucks.*

That evening on my way into the Welcome Reception, I noticed a handsome blond man, just outside the door, beer in hand, looking off into the distance.

"Chris, is that you? I love how you write about your wife in Widow's Voice. My name is Anne Marie and my husband Tim was also my soul mate. New Year's is my worst holiday now, too." I'd remembered Chris' heart wrenching blog describing his first New Years without Maggie.

Chris smiled and acknowledged my compliment. We both drifted to our own thoughts as cherished personal memories flooded in, then I returned to the moment and asked, "Are you coming inside?"

"Eventually," Chris said with a far away look in his eye. "I'm not into meeting a lot of people right now."

But at one o'clock in the morning, Chris, Nikki, Cassie, Roy, Kay and myself, all "first-time campers" were still in the bar sharing stories and forming bonds of friendship through our sorrows. "My Maggie was only 33 when she died from colon cancer. My Mike died from a disease called sarcoidosis; he was only 38. My Dave died six days after contracting an infection that attacked his heart; he'd just turned 36. My Cheryl was 34; her trachea was scarred from a childhood illness and she stopped breathing. Soon after his 44th birthday, my Joe drowned when his car skidded on ice and went into a lake."

Each story had its own horror and aftermath of devastation. And so, the weekend continued for more than 250 brave widowed souls who opened their wounds, their hearts and trusted enough to share our stories in the club not of our choosing.

On Saturday morning, when Michele Neff Hernandez stood at the podium for her keynote address, I was in the front row beaming a smile even Timmy could see. Being amongst so many grieving widowed people helped me realize I was not alone.

Tears replaced my smile as Michele told how on August 31, 2005, an inattentive driver took her 39 year-old husband Phil's life on his evening bike ride despite his helmet and strict adherence to bike safety. Unable to find many other young widowed people to relate to, she started Soaring Spirits Loss Foundation in 2008 and Camp Widow in 2009 as a way to connect and heal, finding hope through sharing our journeys of grief.

I drifted back to when I whispered the word *Hope* to my white stone at The Spring's New Year's ceremony. It was a word I dare not say aloud, fearing it would never exist in my life again. And yet, here was Michele saying it loud and clear, declaring Hope to be a beacon for us to believe in, even through the devastation of our losses.

Michele encouraged us to find our own "voice" after our loss of the "unified voice" shared as a couple. She recounted her own story as a young widow and the slow process of rebirth that occurs as you discover who you are without your beloved.

And then Michele pointed to the large screen behind her, "Here are some amazing, brave widows and widowers who are learning to find their unique new voice. Join us on this road to finding your new voice. We will be right by your side."

As the title *Standing Up, Giving Widowhood a New Voice* flashed on the screen and the song "Stand Up" by the group Sugarland played, I watched pictures flash before my eyes: a widow holding a children's book she'd written; a widower with his two young children: one on his back and another in his arms; a widow proudly holding an Emmy; another with his new puppy; a woman on her wedding day with a newly blended family; another with her newborn baby; another scuba diving with a shark nearby; another getting a tattoo, and on and on and on (Camp Widow "Stand Up" 2011 Video: *http://www.youtube.com/watch?v=E9sDqT3QWoc*).

As the pictures scrolled and the beat of the music played, a newfound feeling of anticipation for the future emerged from my soul. Through this slice of hell called widowhood, I realized I might be on my way to finding my new voice.

Michele invited all of us to move into the center of the room for a group picture. Here I was amongst smiling faces like I saw on the SSLF website. Yes, I said to myself, those smiles are truly real.

Then our group of men and women from 43 states, Canada and one from the United

Kingdom dispersed to workshops tailored to meet various needs from single parenting to finances to dating to moving forward — whatever that meant — I was still figuring it out.

After a long, emotional day, I found myself in my hotel room looking in the mirror at a woman in a fitted, black cocktail dress. As I admired her body and curves I said aloud, "Are you really a widow? Is this happening, or is this a dream?" I shook my head, resigned to my reality and focused on Tim.

Do you like my new dress? Do you freaking believe I'm at a conference filled with widows and widowers who honestly care about me, about us, and all we've been through?

As I walked out the door on the way to the evening's semi-formal dinner banquet, I look backed briefly and a tear escaped my eye as I thought of our hotel room departure ritual. The very first time we left a hotel room, and God knows where and when that was, Tim grabbed me and kissed me deeply.

"Wow, that's a nice way to make an exit," I declared as I pushed my body into his.

"Just making sure our good-byes are as luscious as our hellos!"

On Sunday morning, after another late night of stories and too much wine, I rose at six for the Third Annual 5K Widow Dash to honor our loves. I used to be a runner but after my neck surgery, pounding the pavement was not in the cards, so I walked fast and enjoyed the early morning light. As I crossed the finish line, high fives and smiling faces of widows and widowers greeted me; faces that have seen deep love and immense loss. Faces I never would have known had I not clicked on www.sslf.org.

After a quick shower and suitcase pack, cursing the fact that I had to leave to catch my flight home, I hurried to the farewell breakfast and arrived in time to hear Michele's closing remarks. "Take us home to be with you on your journey and always remember, you are not alone."

With a flurry of final hugs, business cards exchanged, promises to keep in touch and one last good-bye wave, I climbed into the taxi back to my life.

When I asked the US Air attendant to repeat her words, "I'm sorry but your flight has been canceled due to engine trouble; there are no other flights to get you to your destination today. We'll give you a $500 voucher and put you on a different flight home tomorrow," my whoo-hoo fist in the air gesture was greeted with frowns from frustrated passengers in line behind me.

After booking my new flight and reserving the same hotel room I'd just vacated, I grabbed a cab back to the hotel. As I sauntered into the ongoing farewell breakfast, Abigail Carter walked up to me smiling and said, "I thought you'd left."

"Yeah, I did, but Timmy broke the plane. He knew I didn't want to leave."

Each person to whom I told my story *got it*. Widowed people love hearing stories that a loved one had an active role in changing their future. And I got another day to wind down, spend time with new friends, and thank Tim for his gift.

The next day on my flight home, I wistfully looked through my SSLF goody bag filled with handouts and keepsakes. As I reread my notebook, I added bits of memories in the margins and listed my favorite moments. The list grew long and I chided myself for its seemingly limitless boundaries.

"Okay, Anne Marie, come on, you know what you loved best," my logical, orderly brain insisted. "Do I have to come up with the best thing? How about two things?" my indecisive, widow brain argued.

I'd learned the words "widow brain" at Camp. I never knew there was a name for it but we all claimed varying degrees of its forgetfulness, distraction and inability to focus with the fog of grief gripping our grey matter.

"Having lunch with Abigail Carter, talking about my psychic reading with Lisa Fox and showing her my orb pictures--that was memorable. And more exciting was her invitation to come to Seattle sometime!" Then a broad smile lit up my face. "Dancing after the Saturday night semi-formal banquet was my best memory of the weekend."

I drifted back. The festivities started with a cocktail hour and hysterical photo booth with props, followed by dinner and group pictures of "widdas" in our beautiful dresses and widowers in their dress suits. Then the music began and we filled the floor as the DJ rocked the room heeding Michele's cardinal rule: no slow songs at Camp.

The only time I'd danced since Timmy died was with my sister and nieces at the family wedding in May. I ended up feeling sad because they said how much they missed watching Timmy and me twirling and dipping on the dance floor.

But this was different. As I moved to the beat of the music, dancing with the crowd instead of one specific person, I was transported to a new place in body and mind. For the first time in my life, I was dancing for the sheer joy of feeling it for me and me alone. I finally allowed myself to feel joy without associating it with Timmy. Could I possibly be learning to live again?

CELEBRATION

38

Life is what you celebrate.
All of it.
Even its end.

— Joanne Harris, author of Chocolat

My emotional high from the weekend in San Diego stayed with me for about two weeks until "Camp Crash" hit. I was blindsided by this deeply painful and overwhelming feeling of desolation. Since Timmy died, I always felt sadness after a vacation or a special event and learned to brace myself for it. This was different, more intense, and hit like a ton of bricks.

I've been with over 250 widowed people who get me and now I've returned to my old life without them. How the hell am I going to keep doing this, Timmy?

On top of that, the 33rd anniversary of the day Tim and I met was looming as another reminder that the second year of grieving was worse than year number one. Surviving all of the "firsts" gave meaning to my grief — but this year I felt empty of purpose without a plan for my future.

Tacked to my library bulletin board was a quote by Fyodor Dostoevsky given to me years ago by a grieving friend; I'd never fully understood it until now: "One must love life before loving its meaning, and when the love of life disappears, no meaning can console us."

Trying to bring some meaning back into my life, I thought about how rituals had always helped me get through difficult times. I decided to keep one Tim started on August 25, 1979, the first anniversary of the day we met. I remember it like it was yesterday…

We'd spent a fun day at the New York State Fair. Here we are goofing around in a photo booth:

After the traditional state fair lunch of sausage and pepper sandwiches followed by huge cones of soft ice cream, Tim dropped me at my apartment to shower and change for the evening. Just as I was about to climb into my car to drive to Tim's place, the phone rang. "Hey gorgeous, do you still have that sexy black and white off-the-shoulder top you wore when we met?"

"How the hell did you remember what I wore that night? I didn't think I had it on long enough for it to be memorable," I teased.

"That's true, but I remember it well. And I wore my red linen blazer. Don't be too impressed. I'd just attended my once-a-year father/son golf tournament dinner and wore a red jacket because that's the signature color of Dad's golf group, the Red Bandits.

"Okay handsome, I'll change and be there soon but I expect you to impress me in other ways tonight." When I walked in Tim's door, the smell of garlic and tomatoes filled my nostrils from the lobster marinara sauce he was cooking. He handed me a glass of champagne and we toasted our one-year anniversary with a deep kiss.

Tim disappeared briefly then returned and took me in his arms as Barry White's sultry voice crooned, "Never, never gonna give you up." We danced to the slow beat, Tim in his red linen jacket and me in my sexy top plus the rest of our clothes that didn't stay on for much longer. Every anniversary since, we'd donned the same outfits and danced around the house with memories of that first night swirling in our heads.

I decided it was time to rekindle that ritual again. Thirty-three years later, as the lobster marinara sauce was cooking, I smoothed down the ruffled off-the-shoulder sleeves of my black and white top, put on Tim's red jacket and tied his apron around my waist to keep it from falling off; it was so huge on me.

As I stirred the pasta sauce, my mind drifted to a grief article I'd recently read that suggested a part of healing is to become the person you've lost, at least for a time. It dawned on me that, other than wearing his clothes, I'd taken on many of Tim's routines, partially because I had to (like finances — awful), but others because they helped me feel closer to him. I read the newspaper in his chair and prepared roast chicken exactly the way he did. I've kept up the house and gardened as best I could, even though I killed the tomatoes, but I found that doing things the way Tim did grounded me and helped me feel safe and centered.

I even started to look like Tim. My body became lean like his having maintained my rapid weight loss of 15 pounds from when he was diagnosed until his death. It's amazing what stress and grief can do to a body. I'd lost my "menopausal middle" and now had a flat stomach and more muscular-looking legs like Tim's. Keeping our daily workout routine helped mold my body and heal my psyche.

As a couple, we prided ourselves as two independent people with a deep sense of mutual respect walking side by side in life. But when Timmy died, it was as if I had taken him and shoved him deep inside of me, integrating him into my being. My problem now was how to take him back outside of me.

Staring at his picture, I said, *Boo, I'm trying to figure out who I am without you; all of my future desires and plans included you. I met widows and widowers at Camp who've created new lives and even remarried but damn, I don't know what I want. It's so freaking hard to start over.*

My heart skipped a beat when the doorbell rang. "Amy, WTF are you doing here?"

My dear friend handed me a bottle of Prosecco and declared, "I didn't want you to celebrate your anniversary alone and besides, I'm wearing my dancing shoes!"

After dinner and much wine, Amy and I laughed and danced around the house into the wee hours to a Studio 54 disco compilation.

"Amy, it was such fun to dance and feel something positive again on this day."

"Annie, it's great to see a smile on your face. I'm sure Timmy is smiling too. He was with us."

When she walked out the door, I thanked her for the wonderful surprise and said, "I guess it's time for me to start celebrating life again."

I sat on the deck with another glass of wine and thought about how far I'd come. Loving that dancing was back in my life, it dawned on me that listening to music had been a part of my healing process from the beginning.

Some widows at Camp told me they couldn't listen to music after their loves died, but I couldn't get enough music. From the moment I woke in the morning until I went to bed, I played all kinds of music: classical, opera, blues, new age, rock and soul. I needed to infuse the air with sound to fill the void left by my inconceivable loss.

When I knew the words, I'd sing along at the top of my lungs. Tim used to tell me I had a beautiful voice and should take lessons. I thought about it after he died and joined a choir but it wasn't a good fit. Besides, I preferred to sing in the privacy of our home.

I'd often sing along with Eva Cassidy or Beth Nielsen Chapman, Corrine Bailey Rae and Loreena McKenitt, all three are widows whose music is devoted to their lost loves. I'd play these female artists' dark, mournful songs as I cried and held Tim's picture to my chest. The sadness of these songs comforted me; I felt safe and understood. Anytime I heard a new sad song in my car on Satellite radio, I'd look it up on YouTube and play it over and over adding to the catharsis of my singing and crying jags. It was difficult for me to listen to "happy music" and unless a song's lyrics spoke to me, I would change the radio station immediately.

After my first Camp Widow, that all changed. I allowed myself to listen to upbeat music and began to move to whatever rhythms pierced the air. Moving my body shifted the flow of my grief. My heart felt full and light as sadness found its way out with each breath, each sweep of my arm, each step of my foot.

Dancing became fun again and I danced often, mostly around the house alone or with struggling, unwilling cat partner, Lucca or Vivi. I imagined myself moving with Tim and it felt wonderful. I could feel his arms around me, dipping me backward and twirling me in circles until I fell dizzy into his arms. The deep pain evoked while remembering our dancing no longer haunted me. Tim and I were now dancing in two realms, our souls forever entwined, living separate but together, joined by the beat of the universe.

With Camp Crash and another anniversary under my belt, celebrating life became my new goal. Of course, saying it and doing it were two different things since my day-to-day life didn't change despite my lofty goal of an attitude change. Happily, Tim had more in store for me to celebrate.

BELIEVE WHAT YOU SEE

39

*Religion is for people who are afraid of hell,
Spirituality is for people who have already
been there.*

— Running Hawk, Lakota Nation

I was looking forward to my annual Labor Day week at Lake Ontario — beach walks, soothing dips to cool my sun warmed body, yummy barbecued meals, watching the sun set into the blue water, star gazing while sitting by the beach fire pit. If it rained, reading mindless chick lit and listening to the waves would fill the lazy time.

Even though I'd grown used to being alone at home, it was too difficult at the lake where I'd spent all my time with Tim, so I invited people to join me. The first year after he died, every moment was filled with family and friends but this year, no one could be with me the entire time. I was not happy, but there was no choice. At least I had my friend, Liz to help me through the first two days. And Lorraine and Paul, who owned the house next door, were there on weekends and holidays.

While I was packing the car to leave Saturday morning, Liz called and said something had come up with her daughter so she couldn't be there until tomorrow. My heart started to pound with dread at the idea of arriving at the cottage alone. The day was hot and sunny. On the hour-long drive, my mind drifted to all of the perfect beach days Tim and I had shared over the years.

Timmy, how am I going to do this? Where ARE you?

I pulled up and choked back tears as I walked in, arms full of food and supplies for the week. As I grabbed Tim's ever-present handkerchief from my purse, I heard a knock on the door. I breathed a sigh of relief to see Paul, Lorraine and their son, Ben, standing there smiling, "Put us to work. We need to get you unpacked so you can join us on the beach!"

"Did Timmy tell you I was arriving by myself today?"

"Yup," said Lorraine with a wink.

Luckily, Lorraine and Paul were like-minded about after death communication, as they'd experienced it with their brother-in-law who died the year before Timmy.

Twenty minutes later, my car was empty and I was sitting next to my friends on their six-person float, wine glass in hand, hot sun beaming down, happy to be alive. After several hours of hanging out, Lorraine and Paul, still concerned, invited me to dinner.

When I walked up the sandy hill between my cottage and their house to get ready, I couldn't believe my eyes; perched on the power line was a huge, gorgeous hawk staring down at me.

Timmy, what the hell are you doing? You knew Liz wasn't coming and wanted to make sure I was okay, huh? Lorraine and Paul have been wonderful. I'm going to change and eat with them, you wanna join us?

Timmy Hawk just looked at me and then out to the water. I hurried inside and got my camera. With shaky hands, I took a few pictures, then the camera lens closed.

What an idiot, I didn't charge the battery! Honey, I'm sure you're not surprised. Don't go anywhere!

I ran next door and told Paul to grab his camera and follow me. Timmy Hawk was patiently waiting. As I talked to my husband, who was somehow inside our favorite bird, Paul clicked away. Lorraine, their son and his fiancé joined us and all were astonished.

"We've been coming to the lake for over 20 years. I've seen hawks soar in the sky or land in a distant tree but I've never seen one on a wire so close to people."

"That's because it's not any hawk Lorraine, it's Timmy!"

"Indeed it is! Hi Timmy, we miss you! We'll take care of Anne Marie, don't worry."

He seemed to be listening as he looked at us then averted his gaze to the lake. The red-orange light of the sun gave his feathers an almost iridescent glow. Paul and I stayed behind while everyone else left to prepare the meal.

What a handsome bird you are. It must be fun to fly. I wish I could die and join you. With those words, he lifted his wings and turned around on the wire. *Okay, I'm not going to off myself, I promise. Don't be pissed, Boo.*

He remained turned while Paul took a few more pictures, then Lorraine called us to dinner on their beach deck. As I reluctantly began to leave, one sharp talon uncurled, turned and grasped the wire then the other followed; Tim was now facing me. Our eyes locked.

My love, my life, I wish this day would last forever. I stood motionless, mesmerized.

Another call to dinner interrupted us and he averted his gaze to the setting sun.

Thank you for being here. I'll always watch for you. I know you are protecting me and guiding my way. As I walked backward, almost falling down the sandy hill, I savored the last sight of him, waved and shouted, "I adore you!"

I ate quickly. Just as the tangerine sun melted into the water, I walked to the edge of the deck, leaned over the railing and looked back. To my surprise, the magnificent creature was still on the wire, basking in the final rays of light. I grabbed my wine and joined him. Paul was not far behind with his camera.

Do you want some of my Chianti, Boo? We just had yummy BBQ pork loin, potato salad and roasted corn on the cob. Do you miss drinking wine and eating human food?

I raised my glass and he averted his gaze to meet mine. A chill ran down my spine as I saw a hint of blue in his eyes in the last glimmer of the day.

My love, it really is YOU! Hey, you have the same initials in your afterlife animal, T.W.H. — Thomas Wentworth Higgins a.k.a. Timmy Wild Hawk, how cool! Or do you prefer to be formal and go by your birth name, Thomas? No, I always liked Timmy better. No one else knew about your wild Timmy side that you showed only me, that's what I miss most, other than gazing into your blue eyes.

As a tear escaped my eye, everyone returned for another look. Then Lorraine invited me for dessert and a game of cards. Paul clicked one more photo and as he walked into their house chuckled, "I'll leave you two lovebirds alone."

I wanted time to stand still but dusk turned to dark and mosquitoes started their incessant attacks. As difficult as it was to leave, I relented and bid him goodnight. *I will always love you.*

I woke up at 6:30am, late for me, but I was on laketime. I walked into the kitchen and saw that the flashlight I'd used to check the wire at 1:00am was still lit on the counter. What a goof I am, now *another* battery will probably have to be replaced!

September 3, 2011—
Want to share some of my wine?

I looked out at the power line; my TWH wasn't there. Disappointed but not surprised, I made coffee and breakfast and let the events of last evening sink in. As the rising sunlight streamed into the back door window, I turned to witness the dawning of the day.

"Holy freaking hell, Timmy! What are you doing back there?" I yelped. I opened the door and stepped outside to the amazing sight of him comfortably perched on the roof of the storage shed. *Is that where you spent the night? I didn't see you on the wire when I stumbled in. I thought you'd left!*

September 4, 2011 — Are you thinking about driving? Isn't flying more fun?

September 4, 2011 — I'd love to let you into the cottage!

I grabbed my camera with a fully charged battery and clicked away. He flew from the shed onto my car. *What the hell! Why would you want to drive when you can fly? Hey, no bird crap on the window, please.*

I stepped off the cottage stoop to get a better camera angle and he flew to the ground, walked along the cottage foundation and hopped onto the stoop. He took a few steps and stood next to the door.

Believe me, I would love to let you inside and into my bed but I don't think the owner would appreciate a bunch of hawk feathers all over the place.

I sat on the grass and talked with him a few minutes, then he flew down the driveway. My heart sank. I assumed he was leaving. I followed and found him perched in a tree. Relieved he had not flown away, I began my burning questions: *So what do you do with your time in the afterlife? Are you busy or bored? Do you miss me? Are you always a hawk or an orb or an angel or what the hell are you?*

TWH just looked at me from his perch, as my wished-for answers did not arrive. I was quite content to sit on the grass and just be in his presence.

Boo, do you remember years ago when that hawk in the zoo flew down and grazed my finger when I leaned on its cage? I just learned in a class on power animals that the hawk "chose" me to serve as my spirit guide and protector. Sometimes your power animal will "attack" you to make itself known. This is especially true of birds of prey, that they "take you" to speak to you. But I wasn't hurt or frightened. He certainly got my attention though, just like you are, my Love.

After awhile, my cell phone rang. Liz said she would be there by lunchtime, daughter crisis resolved. Always worried about everyone's stomachs — it's the Italian in me — I said, *Boo, I'll be right back. Please wait. I've got to go prep the barbecue now that you can't do that for me. You really did spoil me.*

I hurried to the gas grill on the beach deck. "Oh great, the freaking propane tank is empty. I'm gonna kill the last selfish renters for not re-filling the tank. Paul, help!"

I'd spied Paul out of the corner of my eye getting their beach chairs set up for the day. He came to my rescue, unhooked the gas tank and put it in my car as I cursed the previous renters.

I drove to where Timmy's spirit inside this glorious bird was perched and implored, *Boo, please don't go I have to get this damn tank filled. The last renters were total asses! I'll be back in ten minutes!*

I prepared myself for him not being there when I got back and thanked him and the universe for yet another miracle. I filled the propane tank at the local gas station and raced back. Had there been a state trooper on the highway, I definitely would've been fined.

When I turned the car into the cottage driveway and craned my neck to look into the tree, I breathed a sigh of relief to see TWH patiently waiting. Just the sight of him calmed me and I knew I'd be okay. I rolled down my window, leaned out and said, "My love, Liz is on her way. I'll be fine now. I won't be alone."

And with those words, Timmy Wild Hawk looked at me then soared off into the clear blue sky.

September 3, 2011—Chills ran down my spine as his piercing blue eyes gazed at me. Two months later, I showed these pictures to Lorrie Schumacher, master falconer (wild bird trainer). She was shocked that a wild hawk came and stayed with me for almost 24 hours. She was also shocked at the blue color of his eye; this is not a characteristic trait and she had never seen it before.

September 3, 2011— When TWH turned away, we did not see a dragonfly perched on his shoulder until we looked at the photo. I showed Lorrie and she said hawks eat dragonflies so it was beyond her comprehension that the insect sat on his shoulder unharmed. I later learned that Native Americans believe dragonflies are souls of the dead and represent immortality. I guess Timmy brought along a spirit guide or maybe it was another relative.

More hawk photos are on my website: www.dancingintworealms.com

ANTICIPATION
40

Anticipation, which is a mortar to desire, the ability to imagine it as if it's happening, to experience it as if it's happening, while nothing is happening and everything is happening at the same time.

— Esther Perel

T immy Hawk's lake visit was certainly cause for extended celebration. After Liz left, I enjoyed two days alone basking in warm memories.

Then I shared my joy with friends John and Mary Lou and Diane who joined me for the rest of the week. When I showed them pictures of TWH, my like-minded buddies believed their eyes. Because they all knew Tim, they understood he wouldn't want me to arrive there alone and would wait to make sure I was okay.

When I returned home, the depression I usually experienced didn't come. TWH's visit energized me and gave me new hope. Grateful to have turned a corner in my grief process, I embraced celebrating and working on the goal of "whatever the hell I was supposed to do with the rest of my life." (Become a hawk trainer maybe?)

You need to talk to Lisa again. This thought greeted me when I woke one morning in late September. I wasn't sure if it was Timmy or a dream, but with my first cup of coffee in hand, I was checking flights to Seattle. When I saw the ticket cost $500, I remembered the voucher for that exact amount from my cancelled flight in San Diego after Timmy broke the plane. *Hey, Boo, did you plan this trip all along?*

Lisa Fox had said when we spoke in March that I would know when the time was right for another reading, and I felt this in my bones. I contacted Abigail Carter and asked for Seattle hotel recommendations but instead she offered her weekend retreat on nearby Vashon Island.

Several emails later, my flight and rental car were booked for October 27-30 and my second psychic reading was set with Lisa at Abby's house. Since Lisa lived on the same island, I just needed to be there with an open mind and digital recorder! The anticipation of my upcoming trip kept my emotions on overdrive as I counted the days.

In the meantime, I had several anniversary dates to get through.

As I drove to Lake Ontario for Columbus Day weekend, I had no illusions that the second anniversary of Tim's toe stubbing would be easy. After my ritual of touching my kissed fingertips to the stair step where this horrible saga began, I was ready to enjoy the rest of the time. I'd invited Annie, who'd made Timmy's urn, still preferring overnight company to being alone at the lake. The weekend was lovely, unseasonably warm and we even swam in the tepid water.

On Monday morning, Annie and I took a six-mile beach walk and saw flocks of gulls, terns and geese line the beach then fill the sky when we got close. "Annie! Look at that weird seagull with pink feet. None of the others have pink feet. It must be Timmy. You know how we joked about his feet."

"Yeah, too bad the bird doesn't have Tim's flip flops on! Oh shoot, I wish I'd brought my camera."

"Annie, this reminds me of a beautiful quote by Pablo Neruda that I found soon after Timmy died: "But I love your feet, only because they walked upon the earth and upon the wind and upon the waters until they found me." It was bookmarked in one of Tim's poetry books near his reading chair. I felt like he wanted me to find it, like he was talking to me."

"What a perfect quote. Timmy speaks to you in so many ways."

"Yes, he does. Hey Timmy, are you trying to tell me something?" I asked as we took in the last sight of the pink-footed seagull before he flew away with the rest of his yellow-footed flock.

Clouds started to form when we got back to the house. After packing our cars and hugging good-bye, I noticed my feet hurt. I didn't think much of it and planned a soak when I got home. About two hours later, after driving through a rainstorm and unpacking, I settled into a warm bubble bath. Rubbing my weary feet, I yelped when I touched my toes and saw that both of my big toenails were black. My mind jolted back to the same ugly sight two years ago when Timmy was hurt. *So now it's MY turn? This is too freaking weird!*

The next morning when the podiatrist's nurse booked me for their only available appointment, the irony did not escape me. Two years to the day, I found myself in Dr. Conti's office having the same procedure as Timmy but mine was *both* big toes being drained of blood.

"So do I have to worry about being diagnosed with leukemia now?" I said half-kidding and shaking my head in disbelief.

"I don't think so; this is just an unfortunate coincidence, probably friction from your sneakers on that long beach walk. You'll be fine. In a month or two you'll probably lose both toenails but they'll grow back," Dr. Conti predicted.

"What? Timmy didn't lose his toenail but then again, he only lived 19 more days after you saw him."

As Dr. C. finished wrapping both toes with gauze and tape, I was glad I'd worn sandals. He looked off in the distance and said, "I still remember that day; we never imagined Tim was that sick since his bruised toe was his only symptom."

"And now I have the same damn minor surgery plus unrelenting grief. Is this like Christ's stigmata to document my wounds of suffering?" I retorted.

Dr. C. frowned and crinkled his bushy eyebrows. Maybe I hit a nerve in his Catholic-Italian psyche. "Okay, I'll cut the drama. I thought you might laugh at my irreverent humor."

"Your humor is refreshing and impressive for all you've been through, Anne Marie."

"Believe me, laughing just postpones my tears."

After a hug from Dr. C. and his nurse, my held-back tears finally streamed down my cheeks as I waddled out the door. Memories permeated my brain of walking out that same door with my one-toe bandaged husband and our naiveté that we had all the time in the world.

As I stared at my aching toes before falling asleep that night, I didn't think to ask Timmy why this happened. The great mystery of life and death, even with all of the signs and positive coincidences still left me alone and baffled. I'd learned the hard way that some questions have no answers and accepting what comes your way is sometimes all you can do.

The next morning, the second anniversary of diagnosis day arrived. These dates have their way of bringing up the deepest emotional pain and now I had physical pain on top of it. After an uncomfortable night, I woke at my usual time, but decided bike class was not possible. I fell back to sleep.

Lucca made an executive decision that 6:20am was the best time to pounce on my chest and remind me his breakfast was a high priority. Groggy, I climbed out of bed, kissed Tim's urn and gathered Lucca and Vivi into my arms.

Looking out the window at the star filled sky and hint of morning sunlight on the horizon, I thought back to all of the sunrises we'd witnessed from many places in the world. None compared with the sunrise in our own bedroom. We owned these special rays of dawn witnessed day in and day out from our personal sanctuary.

My love, my life, how is it possible I am still here and you are there? And speaking of there, where the hell are you?

I breathed deeply knowing the answer would not come. Despite all of his signs over these two years, I hadn't heard a satisfactory answer for where Tim was. I loathed the "spirit realm" where he apparently existed, but I could not reach. While there was comfort in knowing he was "somewhere, out there" I wanted to be able to see, smell and touch *him*. My desires and yearning overwhelmed my daily existence and I'd thought many times of joining him.

Don't worry Boo, I told you I'm not going to kill myself. I have to live for Lucca and Vivi. They depend on me and I on them, but I'm still figuring out how to do it. People say, "you're so strong." I hate those words because with them come judgments and unrealistic expectations. I don't feel strong. I feel exhausted most of the time and resigned to circumstances beyond my control. One never knows all that can be endured until there is no choice.

The next seven days were filled with Timmy signs: three hawk sightings, a great blue heron flying low over our backyard and the cats acting particularly protective and odd. Whenever I left the house, they both ran to the door and cried, trying to follow me out the door. Upon return, they jumped into my arms and wouldn't let me put them down. They were always nearby and frequently begged to be picked up, but this was different.

So Boo, what's up with Lucca and Vivi? Are you in them now? Lucca's almond shaped blue eyes so remind me of yours. If I can't have you, our kitty kids are the next best thing in my life that I can touch and love.

The next morning as I was getting ready to leave for Seattle, I heard Vivi crying. I walked into Tim's bathroom and found her staring at his shower door. I noticed the shower ceiling light was on.

Okay Timmy, playing with the lights again, huh? I haven't used your shower since you died; the idea is too painful.

Vivi kept crying, so I opened the door. As she walked into Tim's cavernous nine by five foot shower, the ceiling light started to flicker. She looked up at the light, stared at the black tile walls, meowed a few times, and then sat down near the floor drain.

"Vivi, you miss Daddy too, huh?" I stepped inside and picked her up for a cuddle. I smiled as I reminisced about the times Tim and I shared his shower, playfully washing each other's hair and bodies.

Maybe you'll join me in the shower on my trip, Boo! You'll be there with me right?

Even though I was filled with anticipation about what was to come, I was nervous about why the cats had been acting so strange. Did they know something I didn't?

BE CAREFUL WHAT YOU WISH FOR

41

We plan, God laughs.

— Yiddish Proverb

W hen I parked the rental car at Abby's Vashon Island haven, I was in awe. Once owned by Betty MacDonald, author of the beloved *Mrs. Piggle Wiggle* series, the 1940's rambling house of dark brown horizontal wood planks is perched high on an evergreen-treed cliff overlooking Puget Sound.

"Abby, this house feels like a living creature," I told her as I walked through the carved wood entrance door.

Floor to ceiling windows brought in subtle daylight filtered through thick foliage that surrounded the house. As I walked past the brick fireplace in the kitchen through the long, rectangular dining room and into the great room with an even larger fieldstone fireplace, I felt transported back to a time before I was born. Yet it was also oddly familiar.

My eyes caught light streaming into the room through a glass door etched with white swirling images and figures. I walked over to it and said, "I've seen this door before, maybe in a dream? No, I know where, it looks like the strange white images in the cottage door windows when Timmy hawk was there."

I showed Abby the picture on my iPad. "Those are clear glass windows in the cottage. What the hell is in them? They look like weird, bizarre faces to me. At the time, they kinda' freaked me out. Now look at your door, similar weird faces."

 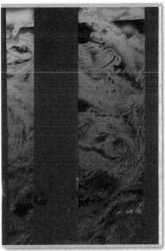

"In comparison, they're really cool. Not exactly alike, but still cool."

"Ab, I know it sounds crazy but Timmy wanted me to be here."

"Looks like it, so enjoy your time! I've got to go back to Seattle for my kids' school event but I'll see you tomorrow. Relax and see what Timmy has in store for you!"

After I unpacked groceries we'd picked up from the local supermarket and poured a glass of wine, I decided to explore. I was tired from the cross country flight, twenty minute ferry ride from the coast and three hour time difference, but I wanted to take in every bit of the fading sunlight and breathe the ocean air.

I walked onto the deck and looked at the inky blue Puget Sound water below. Directly across, emerging from the previously cloud covered sky was snow capped Mount Rainier. I was mesmerized. The setting sun pierced the eastern sky and made luminous the majestic white-capped mountain. Even though it was inland hundreds of miles away, the immense mountain seemed to be jutting up from the mainland within arm's reach. I stretched my arm out to touch the illusion before me.

I feel like I'm in a dream, Boo. I can't wait to talk to you.

The next day Abby arrived early and we spent the morning sharing stories about our husbands' untimely deaths. As she spoke, two thoughts came into my mind: her long wavy chocolate hair matched the color of her house and her hazel eyes had seen a whole different level of horror at the ripe young age of 36 when her husband and so many others were killed in the World Trade Center attacks.

I'd never known anyone widowed by 9/11 and haltingly read her book, *The Alchemy of Loss,* after we met at Camp. I recall having to read it in spurts as her words churned my own grief. "Your memoir was an incredibly moving and powerful read, Ab."

"Thank you and speaking of, good luck with your psychic reading. I can't wait to hear about it!" Ab said as she donned her jacket knowing Lisa was due to arrive soon.

"I can feel your Arron here and hope he brings Tim along."

"Oh yeah, Arron is definitely here. I felt him when I first looked at this house. I'm sure he helped me find it."

"This place is so spiritual, it seems otherworldly."

"It is indeed." Abby smiled as we both glanced out the window and a white mist enveloped the deck.

I had seen a guest book with lovely sentiments written by previous visitors and asked, "Do you rent this house?"

"No, other than when I spend time here with my family, this house is a respite and retreat for grieving people. I want to provide a peaceful space for healing."

"Wow, you're amazing Ab!"

"Thanks! See you later, we'll celebrate your reading and who knows what else?" With a wave, she was out the door.

As I centered myself in preparation for Lisa's arrival, I heard my cell phone ring. "Hi Ab, what's doin'? You just left a few minutes ago."

"Yeah but Arron and Timmy haven't, go look outside."

I walked onto the deck. The mist had cleared to reveal huge double rainbows arced over the Puget Sound sky.

"Wow Ab, a sign from the divine!"

"Yup, our guys are definitely with us!"

October 28, 2011—Arron and Tim Signs—Double Rainbows over Puget Sound.

A few minutes later, Lisa arrived in a flurry. "I'm sorry, I was in Seattle and caught a late ferry."

"No worries, Lisa!" *Wow Timmy, she is so pretty, no wonder you like talking through her,* I thought to myself knowing Tim could hear me.

Her shoulder length auburn hair framed her face and her warm grey-green eyes took me in. She was taller than I'd imagined about 5'10" and fit, I thought, after hugging her muscular shoulders, a cross between Julia Roberts and a female superhero.

"Timmy has been popping in and out all day, he is so excited you're here! Let's get started, so I can tell you all he wants to say!" Lisa beamed.

"Is there a best place in the house for us to connect to Spirit?" I was anxious to make sure Timmy would like where we chose.

"He's everywhere but let's go into the living room where Abby and I have talked with Arron many times."

As I sunk into a large leather chair, I wrapped Timmy's green sweater around my shoulders, put his lovebird tie on my lap and surrounded myself with his pictures and travel urn.

"I love it that you brought Tim's things with you."

"I even have on his bikini underwear, they are big in the front but they feel comfy."

Lisa chuckled, then took a deep breath. With eyes closed, she spoke as Tim, *I love you Anne Marie with all my heart and soul. You are my golden girl, the love of my life and all eternity but it's time for you to move forward and find new love in your life.*

Jolted, my eyes welled up with tears and then anger. *What the hell does that mean, Timmy? This is what you've been excited to say to me? What if I'm not ready?*

Lisa continued to speak as Tim, *I cannot return to your realm. You're on the physical plane and you need physical love.*

But I'm not ready to let you go!

You don't have to let go of me but you have to move forward; it's part of our plan and I have to move on too, but I'll never let go of you.

I sat on the edge of the chair, my fingers digging into the arm rests, imploring Tim to stay, *Move on, where are you going? I can't have you leave me twice. Please don't go, wherever the hell you are going!*

I'm not going anywhere; I'll always be with you. I'll keep coming in animals and send you coins and other signs. But please be open to finding new love, someone who'll care for you in a way I can't anymore.

Lisa opened her eyes and with a gentle smile said, "Tim has so much love for you, it's quite extraordinary. I've seen a lot of love in two realms but yours is amazingly powerful. Don't worry, your soul mate bond will never be broken, but you have to live the rest of your life in this physical plane."

"So, now you're *both* ganging up on me huh?"

"Well sort of," Lisa laughed. "Anne Marie, he needs you to let go so he can go as well."

"I can see myself in the ICU holding his legs down while they intubated him and he gave up his last ounce of freedom."

"That's a perfect metaphor. You are holding on and refusing to let him be free, but he needs you to allow both of your spiritual paths to progress. It's all about love and the unity of all souls. In our pure form, we are soul energy and light. Tim is an evolved soul and your love is a form of bright light, after his body melted away, his soul now aspires to become even brighter."

Damn you, Timmy, so you go off and become brighter while I live in this dark hole of suffering!

Lisa closed her eyes and returned to speaking as Timmy, *I'm sorry it's been so painful for you but it's time to let go. I'm in a place with more dimensions than I ever could have imagined and I need to move forward as do you in your dimension of human time and space. We are in different places but they are parallel universes. I'm just a breath away. We still maintain a connection; continue to look for me in hawks and herons.*

So the herons I've seen are you! Their symbolism means independence and self-reliance. I've been both, I've had no choice. But I NEED your signs; they help me feel connected to you.

Lisa chimed in, "Anne Marie, spirits are given the gift of returning for awhile but the longer he is gone, you won't see him as much."

Frantic at her words, I implored, *Timmy please, I need you to stay. I'm not ready to let you and your signs go!*

Lisa said, "Tim understands you aren't ready but sometime after the next two years, if you are willing, you'll meet a man who lost his wife to cancer. You're supposed to meet but you need to get out and be involved in things you love like literary and art events. Go to fundraisers and social events like a holiday gala."

Lisa smiled, Tim just said, "Dress to the nines and step out in your beauty."

"Sweet Timmy, he loved it when I got dressed up. He was quite the dresser too! But Lisa, I don't understand the part about if I am willing."

"Anne Marie, we all have free will. You have a destiny but you also have choice."

"Okay, I choose to have Timmy come back."

Precious Pie, I can't come back. I want you to live. You're a passionate woman, full of life. I'm glad you're dancing again.

I had to catch my breath when he called me Precious Pie, one of our many pet names Lisa could never have known. I thought, maybe I should put away my skeptical brain but that's part of my humanness that can't be denied.

Lisa interrupted, "Oh how lovely. Tim just showed me a vision of you dancing, his hand is at the small of your back and he dipped you and kissed you. What a delightful man!"

"Exactly, I don't want another man! I want my Tim!" I envisioned myself stamping my feet like an obstinate child.

Lisa returned to speaking as Tim, *Be open to life and open your heart to another. Don't keep a closed sign on your heart.*

Timmy, my heart is not closed, it's ripped open, bleeding and pissed off that we can't be together.

Timmy, my heart is not closed, it's ripped open, bleeding and pissed off that we can't be together. I wanted to throw something out of frustration but resisted the urge.

You'll join me someday but you still have to live your life. I love you. I adore you. Stitch up your heart and live.

Lisa returned to speaking as herself and said, "Anne Marie, do you have any questions?"

I assumed she was getting tired of this back and forth stubbornness on my part. Tears rolled down my cheeks. I didn't understand or want to hear Tim's message of moving forward but I gave up and asked, "Yes, I have a family member managing my money and I don't always agree with his philosophy. What should I do?"

"Timmy said there is a woman in your future who can better manage your money. You'll have some hurdles to turn the money over and detach from your family member with love, but go with the woman."

Okay, Boo. I wish I didn't have to think about money and could just retire and leave my crazy workplace but I'm too young.

Lisa took over again, "Tim is saying he wishes you didn't have to work either but he sees something else, another job opportunity within your same group but in another place."

My skeptical self reappeared, "Yeah, don't I wish!"

Lisa continued, "Tim says to just keep your options open because there are people at work, one woman in particular who is not trustworthy and is not a team member. Stand your ground and don't give away your power. She's an energy vampire. You'll learn lessons though, and the tools will come for you to let go of things that aren't serving you. This will make room for another opportunity. Tim tells me he likes your boss. There's an amazing story that is yet to come for you and your boss in the next two years."

I thought back to when Alex told me we both were going to be leaving work and here it was again. "Gee, a lot is going to happen in these next two years, huh? Well, I love my boss so at least I don't have to give him up!"

Remember sweetie, I'm never, never gonna give you up.

Startled once again by something only Tim would know, I was transported back to our anniversary dance and Barry White's song. My heart ached and was comforted at the same time. I told Lisa I was having a really hard time with the concept of moving on.

She said, "Tim wanted you to begin to move on not because he rejects you in any way, but *because* he loves you so deeply. He has a completely different perspective now of divine love but you are still in the physical. He can't meet those needs so he wants you to find happiness but only when the time is right. It is really the most incredible message for him to push gently in this direction. I hope you'll understand this soon, when you are ready."

"It's difficult for me to imagine another love when Tim is so fully present. It's confusing to have his love and be encouraged to find another."

"Please know that you are so very loved by him and he only wants your best. He is *not* rejecting you nor did he plan to abandon you by leaving this earth plane. He was simply called home and to a higher service. He is a truly powerful light now!"

"Thank you Lisa. I need time to let this all sink in. I'm off to meet Abby in Seattle for dinner."

"You're so welcome. Thank you for the pleasure of meeting with both of you together, I enjoyed the energy. I'm here if you need me."

On the flight home from the West Coast, I was not in a celebratory mood. Even with the reassurance from Lisa, I was pissed and sad that the main message from Tim was to move forward when I still had no clue how.

Well Boo, it sounds like changes are in my destiny so I guess I'll just go with the flow and see what comes up. Plus, I have at least two more years before I find a new partner so I'm gonna hang out with you. You're free to go do whatever you've got to do in your realm but please come around every once in a while like you promised. In the mean time, I have a surprise for you…unless you already know.

PREYING
FORWARD
42

When you walk to the edge of all the light you have and take that first step into the darkness of the unknown, you must believe that one of two things will happen. There will be something solid for you to stand upon or you will be taught to fly.

— Patrick Overton

I wanted the second anniversary of Tim's death to be upbeat and fun — what better way to celebrate than to have a possible relative of TWH visit!

As 28 curious friends and family gathered on an unseasonably warm early November day, wild bird handlers Lorrie Schumacher and her daughter, Talon Skye, of *Talons Birds of Prey*, placed five large wooden boxes throughout our backyard.

One by one, the boxes were opened. To the delightful squeals of children and "ahs" of adults, Lorrie and Talon revealed their contents: Tilly, a small barred owl was placed on top of a blanket on the ground; Jewel of the Nile, a large black raven was put on her perch on top of her box; Big Mama, an enormous eagle owl sat on my wooden bench with watchful Talon nearby; Aurelia, a grey and peach feathered Saker Falcon rested on top of her box and finally, Machu, a dark brown and chestnut feathered Harris's Hawk curled his talons around the top of my wooden chair.

For the next two hours, we learned about each bird's habitat, life history, diet, and hunting abilities during what Lorrie refers to as their *Hawk Walk* experience. Then I got an amazing thrill, I held Machu and had him feed and fly from my thick leather gloved hand.

Machu, the Harris's Hawk, ready to show us his soaring talent. (Tim told me to wear his rust colored sweater around my shoulders that day. I guess he wanted Machu and I to be color coordinated.)

As Machu gracefully flew off my glove into the bright blue sky, I thought back to four years ago when Tim and I read about the *Birds of Prey Hawk Walk* in the newspaper. Unfortunately, we had plans to be out of town when Lorrie and Talon were scheduled to perform with their wild birds at an outdoor art park near Cazenovia, about 20 miles east of Syracuse.

Then, seven months after Timmy died, when I read about another wild bird performance, I knew I had to go. Even though Tim had already come to me in a hawk flying by my car, in my backyard, and high in the sky, I wanted to see one close up. (At that point, my own TWH event at the lake hadn't happened.)

I remembered this was the first time after Timmy's death that I went to a social event alone — up until then, I needed a friend or family member to join me. I'd feared doing something on my own, partially because I could break down in tears for no particular reason. If that happened while driving solo, it might not turn out so well.

With no one else in my car, I steeled myself, drove without incident and arrived ready for the close encounter. For the next hour, I watched Lorrie and Talon skillfully handle their birds of prey in various displays of hunting and acrobatic flying. No one was allowed to touch the birds at this public show but being close to them gave me comfort. Afterwards, I spoke with Lorrie about my husband and hawk sightings. A knowing smile spread across her face.

"Lorrie, you don't think I'm crazy to say my husband comes to me in hawks?"

"Absolutely not, Anne Marie; it's not the first time I've heard about spirits inhabiting birds. Your sightings have been unusual, especially the time the hawk flew next to your car window twice in one day. A hawk would never put itself in harm's way being so close to a car but I believe what you're telling me."

My mind returned to my own ongoing backyard show. After the birds were returned to their enclosures and my guests left, I showed Lorrie and Talon pictures of TWH at the lake. "Anne Marie, this is impossible, a wild hawk would never be so close to you and stay almost 24 hours, let alone perch on your car, your cottage porch and sit near a broom...hawks are afraid of brooms." Lorrie said emphatically.

"Really? Cool. Look at his blue eyes; they're like my Tim's. I Googled and found that hawks eyes are not usually blue but yellow or brown."

"I've never seen a hawk with blue eyes; it's not a characteristic trait. And the dragonfly perched on his shoulder, that's crazy. Hawks eat dragon flies."

"Maybe Timmy didn't want to eat another spirit relative."

Excited to confirm each of my hawk experiences, I handed her my next treasure, "Lorrie can you tell me what kind of feather this is?" I told her the horrible story of when I ran over the dog, Diego and found this dry feather the morning after on the soaking wet pavement.

"That's definitely a hawk underbelly feather. Your husband certainly finds ways to bring you comfort in your sorrow. Thank you for sharing your Tim with us."

That evening, I relaxed on the back deck feeling peaceful after another fulfilling anniversary event in honor of my Tim. A soft breeze caressed my left ear and I knew he was there.

Hello my love, I've wanted a sign from you about where to go and what to do with my life. Even though I was upset, I knew your message to move forward was what I needed to hear. Lisa said your love is a form of bright light. Holding Machu today with his wings spread in anticipation felt like you sending your guiding light. Let's see what unfolds as I take flight.

PROGRESSION

43

How people treat you is their karma, how you react is yours.

— Dr. Wayne Dyer

After the elation of the *Hawk Walk*, I was *not* looking forward to returning to work. I hadn't been there since I went to Vashon, preferring solitude so I could process what I'd heard from Timmy through Lisa.

As I reluctantly walked to my office, I thought about the end of the bird show and a smile came to my face. While Lorrie and Talon packed up their birds, I thanked everyone for coming and handed out bubble wands. As luminescent circles of color filled the air, I said, "Let your wishes soar like Machu and when your bubble breaks, Timmy has heard you."

I'd sneaked in two wishes with one big bubble and asked Tim to continue to send signs and help me deal with my workplace drudgery. Yet when I sat down at my desk, a feeling of dread washed over me as I thought about what Lisa said about my toxic work atmosphere and untrustworthy officemates.

A few months earlier, after entering the lunchroom filled with chattering women who just went silent when I walked in, I'd told a remaining supportive colleague that I felt so uncomfortable I wanted to quit. In the past, I would let this kind of office clique crap roll off of my shoulders because I had Tim to kvetch to every night. But without his understanding ear, I was done. On top of the exhaustion of trying to survive each day, I hated being exposed to women who gossiped behind my back about how I was dealing with my grief, my life and God knows what else. Plus, I'd never fit their mold to begin with.

My colleague said, "These women have no clue about the depth of love you and Timmy shared. One of them would like to shoot her husband, another is getting a divorce and another has never been married and is miserable. In fact, they're all miserable. They've been jealous of you for years. They're not worth your time. Ignore them and keep doing what you do best, taking care of your patients and maintaining your personal and professional standards. You're doing an amazing job under difficult circumstances. Stay with your integrity, and don't stoop to their level."

"Easier said than done. Since I have my own office and my job has nothing to do with theirs, at least the only thing I have to share is this office suite. But I think I'll ask my boss to have someone from Human Resources come in and talk about toxic workplaces."

Before that could happen, I was called into Human Resources instead because my office mates were "worried about me." I was furious after hearing why they were worried — "because I was not at my desk at 9am and often came in late."

"That's *BULLSHIT!*" I said to the befuddled HR supervisor. "My job is a separate clinical practice in a shared office suite but it and has nothing to do with theirs. I'm awake before 5am and answer emails from patients and health care practitioners in my genetics field. Plus, I often work in the evening and on weekends because many of my contacts are in different time zones. I'm a professional and don't punch a clock. These women are not my superiors. I insist you call my boss who is fully aware of how much time I devote to work in and out of the office. He's the one who approved my flexible arrival time."

After the phone call to my furious boss, the HR person said, "I'm afraid we made a mistake, we're very sorry."

"If you're so sorry, then take it up with those "worried" people and tell them to mind their own business."

These officemates were supportive when Tim died, but that lasted about six months. I didn't even get the mythical "one-year" to get over my husband's death. Maybe I should have worn black like my Sicilian relatives. And I shouldn't have cried when a memory overwhelmed me or come to work without make-up for fear of a mascara-stained face.

When you open yourself up to others out of neediness, their support is welcomed. But that openness invites judgment when you don't follow others expectations of how you "should" grieve. The sad truth is, unless you've been widowed, you *cannot* possibly understand that unique kind of pain. I certainly had no clue until it happened to me. So I had to deal with others' primarily negative judgments about everything I did while trying to understand, knowing they were clueless. But that was difficult when their actions spoke louder than words and they'd ignore me rather than lend a needed tissue or kind word.

When I told them I was having a rough day, their answers revealed everything: "You just need to get out more or stop dwelling on your husband so much. You were too close." I quickly learned these were not people to confide in. Since I didn't associate with them outside of work, I didn't count them amongst my losses.

Thankfully, after the HR incident, people did mind their own business. I remained my gracious self and came and went as before, working closely with my boss and doing my job.

As I sat at my desk that morning, reliving those memories of the last two years was painful, but I was becoming expert in my ability to cope with people and things not in my control. As Tim taught me through Lisa, keeping the "energy vampires" at bay was critical, while understanding I was learning powerful lessons in my life.

Well, Boo, I'll chalk all of this crap up to moving forward and know this too will pass. As they say, "Living well is the best revenge."

With that thought, I was glad I had my St. Bart's vacation to look forward to in three weeks. Unfortunately, no friends would be able to join me this time. I was about to have a crash course in *Widow Traveling Alone 101.*

NO
EXPECTATIONS

44

Let your dreams outgrow the shoes of your expectations.

— Ryunosuke Satoro

The day before my St. Bart's departure, I pulled my empty travel purse out of the closet and set it on a chair. When I grabbed it to put my passport in, it fell on the floor and a 2011-D penny and 2002-P dime rolled out of it.

Boo, I love it when you give me coins. Thanks for letting me know you're here!

Later that evening, while sautéing garlic and kale, I thought I felt Lucca rub against my leg. I looked down and by my foot was a four-inch long white feather.

Wow, Timmy, thanks again! You must be growing as an angel; this white feather is much bigger than the last on one you gave me!

I placed the feather, penny and dime in my purse and breathed a sigh knowing Timmy would be with me on my solo expedition. Even though these events were

November 26, 2011—Four-inch Feather found on the kitchen floor the day before my trip to St. Bart's.

somewhat calming, I was still filled with angst. As familiar as I was with St. Bart's, I decided to have *no* expectations because when I imagined being there alone, fear rose in my gut. It wasn't so much being afraid of anything real or tangible; it was fear of the unknown that took my breath away.

When the small plane descended on the St. Bart's runway, a hawk appeared flying low by my window then veered off to rocky cliffs near the airport. I was shocked. I'd never seen a hawk in all of my previous trips there, but he was definitely soaring in the sky.

Even if I'd allowed myself to have expectations, this would *not* have been on my list.

When I pulled up to my villa, what I assumed was the same hawk swooped out of the sky and flew over the pool. *Did you follow me? You gonna take a swim? Let me get naked and join you.*

The first week passed with no more TWH sightings. I tried to stick with my original plan and not expect anything. I went about my routine of indulging in sun, sand, delicious seafood and wonderful French wines.

I splurged and ate lunch at a different restaurant every day. Some of the wait staff remembered me from our previous trips and were always welcoming. Then they would ask if my husband would be joining me. I explained the situation and pointed to his memorial card I always put on the table. Some people were appropriate and others just shied away. Death doesn't make for nice conversation in tropical paradise.

With no designated driver after sunset cocktails by my pool, evenings were spent at the villa, reading, writing and enjoying simple meals with occasional stray cats to keep me company. I was amazed at my resilience doing it all alone.

Henry called from France to check on me and make sure all was okay at his house. "If you buy any paté there, be sure to pack it in your suitcase," he teased.

"Don't worry Henry, I don't have you to rescue me, unless you and Anne-Marie want to hop a plane and join me! Although I have to admit, I'm doing okay here on my own."

Nine days into the trip, while taking an early morning walk on St. Jean beach, TWH startled me as he flew low out of nowhere. He circled a few times over the crashing waves, flew over me again then disappeared. *You scared the crap outta me, Boo! I thought you were going to land on my head. Thank you for returning, though.*

Four days later, with my suitcase packed for departure the next day, I was getting into bed and noticed the night movement floodlight was shining on the driveway. The villa is the only house at the end of a long dead end unpaved road so anyone who arrives has to be either lost or worse.

Thinking the worst, I locked my bedroom door. With my back against the wall, I peeked sideways out the window trying to stay hidden. A tall figure emerged from under the light; face forward, eyes glowing. Unable to make out the image, despite being scared out of my mind, I turned myself full view and looked out the window. Fifty feet away stood a huge white peacock, feathers folded down, neck fully extended with its beak reaching for the light. Its curiosity satisfied, the light dimmed as it sauntered into the night and my heart went back into my chest.

Timmy, remind me to look up peacock symbolism and if you ever decide to come to me in a different bird again, please do it in the daytime.

As I boarded the plane for home, TWH flew by the cliffs near the airport where I'd first seen him. I breathed a thankful sigh, *You're such a handsome hawk but miniature compared to the ones at home. Maybe you don't need so many feathers in this warm climate!*

I later learned the species in St. Bart's was a broad-winged hawk, with similar coloring but much smaller than the red tail ones I spotted in the Northeast.

After surviving two weeks alone that were surprisingly pleasant — even with bursts of tears and sadness — I returned home to face the dreaded holiday season. Since my rule of "no expectations" kept me in good stead while away, I decided it might be a good way to proceed. After all, you can't be disappointed if you don't expect anything.

Christmastime with my family went by fast. Another sad holiday in my childhood town; all previous happy memories clouded by my sorrow. As I drove back home during a blinding snowstorm, I especially missed Timmy's safe, strong arms at the steering wheel.

I hate driving through this! Timmy, please keep me safe so I can get back to missing you with Lucca and Vivi in my arms.

Hoisting my own suitcase and all the airplane and car travel did a number on my body. Ever since my neck surgery, I've had chronic neck and back pain so frequent massages and visits to my chiropractor, Sandi, have become a routine part of life. Two days after my intense drive home, as Sandi was calming my weary back, she told me a story about her son Zak that soothed my weary heart even more.

I knew that her six-year old son has been intuitive since he was two when he announced he saw his great grandpa, Sammy, in his dreams. Sam died when Sandi was a teen, but Zak knew his name and could describe what he looked like, even though Sandi swore she'd never spoken about him.

When Timmy died, Zak begged his mother to go to his calling hours at the funeral home. Zak had only met Timmy once, but said his grandpa Sam told him to go. Since then, Zak has kept Timmy's memorial card on his bed stand and has spoken often of visiting Timmy and Grandpa Sammy in heaven.

In fact, just before I'd left for St. Bart's, Zak told Sandi, "Timmy takes the bad men to that other heaven, you know, the one with all of the gold. He's like a policeman, but he's different. He helps a lot in heaven and has a special job like he did when he was here." Zak had no idea Tim was a judge in real life.

I loved hearing Zak stories from Sandi but this new one was the best so far: "On Christmas morning, Zak told us he was going to see if Santa's reindeer ate the food he left for them on the front lawn. He raced out the door and came back with a little bell. He said Timmy left it for him! His dad and I looked at each other and shrugged our shoulders knowing neither of us did it. Zak was so excited, he ran upstairs and put the bell in a special box near his bed where he keeps Timmy's memorial card."

"That's a sweet story, Sandi. Ask Zak to make Timmy into something more interesting than a bell and put him under my pillow please!"

It was dusk when I pulled into my driveway, back and neck adjusted for now. A fresh coat of snow covered the ground. Only my headlights lit the way and out of the corner of my eye, I saw a glimmer near the crabapple tree in the front yard. I parked the car and walked out of the garage to find a strange silver

December 26, 2011—
Zak found this bell where he'd left food for Santa's reindeer. He said Timmy put it there for him.

object lying in the snow.

My first thought was part of a wreath had blown off a neighbors' door but it was unlike any wreath I'd ever seen. Two silver, shimmery six by three inch somewhat triangular shaped hollow objects were joined in the middle so they fanned upward.

My intuition kicked in and I asked, *Is it a heart, Timmy? No, it looks kind of wing-like but what the hell is it?* The familiar confirmatory goose bumps sprouted on my arms and I knew this was something special, now I just had to figure out what it was.

The next day Sandi stopped by on her way to work, excited about my crazy phone call telling her what I'd found the night before. She examined the odd find and said as she rubbed her own goose-bumped arms, "Okay Anne Marie, this is definitely something from Timmy but what the hell is it?"

"You got me by the sneaks; let's ask Zak."

Holding up her cell phone she said, "Okay, I'll take a picture, but I won't tell him anything. I'll show him tonight when I get home and let you know."

I heard Sandi laughing as I grabbed my phone around 6pm, fumbled and almost dropped it in anticipation. "Damn, sorry. Okay, so what did he say?"

"I didn't give anything away. I simply said, 'Hey Zak, look at this cool picture' and he nonchalantly said to me, 'Oh, those are Timmy's wings.'"

"OMG! This is so cool!"I said.

Sandi continued, "I was surprised and said 'Timmy's wings, how do you know, Zak?' He was exasperated with me and said, 'Because Momma, I've seen them in heaven!'"

December 29, 2011 —"Timmy's Wings" found in the snow in my front yard.

I shrieked, "Timmy knows my favorite Christmas movie is *It's a Wonderful Life*. Do you know the part near the end where the little girl says 'when a bell rings, an angel gets his wings?' Well, Zak got the bell and I have Timmy's wings!"

Sandi later mentioned the angel/wing story to six-year old Zak and even though he'd never seen the movie, he said, "Well of course Momma, everyone knows that!"

On New Year's Eve, in front of my blazing fireplace, I thought back to my mantra of how this month began. I raised a glass of champagne and said, *Here's to you my love. Thank you for all of my gifts this month. You certainly have exceeded my expectations!*

DO YOU BELIEVE IN MAGIC

45

The most beautiful experience we can have is the mysterious. He to whom this emotion is a stranger, who can no longer pause to wonder and stand wrapped in awe, is as good as dead.

— Albert Einstein

With New Year's Eve upon me, I focused on positive goals for 2012. I loved The Spring's burning bowl/white stone ceremony and decided I'd burn away "Suffering" and name this year's main intention "Perseverance." I knew in my gut, despite all I'd accomplished, there was a long road ahead. Perseverance was key.

Now, in year number three, I was still figuring out how to keep going down that road. As they say, putting one foot in front of the other gets you over a mountain. Problem was, my mountain path felt like it had too many twists and turns without a clear view around the next corner. Some days I was content to just plant my feet out of bed. Since I was enjoying dancing again, I decided it was time to use my feet for something fun.

I'd seen an article about local dancing classes for women who'd been through trauma and loss. Meeting like-minded survivors of adversity, why not? I couldn't recall the website, but it had the word healing in it, so I Googled "dancing, healing." Although I knew it wasn't the right website, the first title that came up was intriguing, "Welcome to Dancing Drum Healing Arts, www.dancingdrumha.com".

When I clicked on the site, and saw picture of a hawk in flight down a road toward home, I was enthralled. I touched *home* and saw the words "Shamanism" at the top. I scrolled through the info bar and when I saw the words "Soul Retrieval," I smiled and said, *Timmy, I just found the first stepping-stone of my 2012 perseverance path.*

I pulled a distant memory out of my weary brain. A few months after Tim died, I was in a particularly desperate place, walking around the house crying to the air, *Timmy I don't know how to heal from this trauma. I'm split, raw, bleeding.*

Not knowing what else to do, I sat at my computer and googled every derivation of the word "grief" I could think of. I'd grieved the loss of each baby, but this was a whole different level of pain. I found an article that resonated with me: "loss of a significant person in your life traumatizes every cell of your entire being, mind, body and soul."

I got the trauma part right, Timmy. I've been attacked and clubbed repeatedly by a force I can't defend against. When will it stop pummeling me?

No answers came. My googling venture continued. I typed in "healing emotional trauma," and found thousands of links devoted to talk therapy. I already had a therapist and knew I needed something more. As I scrolled down the page, the words "Shamanic Healing" appeared. With a mouse click, a new world opened to me.

Of all the links that popped up, I chose Sandra Ingerman's website, www.sandraingerman.com because I liked her name. Names and eyes have never steered me wrong. As I read through her extensive website, I came across the words "Soul Retrieval" and was definitely intrigued: "It is believed that whenever we suffer an emotional or physical trauma, a part of our soul flees the body in order to survive the experience. The definition of soul is our essence, life force, the part of our vitality that keeps us alive and thriving. The shamanic healing ritual of soul retrieval returns the lost part of the soul."

My soul feels lost for sure. Now how do I find a Shaman to do this getting back my soul thing?

I clicked on www.shamanicteachers.com and was shocked to find a list of practitioners all over the world. *Timmy wow, another slice of life I know nothing about!*

I scrolled down and found a Shamanic healer practicing an hour west of me near Rochester. I emailed her, but after exchanging several conflicting dates, I gave up and decided it wasn't the right time. The idea was pushed into a dusty brain drawer. Since then, the only other time I'd heard about shamanism was this past June's summer solstice ceremony where the shamanic priestess said I had a powerful spirit behind me.

I snapped back to the present drawn in by the picture on Dancing Drum's website. *Boo, I know you've been behind me helping me on my way. And now another hawk is telling me this IS the right time.*

The site belonged to Pat Floyd, shamanic healer, Reiki master and occupational therapist. I saw Soul Retrieval listed as one of her services and picked up the phone. When Pat answered, her voice put me at ease as I told her I was widowed and in need of her help.

"Trauma like yours, Anne Marie, is life changing and debilitating."

Aha, that word trauma again. She gets it. "Pat, I've done many things to heal but it's still so difficult. I read about Soul Retrieval and it sounds like something worth trying."

"We'll find your way to healing together. The soul retrieval can't be done in one sitting. Let's plan to meet at least twice, the first session will be a soul journey and we'll go from there," explained Pat. We scheduled our first meeting for January 6th at her home in Ithaca, an hour east of where I live, and I counted the days.

Luckily, the roads were clear on that cold, sunny morning. I arrived at the top of a steep winding country road. Tall trees stood guard on both sides. I pulled into an almost equally winding driveway wondering where it would lead. Packed snow on crushed stone sang under my tires. With stomach churning, my eyes feasted on an adobe house resting amongst acres of snow-covered fields with forests and hills for miles around. I stood for a few moments, taking in the beauty and stillness, before knocking on the door.

Greeting me with a hug, Pat's crystal blue eyes drew me into her world. We walked through the narrow kitchen to the sunny great room filled with Native American artifacts, leather drums decorated with hand-painted animal figures, rattles, and huge fans made of feathers. A fire crackled in the large stone fireplace.

Pat sat in a comfy chair, hand outstretched to the couch. "Make yourself comfortable for our Soul Journey to connect with Spirit."

A spicy scent emanated from a nearby bowl. Pat explained she'd burned sage to cleanse, purify and protect our physical and spiritual bodies from any negative energy during our journey. I felt wary that we needed protection, but took a deep breath and settled in.

She gave me a hand-held leather drum that reminded me of a tambourine, only larger, and a drumstick. Pat explained we would call forth Spirit together, then picked up her drum, closed her eyes and started the beat. I'd never drummed before but soon our united efforts took me to a calm, centered place. This continued for several minutes. Then we stopped at the same moment as if something magically halted the movement of both of our hands.

I opened my eyes. Pat was smiling. "Your hawk was with me on my Soul Journey, Anne Marie."

"I didn't tell you about my hawk."

"He is your main power animal and he traveled with me and my main power animal, my wolf." Pat pointed to a large painting of a wolf, eyes intensely staring outward as if it was about to jump from the canvas.

"We traveled through a hole in a tree in the forest and found your second power animal, a sea turtle near the shore of a large lake. She was huge and emerged to lay four or five eggs in the sand, then she stayed in the sun and bathed in the light. After covering her eggs with sand for protection, she returned to the water and swam below. She then surfaced and I climbed onto her back for a ride in the water as your hawk flew nearby and my wolf stayed behind near her eggs. The message from your sea turtle is that you are protected. You have many options open to you, once you are free."

Confused I said, "Once I'm free?"

"Yes. Your turtle said to stay afloat; the eggs are your options. Remain open to all of them in your future as you move forward."

"I don't understand."

"You will in time. Also, your husband was with us. He is always around you. When you see your power animals, he is in them. He may not be every hawk or animal you see but they each have a message so watch and listen."

"That's cool. He comes in hawks and this fall I had one visit me

 for several hours at a cottage on Lake Ontario. I now remember a turtle was there as well. My friends and I had taken a hike and kicked off our sneaks to go swimming. When we returned, we found a turtle by our shoes on the concrete patio just outside the door. The cottage is quite a distance from the lakeshore and up on a platform so we weren't sure how the turtle got there. I put it in the sand and it waddled back to the lake and swam away. I felt the turtle meant something but I wasn't sure what."

"Those hawk and turtle visits were to show you the way. Spirit is still with us, Anne Marie. Now it's time for your Soul Journey. Lie down on the couch and cover your eyes with this scarf. May I touch your arm while we travel? I need to stay connected to you."

"Of course, this is cool!" I kicked off my shoes and got comfortable even though being blindfolded felt weird. Pat placed her warm-socked foot on my arm and began drumming.

After a few minutes my mind drifted into a meditative state, but I could still hear and "see" with my mind's eye. I sensed myself traveling, and then I was dancing on the lakeshore around the turtle eggs. Timmy hawk was there. He perched on my hand as I danced. My sea turtle emerged from the water and I noticed the sun was beginning to set. I walked over and joined her in the water. We submerged and swam next to each other underwater while TWH flew above us. A green luminescent light surrounded me. We swam to the surface and returned to the beach. I began to dance again and as the sun set in the water, I heard a voice say, "Be still, you will be all right."

As Pat's drumming continued, I felt something pressing on the bridge of my nose, like a weight was resting on my forehead. I opened my eyes and sensed a shadow passing over me even though I couldn't see through the scarf. I kept feeling intermittent pressure between my eyebrows and knew from my Reiki experience, it was on my third eye chakra, the seat of my intuition. I thought I heard a whisper in my right ear. I reached up; it felt cool to my touch. I noticed my body felt cool as well even though I'd covered myself with a blanket.

Pat stopped drumming. In the next instant, there was pressure on my heart and a whoosh of warm air was blown into my chest. I took a deep breath, feeling a bit shocked, even though Pat had explained what she was about to do. Then a whoosh of warm air caressed the top of my head and seemed to enter my brain. I felt lightheaded. I sat up slowly, took off the blindfold and noticed a hollow piece of bamboo in Pat's hand that she'd used to blow warm air into my heart and crown chakras.

"Pat, did I die and you just warmed me back to life?" I said half-joking.

"No, you didn't die but we journeyed into the underworld, it can be cold there. The warm air was for healing and attunement to bring you back to this middle world we live in."

I shook my head, "I felt like I was in another world." Then I recounted my Soul Journey to Pat.

"You've certainly connected with your Power animals, Anne Marie."

"How did I do that? I've been dabbling in meditation for awhile but I've never had such a vivid experience."

"Yours was a true shamanic journey. Pay attention to your power animal messages until we meet for your Soul Retrieval. It would be useful to have a hawk and turtle image near you throughout your day."

"I already have a hawk feather and wooden statue. I just remembered, Timmy and I found a sea turtle skeleton in St. Bart's years ago and I kept its back shells. How was I to know they would be a part of my future?"

"They are an important part indeed. The hard shells provide protection for the turtle so keep one with you whenever you leave home. Your turtle's message is that you need extra protection right now in your life."

"I do feel vulnerable now that Timmy is gone." Before Pat had a chance to correct me I continued, "now that Timmy is *physically* gone. I know he is with me in spirit and in these power animals."

"Yes, I sense that your Tim is a wise old soul but he's not your only protector. Along with him, I sensed another spirit presence behind you on the couch. I believe you have a Native American spirit who also watches over you."

"That's interesting because during this past year's summer solstice ceremony, another shaman told me I had a wise old spirit behind me. I assumed it was Tim. Today when I felt a whisper in my right ear, I thought it was unusual because Tim comes to me on my left side. I was told by my Reiki master left is my feminine side. So now feeling something on the other masculine side, I guess I'm fully covered," I chuckled.

"You have many protectors who will help you. Listen, watch and allow today's Soul Journey to integrate into your daily life, you will recall and use what you need."

I drove off in a fog, hardly able to comprehend what had just happened over the last intense four hours. That wasn't unusual when I was dabbling in alternative healing modalities. Since I had no frame of reference, I allowed myself to go with the flow and asked very few questions. I wanted to trust the process and so I did.

Ten days later, as I was driving back to Pat's for my Soul
Retrieval, my mind drifted over what had transpired in the interim.
My work life had gotten increasingly worse. I'd walk by an office of
women talking, they'd stop, and then when I passed, they'd start
laughing and close the door. Was I back in grade school? I attempted
to take matters into my own hands. If Human Resources'
interventions couldn't help, I would help myself.

I spoke honestly to three people, an administrator and two staff
members, who'd all previously supported me but then transformed
into snarky actresses in a bad workplace sitcom. Walking into each
of their offices with Margaret Thatcher charm while keeping
Michael Corleone in reserve, I thanked them for their "concern" that
I wasn't at my desk and assured them I was working at home (as if I
needed their approval). I told them there was no need to be worried
about me, but my words didn't penetrate and my intervention
backfired — each one of them was defensive and wouldn't admit
they'd spoken with HR. I knew it was time to leave. Could that be
what my sea turtle was saying about the eggs and all of the options
before me?

As I returned to the present moment, I was so deep in thought, I
almost missed Pat's driveway. I climbed out of my car with armor in
hand. Even though Pat had multiple artifacts at my disposal, I
wanted to be surrounded by my own objects: Timmy's handkerchief
and travel urn, my hawk underbelly feather, a wooden carved
statue of a hawk and five pieces of tortoise shell from St. Bart's.

Pat was pleased. "Bringing your own sacred objects is
wonderful. Make yourself comfortable and we'll start the journey
the same way we did last time."

I lay down on the couch and tied Timmy's handkerchief around
my eyes while Pat touched my arm with her foot and started
drumming. With the familiar pressure on my third eye chakra and
coolness in my body, I began to relax into the experience. My
meditative state was not as deep as before and I didn't encounter
any power animals. I felt in suspended animation surrounded by
the same brilliant green iridescent light that I saw when swimming
with my turtle, but she wasn't there either.

Pat stopped drumming in what seemed like a very short time.
When she sent her warm breath into my heart, this time, my chest

felt very full. And the warm breath into the top of my head seemed to bathe my entire body. When I uncovered my eyes and sat up, I was shocked to see almost two hours had gone by.

Pat smiled and said, "I have much to share." Her blue eyes sparkled and for a moment, I thought I saw Tim in her face. I took him in and waited for her to continue. "I traveled with my wolf and your power animals to three places. The first was a utility closet in the hallway of an office building. You were hiding in the closet and didn't want to come out."

I interrupted her, "That's amazing. There is a utility closet at the end of my hallway. I pass it every time I get off the elevator at work."

She continued, "All of the animals coaxed you out and assured you it would be all right. You were wearing a lab coat and a stethoscope. I took the stethoscope and listened to your heart but it was not there, your heart was missing."

I thought, it's broken *and* missing?

"We walked into an office suite and a man dressed like you was there, it must have been your boss. A cord ran from his heart to where your heart had been. Anytime there is a cord energetically connecting you to another living being, it means soul theft. Your sea turtle and hawk broke the cord with their beaks. Wolf offered the man a gift but he disappeared without it. Wolf handed you the gift, a glowing ball of light. You took it; sprouted wings then shape-shifted into a hawk and flew away. We followed you to a hospital room where a man lay dying. It was Tim. You hovered over him, your wings drooping in sorrow. The moment he died and his soul left his body, a piece of your soul and your heart left to be with him."

Crying, I said, "Yes, I'm sure my heart and soul left with him. I've felt so empty."

"I know. You were so lost without him. But Anne Marie, today when you became a hawk, you flew into the cosmos with the healing ball of light to retrieve your heart and soul fragments that left with him. As much as you miss him, you need your full heart and soul on this physical plane. You can become a hawk anytime and travel to be with him but you must return until it's your time for transition. I don't see that happening for a quite awhile."

I sighed at yet another confirmation of a long life without Tim, but was happy to know I could shape-shift into my own hawk to be with him. This bizarre idea sounded perfectly rational after these experiences with Pat.

She continued, "We then traveled to a classroom and you shape-shifted from your hawk back into yourself as a little girl. Your head was on your desktop covered by your hands. You'd been humiliated by your teacher and unfairly blamed by another girl. The healing ball of light hovered over you and you got up and did an outrageous, uninhibited tap dance on the teacher's desk. You were free and happy without shame or blame any longer."

My gaped jaw shut slowly and I began to retell my story as if I was there. "When I was nine years old, I had a horrible experience with a teacher, Sister Mary Agatha and a fellow student, Nancy Purdy…I'll never forget her name…who blamed me for something I didn't do. A boy was trembling at the blackboard unable to answer her question so Sister "Agony" (my name for her) was mocking and calling him stupid. He started to cry and someone blurted out the answer, fed up with her abuse. When Sister Agony turned and shrieked at the class, Miss Know-It-All, Nancy Purdy blurted out in a singsong obnoxious voice, "Annie Patti said it, I heard her!"

Pat shook her head and said, "So what happened?"

"Agony hovered, yelling at me over my desk. Mercifully, the lunch bell rang; I rushed out the door and ran home. My mother calmed me and after hearing my story, called the school and asked to meet with Sister Agatha. I was scared to go back, but my mother assured me she would protect me. And that she did, because Agony believed me and apologized so I thought I got out of the ordeal somewhat unscathed."

"That was certainly a traumatic childhood event that has stayed with you all of your life."

"Yeah, whenever I've felt belittled and wrongly accused in my life, I jokingly have said I'm back in Sister Agatha's fourth grade classroom. Since Timmy died, I've had a difficult time with cliquey women in my office suite. It feels like I'm with a bunch of bullying grammar school kids who have nothing better to do than to mind *MY* business."

"They are not to be trusted Anne Marie. I can understand why you didn't want to come out of the utility closet but you have powerful spirit protection and your own strength as well."

But Pat, how did you know about that and *everything else*? I didn't tell you I worked in an office building and not a hospital setting. My husband being in a hospital room is obvious, but he could have died at home. How do you know all of this?"

She waited for me to finish and said, "I don't know this. Spirit knows and took us there; I'm simply giving you information shared with me."

I was speechless. Then a concern dawned on me. "I understand how I lost pieces of my soul during traumatic events in my life but I love my boss, there has been no trauma with him. You said a cord between us meant soul theft."

"You and he are very close and the connection with him in that particular setting caused you the trauma, not him. The cord needed to be severed so you could move forward away from the trauma caused by those women at work. They've treated you just like Nancy Purdy in the fourth grade."

"That's for sure. They just added to the trauma of that childhood horror and Timmy's death. For awhile now, I've wanted to leave the toxic work atmosphere but do I have to sever ties with my boss to move forward?"

"I don't think so because the cord was cut and you regained your lost soul pieces as well as your heart."

"You know Pat, my chest feels fuller now and my body feels a sense of wholeness. I still miss my husband immensely, and always will, but I somehow know I'll be okay."

"You can go forward in your life however you choose, your turtle showed you there are many options open to you. Be well. Spirit is always with you as is Timmy. I'm here if you need me in the future."

With a grateful hug, I left hopeful, and ready for whatever the future had to hold.

ILLUMINATION
46

May the bridges I burn light the way.

— Dylan McKay

T he next day, I went back to work with renewed vigor. Just after I arrived, my department chairman called me to meet with him. What now? I thought as I walked across the street to his office, far away from our soap opera. I entered his door and saw his dour expression.

"Anne Marie, I'm devastated; the grant for your salary extension did not come through. We can apply again in six months but in the interim, there is no funding to pay you. We've tried several avenues and have found none. I'm so sorry but January 31st is your last day. Thank you for your exemplary service all these years. I know it's been hard that some people have been insensitive since your husband died, I am so sorry. "

My eyes couldn't have been wider as I thought; NOW you come to my rescue about our toxic workplace. No matter. I squelched a "whoo-hoo" shout. With less than two weeks to go in a job atmosphere I'd grown to hate, I feigned disappointment about losing my job after 31 years at the hospital.

My boss, who was also devastated, couldn't be there during my last few days because of other commitments. I was fine with that because I knew somehow we would continue our professional relationship. The cord that held us together there was severed. The universe and Spirit would provide for us.

On the drive home, I felt elated and frightened at the same time. *Boo, this is confusing but exciting, too. Apparently I have several potential choices before me; my four to five eggs buried in the warm sand waiting for their hatching time. That's cool but I'm beyond scared about how I will survive without my paycheck.*

My practical, survival mode brain kicked in and I realized I qualified for unemployment. Repeating my sea turtle's mantra, "be still and everything will be all right," I knew I'd be okay. I remembered Alex's job change prediction from my astrological chart and her advice about my own awakening.

So is this leaving my job a part of my awakening I so vehemently resisted hearing about? Well, it looks like I get to follow my own path now. I know you're on your own path, too Boo, but please visit mine from time to time, okay?

I chose not to tell the rest of the office about my impending departure. I had no stomach for a fake, happy retirement party. The day before I left, the office suite manager called a meeting to review issues that had nothing to do with me but I attended anyway. Towards the end, when asked if anyone had other announcements, I raised my hand and declared, "For those of you who don't know (I didn't assume my private business stayed private), tomorrow is my last day here." There was stunned silence. Wow, that shocked the crap out of them, I thought gleefully.

For what it was worth, the afternoon was filled with affectionate well wishes that I accepted with graciousness. The next day, I walked out the door at 5pm with head held high, knowing I'd done my best under incredibly difficult circumstances.

Fast-forward seven months and, happily, one of my egg options predicted by Tim through Lisa presented itself on a silver platter. But a lot of incubation had to come first.

CONTEMPLATION

47

Fall down seven times,
Stand up eight.

—Japanese Proverb

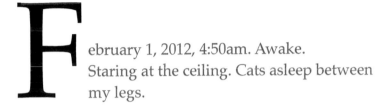

February 1, 2012, 4:50am. Awake. Staring at the ceiling. Cats asleep between my legs.

Here I am with two major life losses in a short time: you, my beloved husband and now my job. On that Life Events Stress Scale, I've hit the top two and then some. I should be in the loony bin by now. At least I had you to help with the loss of our babies. And don't you, or my spirit guides, or whoever the hell is in charge up there DARE take our Lucca and Vivi. You must leave me something to live for.

As much as I was thrilled to leave my toxic workplace, an involuntary departure was not what I had in mind. Why do people wish for more time to do whatever they want? I really wasn't there yet, thinking I was going to retire much later. Now I was free and freaking scared! Scared about money, about what to do with my time, and whether my grief would get worse without a daily routine. Necessity called and I quickly learned to budget money because my cash flow was depleted. But I don't spend much money, except on vacations that are sacrosanct for my sanity — or what was left of it.

My first time-filling decision was starting a writing class at Oasis, an adult education center, exactly one week into my forced retirement. I never imagined those classes would blossom into writing this memoir (one egg incubation started and hatched); I simply wanted to fill my time in a creative way. I also signed up for classes in Jungian psychology, Nia dance and Apple computer courses. Since I had to give back my PC that my boss provided to do work at home, I decided to be adventurous. What the hell, everything else in my life changed so why not? I already owned an iPad but going all Apple added another level of anxiety to my never-before-experienced-world that I was sure to screw up.

But classes did not fill all of my time. Each night I pondered what I needed to do, like feed myself and the cats, versus what I wanted to do now with all the time in the world; I often came up dry. I repeated my Scarlet O'Hara mantra, "After all, tomorrow is another day."

Boo, this starting my life over again has its own grief, and I was just getting the hang of grieving YOU! There's always something to learn on this crazy, unpredictable journey. Maybe instead of Scarlet, I should be channeling my Italian "cousin" Christopher Columbus!

As I navigated the uncharted waters of unemployment and filling my daily existence, I eventually got the hang of life in the slow lane. Recalling the message from my Shamanic journey, I learned to enjoy time to "just be still"— not easy. Yet hours of solitude were a welcomed respite from my toxic work circus and nursing job of taking care of others. It was now time to take care of Anne Marie, a foreign concept at age 57.

The best thing I did for myself was to plan two Camp Widow retreats that year. Since 2009, Camp had been held once a year in San Diego. With an ever-growing worldwide interest and membership in Soaring Spirits, now aptly re-named Soaring Spirits International (SSI) the first Camp Widow East in Myrtle Beach, South Carolina was scheduled for late April and I booked my tickets. I needed my widowed peeps! My first Camp had taken me to a place where I could dance again and feel the sympatico of shared grief. Now I had more to share on this crazy ride.

Boo, I'll be at the first Eastern Camp. It's not cool that I'll be there, but you screwed that up. Still, the resort is gorgeous, right on the Atlantic, and to top it off, Roseann is going! This is her first Camp and trip away since her beloved Michael died so she's anxious. I've met a lot of widows who have a hard time traveling without their husbands but you and I will ease her way.

When I met my "widow match" the summer before, Roseann and I felt an instant bond. We're both half-Italian, in our soul mate relationships for over 30 years, and our wedding anniversaries were different years but one day apart. I was struck by the fact that her dark blond hair and blue eyes reminded me of my Tim. She was similarly amused that my wit was like her Michael's. Our weekly phone calls and frequent emails kept our relationship moving forward, and now we were going to spend more time together.

We synced our Myrtle Beach flight times and shared a cab. When we arrived at the hotel, we were greeted by several of my widowed friends. "Wow, Anne Marie, everyone at Camp is so welcoming," commented Roseann.

"We're all in the same sucky situation so special bonds develop quickly."

Despite a few emotional breakdowns during the workshops, by the Saturday night dinner dance, Roseann was able to relax and enjoy herself.

"You look mahvelous, dahling," I said as she posed in her black lace brocade cocktail dress.

"As do you my dear, what a fun Marilyn Monroe look-alike dress," Roseann said as I twirled in my white, low back halter dress.

"Yeah, I wore black last year and this year white because it's been so long since I've had sex, I'm a virgin again!"

After the evening of fun in the photo booth, eating, and dancing to "only fast songs," the music stopped at 11:30pm. Then, on cue, 114 widowed men and women donned glow necklaces and in hushed silence, our founder, Michele Neff Hernandez led us into the dark night.

It had been raining all day but it stopped just in time for us. Puffy white clouds lent dim light to the starless sky. We walked silently, following a path past the hotel pool and gardens down to the ocean, clutching our precious stashes. When we reached a wooden walkway leading to the wide sandy beach, everyone kicked off their dancing shoes and went barefoot; grieving people side by side visible only by our necklaces and the light of anticipation.

Over the roar of the ocean's rolling waves, Michele's voice pierced our silence, "Whenever you are ready, you will know."

Slowly, in fluid motion, our bare feet greeted the cool, wet sand. Roseann and I, arms wrapped around one another and faces forward to the ocean mist, walked to the edge of the shoreline along with the others. Some were arm in arm, others alone, hugging themselves. We reached the water and waded in to just below our knees. The ocean waves splashed and skimmed our dresses. One glance toward each other and we knew. With tears streaming down our faces, we separated and opened our clenched fists.

In our hotel rooms, hours before, each grieving soul held a gold cellophane bag tied with white ribbon given to all of us at Camp registration. Inside each bag was a two-inch clear glass heart, a five inch square piece of biodegradable rice paper, green raffia twine and this note:

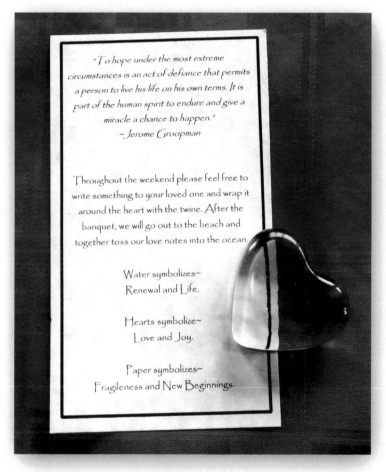

"To hope under the most extreme circumstances is an act of defiance that permits a person to live his life on his own terms. It is part of the human spirit to endure and give a miracle a chance to happen."
~ Jerome Groopman

Throughout the weekend please feel free to write something to your loved one and wrap it around the heart with the twine. After the banquet, we will go out to the beach and together toss our love notes into the ocean.

Water symbolizes~
Renewal and Life.

Hearts symbolize~
Love and Joy.

Paper symbolizes~
Fragileness and New Beginnings.

Getting ready for the dinner dance, in the solitude of my room, I felt Tim's presence. My body was warm and my heart was full as I pondered my note and spoke to him.

My precious Tim, I'm overwhelmed with a depth of love for you that I hadn't experienced when we shared our physical lives. I remember reading a blog called "Transcending Loss" where the author said our love would grow deeper after death. Ashley Davis Bush said that "death doesn't end the relationship, it forges a new type of relationship based on memory, spirit, and love." I refused to believe that was possible. It didn't make sense. It felt like a betrayal of our profound physical bond, and yet, at this moment, I know it's possible because it is happening. As I open myself to new depths of spiritual love, I'll write my message, tie the paper around your heart and meet you later at the beach. I'm wearing your favorite red linen shirt to be wrapped in your arms.

Standing in the water, bittersweet tears found their way to my lips, their salt mixing with the briny ocean mist. I stared at my open palm — one last look. I felt my outstretched arm reel back and with all the strength I could muster, I hurled Tim's note into the depths. Over the sound of the rolling waves my words came forth in a whisper, *I Adore You.*

The experience filled every cell in my body like an electrical current pulsing through me. I was suspended in time and overwhelmed by an intensity of emotion that left me breathless. I felt one with the water, the air, in a dream until frightened shouts pierced the beauty of my otherworld.

"Rick, come back now! Rick, it's time to come back!"

I looked toward the anxious voices and saw several people wading deeper into the crashing waves. I caught a glimpse of movement far out in the water but couldn't tell what it was. I looked to my left and saw Roseann bent over, crying into her trembling palms. I reached to comfort her, but we were jolted face forward by the shouting.

In the next instant, something white appeared in the distance emerging from the water slowly, coming back toward the shore. The white was a shirt and when he got close enough, we saw a man we'd met in our Widowed Without Children roundtable that afternoon. Rick told of his wife's untimely death in her early 30s before they had a chance to start a family. Listening to this man grieve the loss of his wife and children never born was a measure of sorrow I'd not heard before from any man.

As he reached the shoreline, worried comrades surrounded him. One asked, "Rick, why did you go out so far?"

Soaking wet from head to toe, he said, "I wanted to make sure my wife got my message."

Once I centered again, a feeling of elation washed over me coupled with deep sorrow. Roseann and I turned toward each other and start laughing and hugging through our tears. Intuitively, we felt the same emotions: joy and pain, side by side on this seemingly unending grief roller coaster.

Content to leave the brisk air, our cold, sandy feet started back. Roseann stopped a passerby and asked her to take our picture. This — by far — was the best gift our husbands could have given us that night.

Multiple Orbs surround us after our Ocean Message Release, Camp Widow East, Myrtle Beach, April 21, 2012.

An energy healer who attended Camp was blown away when we showed her this picture of so many loved ones there in spirit form. Even though we both knew this in our hearts, the healer told Roseann the large bluish orb above her head was her husband, Michael. And I was thrilled to see my Tim carefully positioned on my forehead over my third eye chakra, the seat of my intuition.

RESOLUTION
48

You must do the thing you think you cannot do.

— Eleanor Roosevelt

Anne Marie Higgins

Whon people asked how I was doing, I often said, "I don't recommend widowhood."

After uncomfortable reactions, I would say, "Widowhood is neither intuitive nor the Kubler-Ross staged orderly process. It's one step forward, a million steps back. It's horrible, relentless, all consuming and much worse than I *ever* could have imagined. It doesn't simply get better with time. You must be doing something to *fill* your time."

Many clueless people thought I should be using mine to look for a new husband. But I was in love with the husband I had! As far as I was concerned, I was still married. Love after death is not expected. *They* tell you to move forward, don't wallow in the past; your loved one is gone. But *they* are wrong. Love after death is intensely deep and intimate. I was shocked by its hold on me. In my wildest dreams, I never imagined our physical and emotional relationship could be deepened by our spiritual, soul connection in death.

I hated people telling me to find someone new — as if that would magically make everything better. In what other relationship are you encouraged to replace the dead person with someone new? When you lose a parent, grandparent or other relative, you don't search for new ones. When you lose a child, people may have another baby but that doesn't replace the one they've lost, neither does a new love. This misguided advice usually comes from the discomfort of others who can't tolerate your pain.

So I continued to find comfort with those who could tolerate my pain *and* fill my time making meaningful memories — my widowed community.

Returning to San Diego, my second Camp Widow that year, the most memorable event was a workshop called "Overcoming Obstacles and Mental Barriers" given by Taryn Davis, founder and director of the American Widow Project (AWP) for military widows and active volunteer for SSI.

I'd been inspired by her weekly messages on the Widow's Voice blog. As I was walking into Taryn's workshop, I thought back to when I'd met her four months ago at Camp East and fell in love with her vibrancy and lust for life.

To honor herself and her husband, Michael, Taryn did things to defy death: skydiving, walking on fire, breaking arrows against her trachea, just your everyday daredevil widow stuff. She shared her crazy experiences with other military widows and now it was our turn at Camp. Her gift to a dozen willing wacky widowed was a parasailing experience.

It was a cool morning on Myrtle Beach and the choppy Atlantic waves looked ominous. But our spirits were high as the first six donned life jackets and climbed onto the multi-person jet-ski that took them out to the parasail boat launch while the rest of us watched from shore.

One by one, Taryn and five others shot up behind the speeding boat and flew high in the sky laughing, thumbs up the whole way. As my cohort climbed onto the parasail launch from the jet-ski, we were energized by Taryn's infectious encouragement, "That was *awesome,* you guys! Go have a blast!"

Waves crashed against the launch and drenched our already wet bodies. As I was being strapped into the harness, dark clouds and lightening came out of nowhere. The boat with the remaining six had to return to shore.

I raised my fist and cursed the air, *Damn you, Timmy! Why ruin our fun?* After a few chuckles from my widowed cohort I said, "Sorry, you can blame my husband. He never wanted me to do anything risky even though I *loved* parasailing before we married. I thought I could do as I pleased now, but he's being a real ass."

Anne Marie Higgins

As we walked to the taxi to return to the hotel, the sky unleashed its fill. Taryn and I huddled under a large beach towel. She cracked up and said, "Ooh, this is fun, Michael and I would snuggle in towel forts and laugh until we cried." When the rain stopped, we emerged from our fun fort ready for our next adventure. Unfazed by the forced cancellation of our parasailing event, Taryn was ready to rock, "Okay all, let's go party!"

I looked at Taryn's huge brown eyes with wonder. How could she be so buoyant and full of life? How can this beautiful woman go on after being widowed at the age of 21? She and her beloved soul mate Michael had been together only five years when he was killed in Iraq. I could barely function some days after our 31 years. But Taryn lived the lesson that it is not the length of time spent with your loved one but the depth of love that matters most. Wise beyond her years and *awake* to her life, she manifested their love in her zest to go on, be in the moment, and not waste *any* time.

My mind shifted back to the present as I walked into the workshop's dimly lit room with eight other widows and one widower. I saw Taryn dressed casually in an American Widow Project T-shirt and jeans, head down, studying her notes, shoulder length dark brown hair tied back from her oval face. Her demeanor was solemn. I spied a piece of canvas blanketing a six-foot long rectangular shaped space on the floor; it looked like it a grave cover. Uh, oh, what did I get myself into?

Taryn began, "Character cannot be developed in ease and quiet. Only through experience of trial and suffering can the soul be strengthened, ambition inspired and success achieved." After reading this quote from Helen Keller, she hinted about "trials" we were about to undergo. The air-conditioned room grew warmer with our added body flushes of anticipation.

We each completed a workbook designed to assess any physical or emotional barriers we were carrying in the baggage of our grief journeys. After a group discussion and centering meditation, Taryn walked over to the canvas blanket and uncovered our first physical trial: "You each will walk this length of broken glass bottles barefoot, I will go first and you will follow. You *will* be fine, this is not an obstacle; it is simply something to overcome."

WTF! I was ready to bolt but talked myself into it after a smiling Taryn demonstrated and emerged unscathed. After a deep breath, with eyes closed and hands held on each side by fellow campers, I placed one bare foot and then the other on the blue and green glass shards. I could hear the glass breaking under my weight but there was no pain. I opened my eyes and walked the path slowly, methodically as Taryn had suggested and when I reached the end, yelled out, "Freaking Wow! I did it!"

We all did it! As we congratulated each other, a grinning Taryn declared, "Now trial number two." After collective protests that trial number one was enough craziness, she handed each of us a one inch thick, twelve inch square piece of solid wood. "Write on one side what you want to break through in your life and on the opposite side, what your life will look like when you've broken through that barrier."

With narrowed eyes and cocked head, I asked, "What the hell do you mean 'broken through,' Taryn?"

With a sly smile she said, "You will each break these solid boards with your bare hands. Break through the old to get to the new. Follow me outside. Overcoming your barrier awaits!"

The sun was shining brightly on the almost deserted hotel parking lot. On the sidewalk, near a wire fence that enclosed the pool area, four cement blocks were spaced several inches apart and stacked, two by two on top of each other forming a platform for our boards. Taryn demonstrated first then we each followed, gathering a cheering crowd of kids behind the fence at the pool.

As I summoned my inner beast, I yelled, "Ahhhhhh," and slammed my right palm downward into the open air for my first practice shot. After two more practice shots, I took aim and with my loudest scream, slammed my open palm downward. In the next instant, I saw my board on the ground, broken in half. Taryn raced to me and after a huge bear hug, I picked up the pieces of my board a transformed super widow!

Minutes later, with a glass of Prosecco in my slightly tingling hand, I read what I'd written on opposite sides of my board to my workshop mates, "I broke through my back pain and disability along with fear of learning new skills that keep me dependent upon others. I opened to goals of fulfilling work and play, spiritual growth, and the possibility of a new love."

A few days after Camp, when our board break video was posted on Soaring Spirit's Facebook page, I proudly shared it on mine and wrote, "When you've survived the death of your husband, walking barefoot on broken glass and breaking a wooden board with your bare hand is *EASY, EMPOWERING and a TOTAL BLAST!*"

Both my splintered board and the arrow I broke against my trachea the following summer at Camp are proudly displayed in my home to remind me of the strength I have found within.

INSPIRATION

49

*We shall draw from the heart of
suffering itself
the means of inspiration and survival.*

— Winston Churchill

After surmounting death-defying feats of breaking boards and walking on glass — okay, not quite, but humor me — I was feeling energized and determined to keep moving forward until my life came to another screeching halt two weeks after Camp.

As I was putting on a jacket before heading to my 6am bike class, I was stopped mid-sleeve by a searing pain in my right arm. I pulled it off and the pain shot up into my shoulder and upper back. Catching my breath after realizing I'd shrieked, I watched Lucca and Vivi skitter in the opposite direction. Ibuprofen and ice didn't touch it. I knew I needed something more and three hours later, I was in an MRI with the working diagnosis of rotator cuff tear.

My orthopedic nurse practitioner read the MRI report with surprise, "Well, Anne Marie it's not what I thought when I examined you, it's a SLAP tear, meaning *superior labral tear from anterior to posterior.* To put it more simply, the cartilage in your shoulder joint is torn. Usually it requires surgical intervention."

"I can't have surgery, my husband died. I have no one to take care of me. How the hell did this happen? I wasn't *doing* anything strenuous!"

"Sometimes it's just wear and tear. With your history of neck surgery, spinal cord compression and chronic pain, you've probably compensated with other muscles for years. Let's get the pain under control and have you start physical therapy, maybe it will be amenable to that. "

"It had better be because this body is not having any more knives in it. I'm still dealing with a precision cut to my heart."

Timmy's death overshadowed everything in my life and this was no exception. As I drove to fill the pain prescription, right arm in a sling, I stared out the window for a hawk to come swooping down to carry me away. *I've had enough, Boo. I'm ready to be with you now. When you die the pain stops, right?*

Committing suicide was not the answer and I wouldn't dishonor Tim's memory by taking my own life. But with the trauma of my last three years of grief and now more physical disability, I could understand why some people take their lives when the pain of living seems worse than the pain of dying.

When no hawk came to rescue me, I realized after two weeks of arduous PT treatments, I had to go this alone. *Damn you Timmy, why didn't you protect me? How the hell am I going to go visit Alex in Brittany this September? My white stone New Year's intention was "perseverance" so I guess I'm giving it a run for its money. Maybe I should have chosen "easy life" instead.*

But that did not come and perseverance won out. On September 7th, I found myself on a plane to France to be with my friend and astrologer with high hopes for answers and solace from my pain.

Alex and her family were vacationing in Morgat, a small fishing village in the south of France and invited me to join them. From my small corner room in her husband's childhood home, I could see a calm gray-blue bay and breathe in the salty ocean air. We took long beach walks and hikes in a nearby forest where beyond the protective bay, we had distant views of the mighty Atlantic. With our shared preference for cooking, we enjoyed meals of local seafood, meat and farm fresh vegetables. This was just the respite I needed.

I was also in need of a plausible reason why my shoulder was injured, even though I'd had no outward signs of trauma. I'd hoped Alex would be able to see this in my chart and tell me why this happened and what else my future held. My skeptical side, ever vigilant, insisted the injury was just overuse but my intuitive side told me it meant something more. "Besides Ms. Skeptical, everything Alex has said has come true, so just shut up and listen to her!"

"Who are you talking to Anne Marie?" Alex said as she entered my bedroom.

"Just my two selves arguing with each other; we do that a lot. Alex, I'm almost afraid to hear my reading. What the hell is going to happen to me next?"

Alex opened her thick astrology handbook and began, "You have had some significant challenges in your past, but I see a new direction and things becoming more stable."

As I breathed a sigh of relief that I'd been holding in for two weeks, Alex continued. "The cartilage tear in your shoulder represents anger turned inward. You were in a situation with people at work that you could not control and that triggered all of the deep-seated emotional traumas and loss in your life. It was like your body was screaming about all of your suffering and something had to give. But it's time to let go of your pain to begin anew, your shoulder will heal and you'll have a new professional start that will be fulfilling, profitable, and totally independent of your previous negative work relationships."

"Alex, did you know my boss and I are beginning our collaboration again? He retired like you said and started a non-profit internet-based organization that provides information for people we used to see at the hospital." Then I told her about my Shamanic Soul Retrieval, my turtle's eggs and how this one had hatched quite nicely. "But Alex, how do you *know* this?"

"Anne Marie, I don't *know* it, it's in your chart. I'm just telling you what is already written."

"That is too wild Alex, so my destiny is in the stars? What happened to free will?"

"You have the power to choose your path at any time, *except* (Alex caught my sly smile and knew what I was about to say) you can't bring Timmy back."

"Aw, what fun is free will, then?"

"You *can* find new love and I see that possibility after two more years."

Another confirmation of what Lisa said. "I'm almost ready for new love. I'm lonely for Tim but as time goes on and the reality of his death continues to beat me over the head, I must accept that he's not coming back, physically anyway."

"Anne Marie, you've been transformed by Tim's death. Your relationship's purpose reached its objective and you're now ready for a new reality. Tim will always be with you and continue to come to you in signs, but they will be less frequent. There will be moments where you will still touch him in an amazing way and *feel* him with you."

"I *do* feel him. I know when he is with me even when there is no overt sign. It's such an intense knowing in my body and soul. It brings palpable comfort." I hugged myself as if Tim's arms were around me.

"Your soul mate relationship with Tim is set in stone for Eternity, it is profound and unchangeable. *You*, however, will continue to change. You're coming out of your mourning and emerging from a dark cave. Tim's death in 2009 was a crossroad in your life that put in motion a seven-year transformation, a rebirth. By 2016, your life will look nothing like it does now."

"This seven year rebirth is interesting. Just before I came here, I read Michele Neff Hernandez's Widow's Voice blog about the seven-year anniversary of her husband, Phil's death in August. She talked about the ways in which trauma leaves a physical imprint on your body. I thought about all of the negative physical things that have happened to me since Timmy died. I feel my grief as a deep physical pain. And now you speak about my body injuries as manifestations of my grief."

"Yes, our minds and bodies are connected, inseparable."

"Michele quoted a scientific article that said almost every cell in our body regenerates after seven years so any trauma we experience in life stays with us on a cellular level for seven years. She interpreted that to mean there wouldn't be any cells left in her body that knew her Phil after seven years. That idea freaked me out. Will I forget what Timmy felt like, sounded like, smelled like after seven years? Is that what this rebirth is all about? That sounds so *empty* to me."

"I don't know if the seven years will manifest itself in that way with you, all I know is, *you* will change but the love you shared will never change."

"Well since my life is already totally different from the one I'd planned, I'll focus on being optimistic for the future because the worst I could've imagined has already happened."

When I returned home rejuvenated from my French retreat and Alex's reading, I was ready to begin anew. Reviewing the Adult Ed Oasis catalog, I chose to continue writing class, Jungian studies and noticed something new that intrigued me.

Boo, I've wanted to be in a Flash Mob since I saw the You Tube video of the one at a train station in Europe. When all of those people filtered out of the crowd and started synchronized dancing in this public place, it evoked such spontaneous joy in the surprised onlookers. And now I get to do one! What's really cool is the last rehearsal is scheduled for November 7th. Dancing my buns off on the anniversary of your transition is a sure sign for me.

A vivacious Oasis fitness instructor choreographed our routine. Lucky for the women who insisted they couldn't dance, her steps were easy to follow. After two and a half months of weekly practice, the instructor decided to postpone an early November performance and wait for a bigger audience. I was okay with that; I still danced my buns off at home to honor Tim's memory.

Five weeks and a few extra dance practices later, our big day arrived. As crazed holiday shoppers scurried about the Destiny USA Mall in Syracuse twelve days before Christmas, we melded with the crowd. When our music came over the loud speaker, fourteen women dropped their coats to reveal Oasis T-shirts and Michael Jackson gloves in honor of the first song *I'm Bad.*

As the crowd parted to give us room and cell phones recorded our performance, I was lost in the movement and beat of each song but it was the last song that got me. As Michael Buble belted out the last verse, *"It's a new dawn, it's a new day, it's a new life, for me,"* my fist in the air "whoo-hoo" echoed in the mall courtyard over the applauding shoppers.

When my mob mates formed a group hug, I told them, "Now I can check that off my Burning Desire List!" I never liked the term Bucket List, it reminds me of cancer; so I came up with my own phrase to build my dreams on.

Check out one of my dreams fulfilled — *Syracuse Oasis Senior Flash Mob* labeled that because all students are over 50 and we are (apparently) "mature adults": www.youtube.com/watch?v=xWCEJ0_aeSk_.

With another solo New Year's approaching, I reflected on what I had achieved on my Perseverance List in 2012: my Soul Retrieval, surviving my job loss and starting a new part time job (one egg hatched), attending two Camp Widows, walking on glass with my bare feet, breaking a board with my bare hand; surviving a Trans-Atlantic trip with a torn shoulder cartilage, the third anniversary of Tim's death, and another wedding anniversary, and my first Flash Mob! I congratulated myself on all my accomplishments. Yet, I still longed for the past. *I guess I'll always yearn for you, my love.*

I hadn't heard from Tim in awhile and was feeling a little abandoned. That's a strange word since death is the ultimate abandonment but Tim's frequent signs for the first two years kept me feeling hopeful and always hungry for more. I reluctantly remembered being warned by Lisa and Alex that Tim's signs would wane over time as they did this past year.

I was grateful though for one on our November 24th wedding anniversary. During a massage from Amy, the ceiling fan started moving on its own over my body. Amy looked up perplexed and said, "Anne Marie, what the hell is going on? That ceiling fan is turned off for the winter. How can it be moving?"

"Oh Amer, it's just Timmy giving me a blowjob." *Thanks, Boo, this feels lovely!*

Anne Marie Higgins

TIME
MARCHES ON
50

Time present and time past
Are both perhaps present in time future
And time future contained in time past.
If all time is eternally present
All time is unredeemable.

— T.S. Elliot

On New Year's Day 2013, as I was looking out the window while speaking with Roseann about missing Timmy, a red tail hawk flew skyward from behind our arborvitae trees. He swooped down and hovered directly across from where I was standing.

"OMG, Roseann, he's here! I want to take his picture but I don't dare leave to get my camera."

My Love, I've missed you. Happy New Year! Thank you for starting mine off with this beautiful gift!

And with that, Timmy Hawk looked at me and flew over the house. I ran and opened the front door to catch a last glimpse but he was gone. It didn't matter. My day was complete.

During my chiropractic appointment two days later, I told Sandi about his appearance. She had a knowing look on her face.

"Zak knew he was coming to you. He said he hadn't seen Timmy in awhile but then a few days ago he came to Zak in a dream. Zak said Timmy is watching you from a special window in heaven and wanted to throw you a coin that said I love you but God said he couldn't."

"That's weird. What could that mean?"

"He also said God gave Timmy a choice to come back but he wants to wait in heaven for you because if he came here, you wouldn't recognize him."

Flabbergasted, I asked, "Does Zak know anything about reincarnation?"

"Not that I know of! He's only seven!"

"Yeah but does he learn about it in church or school?"

Sandi said, "His Sunday school class doesn't teach kids about reincarnation and I don't think the Catholic Church believes in reincarnation, does it?"

"I am a fallen Catholic with nine years of sadistic parochial school under my belt, but I don't recall learning about reincarnation. I only remember the nuns saying that when we die — IF we go to heaven and aren't stuck in purgatory for talking in class — we spend eternity adoring God. I remember thinking purgatory had to be more fun than heaven because adoring God for the rest of time sounded pretty damn boring to me. It's cool that Timmy can adore *me* from his window instead. Oops, the nuns would definitely whack my knuckles for that remark."

"Well he adores you for sure. Zak said Timmy said so."

Through my smile, I was still wondering about all of this. "It's interesting he wanted to throw me a coin because I haven't found any in awhile. I'm still trying to make a decision about changing financial advisors and asked Timmy to help but I'm confused. Maybe the coin is symbolic and holding it back means I have to make my own money decisions. I can't always depend on Timmy. I have to live my own life now."

"I hope you can decide soon," Sandi said, "and feel better knowing that Timmy is always watching you."

"I feel *much* better. Please thank Zak for me. My gut tells me it's time to make a change and come to think of it, Timmy *did* tell me in my psychic reading last year to choose a woman for money management. My lawyer referred a woman to me so I'm off to schedule an appointment with my *new* financial advisor."

With my investments on a new course, my shoulder healed after almost four months of physical therapy and reassurance that Timmy was watching over me, I started the year with a feeling of calm.

I can't remember what negative emotion I burned at The Spring's symbolic ceremony but I took away "Peace" as my white stone

273

intention for the New Year. I yearned for a sense of peace to this emotional roller coaster existence. My widowed life was filled with ups and downs, stops and starts. When I thought I was on track, something would undercut my forward motion.

Boo, isn't it about time I caught a break? I feel like the freaking Energizer Bunny, up one minute, down the next, back up again. Can you ask whoever the hell is in charge up there to leave me alone and go bug somebody else?

After getting through the month of January and my birthday without any downward spirals, "so far, so good," I said aloud, hoping whoever was in charge of my life would hear me. I'd given up thinking I had complete control but stayed hopeful nonetheless. Next up was Timmy's birthday.

We always joked about our age difference down to the hour of our births. I was born January 19th around 5pm in the afternoon and he was born on February 22nd around 5am in the morning. He was 14 years, 11 months, 27 days and 12 hours older. I never rounded it to 15 years, it sounded so much older.

The evening before Tim's birthday, I fell asleep on the couch watching *Sopranos* reruns. I woke with my kitties piled on top of me and noticed the brass clock on the TV cabinet read 12:15am.

Happy celebration of your birth! Well not quite, you weren't born yet, less than five hours to go. I think I'll sleep in. I'll need stamina to get through the day.

After rising at seven, (late for me), I made breakfast and turned on the TV to check the weather. I noticed the clock had stopped at 4:55am. I walked over and saw the metal back was ajar and the battery partially popped out. I thought it was odd because the back of the clock opens on a spring that must be pushed in to release. I pressed the battery back in and rubbed it. The hands were still. When I pulled out the battery, I couldn't believe my eyes: the positive and negative charges were lined up wrong inside the battery casing. I put the battery in the opposite way and it worked.

How the hell did the battery get switched around? Boo, what did you do? You've played with electrical things before, but this is too freaking wild. How the hell did you open the back of the clock and turn the battery around, you don't have hands! But you drew that heart on the shower door, too! So I guess spirits can do anything if they put their mind to it, huh?

Why did you stop the clock at five to five? HELLO! That's the time you were born! Okay, let's have a party!

On all of our significant remembrance dates, I wrote a tribute on Facebook. Underneath a picture of Tim I wrote, "Today is the fourth time I've celebrated my beloved husband's birthday without him by my side. Today I celebrate his Life, our Love and hope he's having a blast someplace in the cosmos!" Little did my Facebook friends and family know Tim was having fun right here with me!

Things went smoothly for the next month and I thought Timmy must have had an "in" with God, Goddess Mama or whoever is in charge out there in Spirit land. Then on March 29th, when I got out of bed, an excruciating pain shot through my left foot. I stumbled and swore. Damn, here I go again. The Energizer Bunny is down for the count!

A few hours later, I hobbled into my podiatrist's office. He diagnosed a stress fracture in my left metatarsal bone due to overuse from my biweekly Nia dance classes, dancing at home and the 5K Marathon I'd walked last week for a benefit honoring Roseann's husband.

"Anne Marie, you can't seem to get away from these foot things; at least this didn't involve blood." Dr. Conti said, trying to make me laugh.

I wasn't smiling. "I've lost my footing *and* my foundation with Tim's death. I keep trying to build a new one but things keep falling apart. What am I going to do? I can't miss Camp East in Myrtle Beach in three weeks!"

"You won't have to miss it. Let's see what can be done to get you to your event."

Twenty-one days later, I was being whisked through the airport on a speeding cart that almost ran everyone over. Thankfully my clunky stabilizing foot boot had at least had one perk!

Since the diagnosis, I'd been careful and followed my doctor's orders. I wore my boot everywhere and took it off only to sleep. When I donned my gorgeous bronze gown with black chiffon overlay to celebrate the five-year anniversary of Camp Widow, the wretched thing had to go! My podiatrist said enough healing should occur during that time of immobilization to wear my dancing shoes at the Saturday night gala. Happily, he was right.

After a pain-free night on the dance floor, at Michele Neff Hernandez's prompt, I walked with 150 other widowed revelers to the beach. Our messages for loved ones were tucked tightly in our palms. When we reached the water's edge, with memories of last year's ocean message release and hope to repeat our orb picture, Roseann snapped our photo. Her camera jammed. Lucky for us, Michael Dare, Michele's new husband and our official Camp photographer, snapped many pictures that showed orbs all around us as did another widowed friend, Diane.

My love, you show up in other people's cameras, too. Fantabulous! How can anyone doubt their eyes?

April 20, 2013—Huge orbs were captured on my widowed friend, Diane's camera while we waited on the beach dock.

THERE ARE NO
COINCIDENCES

51

"Well, look who I ran into,"
crowed Coincidence.
"Please," flirted Fate,
"this was meant to be."

— Joseph Gordon-Levitt

When I walked into my house from my fourth Camp Widow, as much as I enjoyed being away, I was happy to be home. Even though Tim and I had loved to travel, our most cherished respite was here.

Each time I leave and return, I feel more at peace. That was a good intention for me this New Year. Our home is my sanctuary and where I feel your presence most. I'm enjoying solitude more, especially since I've started our memoir. Writing our story deepens my connection to you.

That evening, my ritual of choosing a CD with my eyes closed, to play while I prepared dinner, did not disappoint. I knew Tim was there when Sara McLaughlin crooned about yearning and solitude. I'm learning to be more comfortable living with both side by side. The CD title is a good description of my quest: *Fumbling Toward Ecstasy*. Will I ever know ecstasy again? I'm certainly good at the fumbling part.

Boo, did you pick this CD for me? I remember when Lisa Fox said spirits have the power to pick the right songs at the right time. Well you've got that talent down darlin' and you've been doing it for a while now. Thanks for the welcome home.

From the beginning, I'd called Timmy's non-coincidental gifts "signs," the term most commonly used to describe spirit messages or manifestations. But I'd learned in my Jungian studies that the better descriptor would be that Tim is sending me "symbols."

My inspiring teacher, Kaye Lindauer explained that "signs" are the product of conscious thought and have a factual, recognizable meaning as in a "stop sign." There is no mystery to a sign, whereas, a "symbol" implies something more than its obvious meaning. While symbols may have a conventional meaning — as in the coins Tim gives me — they also possess an indefinable or mysterious quality that carries emotional energy affecting the unconscious. A symbol is always larger than what it stands for and has multiple meanings.

So Timmy, I love how your 'symbols' touch my unconscious mind and intuitive self after, of course, my conscious, skeptical self finally gives up defining what is before my eyes.

I also learned another conceptual phenomenon called "synchronicity" coined by Carl Jung in the 1920s. Kaye explained, "Synchronicity is a belief of spiritual presence within the psyche that gives you exactly what you need at the moment, a very meaningful experience that you need or yearn for. When you are at a crossroads in your life, you are most likely to experience synchronicity."

So Timmy, is that what this grief journey has been, a crossroads? Alex called it that too. When I stand at the intersection looking down each road before me, I see dust and dirt, twists and turns. I've stumbled so many times on the stones, and the curves keep coming as I wend my way, never knowing what is around the bend. It's hard to envision a clear, direct path. Often after fresh pavement is laid by doing something positive, like going to Camp, before it sets, it collapses underneath me. Will I ever be able to pave a smooth road to walk down again?

But in the following weeks, I didn't experience the dreaded "Camp Crash" so that was progress on my road. My foot was almost healed and my summer plans were set for Camp Widow West in late June and Lake Ontario in August. Life seemed to be on more of an even keel but I didn't delude myself that the future would be easy.

Boo, despite feeling more peaceful, I still have moments of sorrow that bring me to my knees. Your signs — oops — symbols and synchronicities help but they aren't YOU. I miss you and who I was with you. I'm not that person anymore. Who am I now? A work in progress. Just like my book, our book. I know you're helping me write it along with the guidance of my fantabulous writing coach, Cynthia Kling. Meeting her through a widowed friend was one of my best synchronicities! Please keep them coming!

Again, Tim did not disappoint...

A warm Memorial Day weekend was predicted and Sandi invited me to dinner to celebrate the start of the season. Plus, Zak told her he needed to see me; he wouldn't tell her why. Sandi had been worried about Zak lately because he'd been having bad dreams and his parents found him in their bed most mornings.

May 25, 2013— TWH perched on Zak's playhouse.

The day of the party, Sandi called me and said, "Timmy must know we're worried about Zak because he showed up here."

"What do you mean?"

"A huge hawk landed on Zak's playhouse in the backyard and stayed most of the day."

"Wow, what did Zak say?"

"He was pretty matter-of-fact. He knew it was Timmy, but was more excited about you coming tonight. He has a big surprise for you."

"Can't wait!" I said.

When I arrived, Zak rushed to hug me. He looked up with his spaced front-teeth grin and handed me a small white box tied with a gold ribbon, "Timmy told me to give this to you."

I couldn't resist combing his wispy blond bangs with my fingers. "That's cool sweetie, when did he tell you that?"

"The other night when I went to heaven to visit him." Zak said in a nonchalant way like this is what everyone does when they go to sleep.

I smiled and glanced at Zak's parents whose dumbfounded looks matched mine even though we'd heard him say that many times before. Yet each time, I needed to reconcile my two selves, Ms. Skeptical and Ms. Intuition, with Zak's reality of visiting heaven.

"Wow!" I gasped when I opened the box and found a shiny copper 2009 Canadian dollar.

Sandi said, "Zak asked me for the box, ribbon and polishing cloth. You did a great job of shining that coin, Zak. Where did you get it, sweetie?"

"Timmy left it under my pillow but he wants Anne Marie to have it."

Sandi and her husband looked at each other again with eyebrows raised then looked to me. I realized then that neither one had put it there.

Canadian Dollar found under Zak's
pillow dated the year of Timmy's transition.

"Zak, this is such a lovely gift. Are you sure you want to give it to me?"

"Yes, Timmy wants you to have it," said beaming Zak.

"Wonderful! Now I have something special for you from Timmy and me."

Zak squealed when he opened his gift — a turtle-shaped pillbox with some of Timmy's ashes inside. As morbid as it sounds, he'd been asking for them for a while, but I'd hesitated. After his parents gave the okay, I started looking for something to put them in.

His almond-shaped blue eyes widened. "A turtle! Did Timmy tell you they are my favorite?"

"Yes, he did Zak!" I thought back to when I was in the Hobby Lobby store trying to find something a seven-year-old boy would like. When I found various animal shaped pillboxes, my hand went for the turtle, my other power animal. My Timmy voice told me I'd chosen the right one.

"Momma look! Timmy knows I love turtles and I didn't tell him!"

As his mother smiled, I continued, "Turtles have protective shells and hawks have protective eyes that always watch over you. Timmy is with you and will keep you safe in your bedroom."

With an ear to ear grin, Zak declared, "Momma, I'm gonna sleep in my own bed tonight, I have Timmy *and* his turtle!"

Later that evening when Sandi and I were getting dessert ready, she said, "Anne Marie, I'm thrilled about the turtle and your great way of helping Zak not to be afraid, but that coin is amazing!"

"Yes it is! It's not like Canadian dollar coins dated the year Timmy died are easy to come by! I've asked if he had a stash of coins in heaven or wherever the hell he is…oops, is that an oxymoron? How'd he get a coin from another country? I wonder if he needed a special spirit passport to get it?"

REGENERATION

52

Deep unspeakable suffering may well be called a baptism, a regeneration, the initiation into a new state.

— Ira Gershwin

After tucking Zak safely into his own bed, I felt my usual two conflicting feelings at once: exhilaration and confusion.

On my drive home I mused, *Boo, this coin is incredible. I'll take it as a message that my decision to change financial advisors was correct. Even though I'm feeling settled about money and at peace with my solitude and writing, I struggle with the "bigger picture." Despite all I've accomplished, I still don't understand why you had to leave and what I have left to do. Lisa, Alex and Patsy told me that I've not completed all of my lessons in this life. WTF? I thought I finished school with my Master's degree. Do I have to get a Ph.D. in lessons and suffering before I freaking graduate? Then what? Do I die and join you? Were you done with your life lessons when you died?*

Leaving unfinished one of my many existential conversations with Tim, I walked into the house to the cats' usual protests that I'd left them alone. As I gathered them into my arms for a reassuring hug, I checked my computer before falling into bed. An unfamiliar website was on my screen: www.yoursoulsplan.com.

What the hell is this? Timmy, were you in your window in heaven listening to me? I think I saw this website during a Google marathon and forgot about it. Is that why it's on the screen right after I asked you what the hell I had left to do in my life?

As I read the homepage, I thought, this is some wacky stuff: "Before you were born, you planned the specific experiences, relationships, and challenges you have had or now have in your life. Why did you choose the particular people who are in your life? Why did you plan your most difficult challenges? What is the deeper spiritual meaning and purpose of those relationships and challenges, and how can you best utilize them to learn and grow?"

I saw the words "Pre-birth Planning" and remembered Patsy told me about it but I dismissed it as being too *out-there*. Yet, here it was again. This time, it sounded interesting, at least in terms of the questions I'd just been discussing with Timmy.

The website's author, Robert Schwartz, certified therapist in past life and between lives soul regression offered online sessions but I wasn't interested in going backwards. It was hard enough living in the present and figuring out how to move forward. But his offer of "Spiritual Guidance" sounded like what I was looking for: "This session will help you understand the deeper meaning of your life: why you are here; what you hoped to learn in this lifetime; the purpose served by the major relationships in your life; and why certain patterns may reoccur."

What the hell, I've sought answers from psychics, shamans, astrologers, Reiki masters and spiritual healers, so why not give this guy a try? Thanks for the tip, Boo!

After a few emails, our Spiritual Guidance session was confirmed. But on June 12, 2013, something was wrong with Robert's Skype so we had to do a telephone consultation. "Sorry about my computer glitch, Anne Marie."

"That's okay Robert, the same thing happened when I tried to Skype with a psychic two years ago; must be my husband or spirit guides don't like videoconferencing."

"So your husband has made his transition?"

"Yes, unfortunately, in 2009. It's so hard to go on without him. I'm left with questions about why I'm still here."

"I'm sure it must be difficult. I'll try to help you."

"I'll take all the help I can get," I said, anxious for any new information.

"In my research, I've found a number of divine virtues that we seek as souls to cultivate and express on the physical plane. Before birth, most people plan to develop between two and five of these qualities, and life's difficulties play an important role in this process. Your major challenges were planned by you in order to foster those virtues that are most important to you at the soul level."

"So how do I figure that out Robert?" I said while holding back Ms. Skeptical's sarcasm. It was a good thing we weren't on Skype because my eye-rolling was a giant give-away of how I was feeling.

"Get a piece of paper, number these thirty virtues in a row down the page, but leave space at the top."

As I listed the virtues, starting with "Trust" and ending with "Attentiveness or being in the present moment," I was struck by my reaction to several of them: "Faith, Patience, Forgiveness and Equanimity (staying calm and balanced regardless of what happens around me)" all made my stomach churn. I knew I'd not fully fulfilled those virtues.

"These are interesting, Robert. Forgiveness especially sticks in my craw. I'm Sicilian so it's a difficult one, even though I was raised Catholic."

Robert chuckled, "It's hard for many people. Now list across the top of the page the major challenges you've had in your life."

"That's going to take more than the hour session."

"Only list the major ones, most people have between three and five. If people have more than five, they've had a particularly difficult life."

I thought about my life as having been difficult but also filled with joyous experiences. "Okay, my major life challenges were my neck surgery when I was 29 and the continued disability and pain, my infertility and loss of seven babies over ten years, and the loss of my beloved husband."

"Now go through each of the thirty virtues and rate how each of these life challenges have helped you cultivate or express that particular virtue. Zero is 'not at all' and ten is 'as much as you can conceive of.' Rate them in this present time, not when they happened to you."

"How I feel *now* versus when they happened to me? That's thought provoking." When I finished, I was surprised that many had higher numbers. But I was not surprised that I rated "Forgiveness" low. I chuckled. I had to work on that one.

"Now tell me the three to five you rated the highest."

"Perseverance, Courage and Intuition are my top three. Self-love and reverence for life are also high."

Robert explained, "Those virtues are the ones your soul came here to cultivate through the challenges you planned."

"*What?* I thought it would be the low scoring virtues I had left to work on!" I stared at my list again.

"No, Anne Marie, your spiritual awakening happens through your life challenges. When you experience these challenges, you get at the underlying lessons."

"Here we go again with these damn lessons! Oops, sorry, I'm a bit skeptical about all of this. So you said I *chose* my major life challenges?"

Robert's voice was straightforward and matter-of-fact. "Yes, in your pre-birth planning, you and your husband chose those challenges together to foster each other's growth and master lessons from a previous life."

"I was told we pre-planned our lives by my Reiki master but honestly, those concepts are difficult for me to wrap my brain around."

He wouldn't let me side track him. "And yet, how do you feel about the three main virtues as they have been manifested in your life?"

"Well frankly, I *do* feel that I've persevered and it has taken a lot of courage to get through my major challenges and losses."

"You may have had children in a previous lifetime but in this one you chose not to. You wouldn't have been able to cultivate your other virtues fully had you and your husband had children." Robert's voice had a sympathetic tone.

I remembered that Alex told me that as well. Feeling that familiar lump in my throat when thinking about our unborn children, I pushed it away with, "I have my precious cats though!"

"Yes, our pets are here to support and help us handle our challenges. They teach us to love ourselves unconditionally."

"My fur-babies have saved my life more times than I can count. And I know I couldn't have gotten through all of my losses without a healthy sense of self-love. If you can't love yourself, how can you learn to love others? Even the Dalai Lama believes that, I heard him speak recently."

"Exactly. All love must start with self-love. And how do you manifest reverence for life?"

"My reverence for life is in my love for people but I love all animals, even insects. I won't kill an insect inside my house; I always catch it in a jar and let it go. I've been that way since I was little. Wait, I take that back, I'll kill an attacking mosquito. I'm not sure why they are here except for bat food."

Robert chuckled, "As far as your neck surgery and your disabilities, this is about the law of attraction. We attract illness into our lives partly to teach us about suffering, but also, in your case, to develop your courage and perseverance. Choosing these disabling life events as part of your pre-birth plan was very intuitive of your soul."

"Oh great, I'm so glad to know my physical and emotional suffering has served a purpose. Seriously though, I've always had a measure of intuition and my husband's death has cultivated it even more. I've noticed that whenever I go against my gut, I make the wrong decision."

"Intuition or self-referencing is to see oneself as the ultimate source of knowledge to make our own decisions in life. It's good that you listen to your gut. It won't lead you astray."

"Yet I struggle when my skeptical brain and intuition don't agree. My husband speaks to me and has come to me in animals and other strange phenomena like orbs in photographs. He even knows when it's an anniversary date. It feels like I'm living in two different worlds torn between a logical explanation and believing my senses."

"This is common when a loved one is in the non-physical realm and you're trying to make sense of everything you're experiencing in their after-death communication. What's important to understand is that one's personality continues forever, it is eternal. So your husband would choose to communicate to you in a way that would make sense to you."

"Yes, it's lovely." My moment of appreciation faded quickly as I was overcome with frustration, "but I'm still miffed that I have to continue to endure more challenges in life. When am I done and how did he get off so easy?"

"Your husband chose to leave and return to spirit as part of both of your plans. Death is always a choice. It's suicide on a soul level. He completed his life purpose in his love for you and his death fosters continual growth in your life."

"Oh this is just too hard, can't I take it back? I must have been crazy to agree to this plan. I often say I must have killed someone in a previous life to have experienced so much loss in this one. Do I have bad karma or something?"

"Karma is nothing more than balancing your energy from one life to the next. Perseverance is an older soul's work so that's a positive sign you're balancing your soul's path through these losses."

"I'm an old soul, huh? I was told my husband is an old soul, too. How sweet, two old souls persevering through eternity, separately but together." I said in a singsong cynical voice.

Robert didn't get my sarcasm or chose to ignore it. "Your courage to persevere on your life's path and follow your intuition will help you learn more about your soul's path. Through self-love and honoring all life, you will further develop your main virtues and nurture the other ones on the list. Keep your heart open and allow divine love to flow and lead your way."

When we hung up, I felt encouraged in the validation that my life experiences cultivated particular virtues that have served me well. But I was also discouraged; if this was all pre-planned then why the hell bother?

Boo, I'm not quite on the same page with the idea that we came up with this crap ahead of time. And even if we did, the million-dollar question remains, what the hell do I do with this information, let alone the rest of my life? I'm going into my Scarlet O'Hara mode with a glass of wine. Maybe each swallow will add clarity to my muddled widow brain.

TRANSCENDANCE
53

Dance, when you're broken open.
Dance, if you've torn the bandage off.
Dance in the middle of the fighting.
Dance in your blood.
Dance when you're perfectly free.

— Rumi

When Michele Neff Hernandez told me a Widowed Flash Mob was scheduled for June 29th, the Fifth Anniversary of Camp Widow West, I was elated! She said I'd inspired her when I posted my Oasis "Senior Flash Mob" on Facebook last December.

To choreograph the routine, Michele recruited AnnMarie Ginella of *Widow-Speak* (www.widowspeak.org), and Kris Freewoman of *We are Women on the Move!* (Facebook group). Their goal was to "express grief while dancing into renewal."

When I first saw the dance tutorial performance posted on YouTube for our pre-Camp practice, I cried for five minutes straight, my deep grief aroused by their movement and music. It took me several days of trial and error before I was able to dance through the entire sequence without crying. After two more weeks of daily rehearsals at home with two wary cats that dashed away each time my arms and legs moved in different directions, I was ready. When I checked into the hotel in San Diego, I had the routine imprinted in my brain.

While volunteering at Camp registration, I met one of the Flash Mob choreographers, AnnMarie Ginella, a slender woman with silver wavy hair flowing down her back. I told her I was excited about attending her rehearsal later that afternoon.

I arrived early and we talked about our similar names and Sicilian heritage. I asked AnnMarie where Kris, her dance partner was.

"She's not widowed but wasn't able to be here anyway so I guess I'll dance alone, unless you'd like to do it with me. Do you know the routine?"

"In my sleep!"

With high fives, Ann Marie and I agreed, "Let's do it!"

After rehearsals over the next day and a half with several willing widowed campers, the time to perform arrived. We walked out of the hotel into the warm sunshine. As we meandered onto the lawn in the crowded pool area, none of the swimming or sunning guests noticed us in our Soaring Spirits T-shirts.

The music started. My rapid heartbeat calmed as AnnMarie and I lined up to lead the dance. As my body moved with the music, I was mesmerized, enacting my devastating journey of loss with widowed kindred spirits. Thirty-one women and two men of various ages, shapes, sizes and colors, came together to show the world we had survived.

We started in prayer pose, bent over, faces covered, feeling our deep sorrow, then slowly rose to the soulful *I'll Be Missing You/Every Breath You Take* by P-Diddy and Sting. Standing tall after being beaten down by our loved one's deaths, we began moving through our grief, one foot in front of the other. I sang my heart out to Tim with each motion, enacting the bond broken by death juxtaposed with my need to keep moving forward:

> *"Every step I take, every move I make, every single day,*
> *every time I pray, I'll be missing you. Thinking of the*
> *day, when you went away, what a life to take, what a*
> *bond to break, I'll be missing you."*

As we touched our hearts, our arms reached hungrily in mournful yearning for the past but the call to continue our lives takes over. As Natasha Bedingfield's *Unwritten* filled the air, we cut through our grief with our arms and legs jutting outward against the forces of pain that have gripped our lives. We continued to move purposefully, faces and arms stretched upward as the lyrics encouraged us to feel sensation with the skin that still hold's our loved ones' touch, and to speak our truth in the aftermath of loss. We reached forward with open arms as these words propelled each of us into our unknown paths yet to be forged…

"Feel the rain on your skin
No one else can feel it for you
Only you can let it in
No one else, no one else
Can speak the words on your lips
Drench yourself in words unspoken
Live your life with arms wide open
Today is where your book begins
The rest is still unwritten."

Then we each partnered with another briefly in the solidarity of our shared grief, palms clasped as we looked forward past the grief that clouded our view of the future...

"Staring at the blank page before you
Open up the dirty window
Let the sun illuminate the words that you could not find"

We separated and grasped the open air with hope and relish for whatever awaits each of us in our unwritten lives...

"Reaching for something in the distance
So close you can almost taste it"

Then in anticipation of what is to come, we took deep bows and rose with triumphant arms wide open to the sky as we proclaimed:

"Release your inhibitions!"

Our shouts of joy filled the air. A transcendent inner peace warmed my heart. Another Burning Desire fulfilled.

June 29, 2013— Group picture of the first widowed flash mob!

Check out the Video: Widowed Flash Mob: Camp Widow San Diego 2013: http://www.youtube.com/watch?v=q02_MiozNZg.

TRANSFORMATION
54

*The Coming to consciousness is not
a discovery of some new thing,
it is a long and painful return to that which has
always been.*

— Helen Luke

On my return flight, I pulled out my iPad to collect my thoughts. Back at my first Camp in 2011, I remembered Abigail Carter saying, "Losing my husband was a gift," during her workshop on *Resiliency through Creativity*. I was horrified by her words at the time, but now I understood what she meant. I've done things I never would have had Tim still been alive.

In this unchartered path of transformation, I've received *many* gifts and will continue to pay them forward, as they say. Volunteering at Camp Widow has been fulfilling, but I'm even more excited about continuing to spread the message of hope to other widows and widowers by becoming a Soaring Spirits regional support group leader in my town.

I suddenly realized these choices of "helping to support widows" were predicted in my astrological and psychic readings a while ago. In the past, my skeptical brain would have never considered consulting the stars or a medium but I'd become open to looking for answers wherever I could find them.

When I got home, I felt a profound sense that something had changed deep inside of me. I said aloud, "I am not the same person I was when Tim was alive. I'll never be that person again." I thought about how grief had forged a new path in my heart and soul forever altering the flow of my life. It was late and I was tired from traveling but energized by the recognition of my personal transformation.

I put down my suitcase as my kitty kids greeted me with their usual, "Where the hell have you been?" meows. Lucca sniffed my suitcase then lay down on the rattan floor mat for a tummy rub. I glanced at the mat's imprinted picture of ruby red slippers with my favorite saying from the *Wizard of Oz*, "There's no place like home." No matter where we went on vacation, at some point Tim and I agreed we missed being home so I'd channel Dorothy and say, "Let's close our eyes Boo and I'll click my ruby slippers."

Another "aha moment" appeared in my mind. I went to the refrigerator, poured a glass of wine, sat down at my computer and typed these words: **What does it mean, 'returning home' and where have I been?**

I thought back over the odyssey of my wandering grief journey that always led me back to this safe haven. I thought about the irony of the ruby red slippers that, according to Glinda, the Good Witch, always held the power to take Dorothy home — she just had to discover that for herself.

Tim's ruby red shoes came to mind next, with all of our shared dancing memories. I fast-forwarded to my last memory of taking his red shoes home with me after his funeral because I couldn't bear to have them cremated. Shoes are a symbolic vessel: we stand in them to take us forward, out into the world, plunging us into our life journeys. They also take us back to our foundation: home.

In the past, this word meant us as a couple, and the time we spent together in our sanctuary. But it wasn't just *our* house — the physical structure. Home had been anyplace Tim was. He was the solid base upon which I'd built my life. As long as we were together, I felt safe, protected, loved. Losing that foundation had rocked me to my core and challenged my trust in everything I knew and believed in.

What was home now? It was more than a place filled with the memories we made. It was about *my* time, *my* solitude, *my* life. I'd been on a saga of self-discovery after a cyclone of grief had crash-landed me in a frightening, unfamiliar world. In my four year, eight month journey down my own yellow brick road, I'd met with incredible obstacles and found *myself*. I was just like Dorothy, who realized she didn't have to look any further than her own backyard to *know* what was inside all along.

A third "aha" moment hit (it was definitely a night of "aha-ing") and I checked the rough memoir outline I'd scribbled down months ago. I found a note to include a quote from Joseph Campbell, the famed mythologist and storyteller, "You must give up the life you planned in order to have the life that is waiting for you."

I could see Timmy's smiling face as he read those lines to me from one of Campbell's many books that lined our shelves. It was a quote I never paid much attention to until we finally accepted we weren't going to have children. After that, I had just the life I wanted with Tim — nothing else mattered.

Boo, I loved when you read to me, sharing insights from Campbell's books and watching Bill Moyer's PBS series, "The Power of Myth." These were amongst our favorite past-times.

Tim was an avid reader while I was an avid "experiencer." After dinner, if we differed about how to wind down the day, he'd sit in his chair with a book while I played with the cats, looked out the window, puttered, read the newspaper, watched TV, or surfed the 'net. I preferred reading books on vacation.

Sorry Boo, I haven't read all of Campbell's works you left behind but I have a deep sense that we've entered and become characters in those books. I certainly gave up "the life I had planned," and so did you. I'm still not convinced about that pre-birth planning thing we supposedly did. If it's true, we must have been stoned on some really intense cosmic hallucinogens.

Reflecting on all of the alternative healing modalities I'd dabbled in, I felt a gnawing pain in my heart and confusion about all of the strange concepts I'd never heard of in my neatly planned life that had gone totally off course. After a deep sigh and sip of wine, I continued my conversation with my husband.

Remember that other famous Campbell quote, "Follow your Bliss?" We used to say you'd found your bliss in me and I in you. Now my bliss is a mystery. I guess I'll find it in "the life that is waiting for me." My as-yet unwritten life.

Even though it was close to midnight, I was wide awake. I thought more about Dorothy, Home, and Joseph Campbell. Then it hit me.

Boo, I've been on a Hero's Journey, like timeless mythological figures enacting the universal human themes that Campbell wrote about. Even though these were historically written for the male's journey, I can relate to parallels with female protagonists in The Wizard of Oz, Alice in Wonderland *and* The Snow Queen. *Fairy tales, operas, plays, even TV shows depict the hero's journey, the archetypal quest for Self.*

I scoured the bookshelf, pulled out Campbell's *The Hero with a Thousand Faces* and found the description of this journey:

"A hero ventures forth from the world of common day into a region of supernatural wonder: fabulous forces are there encountered and a decisive victory is won: the hero comes back from this mysterious adventure with the power to bestow boons on his fellow man."

When my cozy world was ripped from underneath me, the bereavement process propelled me into an alien land. The additional "supernatural wonder" of Tim's symbols and synchronicities pushed me further into this mysterious world. My logical, skeptical brain would never have gone on this journey. Thankfully, my intuition won out. I thought about my Shamanic Soul Retrieval that felt so supernatural. Truthfully, all of the alternative healing modalities I tried along the way — astrological and psychic readings, qi gong, hypnosis, Reiki, vibrational healing, spiritual guidance — felt wondrous to me.

I continued to pick apart Campbell's words. The "fabulous forces" I've encountered on the way are numerous, but a few stand out. Having to become independent is something all widowed people face in some form. I'd always joked Timmy had been my wife because he did everything for us. I was capable of the tasks, but loved being taken care of even more — who wouldn't? When I had no choice but to care for myself physically, emotionally, and financially in a new, frightening world, I found strength I never knew I had.

Boo, this reminds me of what I learned about the process of Individuation or "coming into the fullness of one's own being." Those words from my teacher Kaye Lindauer quoting Jung have stayed with me. I remember feeling sad when I heard them because I didn't believe I could become "full" without you beside me. Honestly, I thought I was full before, but I see now, that your leaving has forced me to grow up. That is a victory every day.

Losing my job forced me into a new scary place. I see how the betrayal of false friends was a gift because my life has flourished since I left them all behind. I remembered the psychic, Lisa Fox telling me, "The most difficult people and situations in our lives are the ones with the most opportunity for our spiritual growth. We are brought into darkness to illuminate our path." I had not realized the truth of that statement before, but I do now.

Boo, what's that other Campbell quote with the word abyss in it? I remember hearing the word from my sister Camille after she endured years of chemotherapy for leukemia. She said the experience was like being at the edge of an abyss, it was so horrible. Boo, you only got to experience nine days of chemo. I guess missing the abyss was a good thing?

Another time, I heard the word from your colleague Langston about a month after you died. Recollecting his experience of losing his wife to cancer, he told me I was on the edge of an abyss and I had no idea what I was in for. He was so right.

My Google search for "abyss and Joseph Campbell" gave me my answer: "It is by going down into the abyss that we recover the treasures of life. Where you stumble, there lies your treasure."

My treasure, eh? I'm not sure I'm at the treasure stage but I know about stumbling. Oh come on Anne Marie, I silently chided myself; you must admit you've discovered many treasures in your life. Okay, some treasures remain from our shared life that I have a renewed appreciation for: Lucca and Vivi, our families and friends who have loyally stayed by my side, our home and all of the comforts of the familiar that keep me grounded.

I have other treasures that have come out of the abyss: new relationships with widowed and non-widowed people, honing my skills of self-care, a deeper sense of compassion for others in pain, profound spiritual growth, a richer connection to nature, a renewed appreciation for solitude, a knowledge of the metaphysical world and the wisdom gleaned from various readings and alternative spiritual practitioners.

But my greatest treasures are your symbolic messages and knowing you are still with me, Boo.

I returned to the description of the Hero's journey and continued to pick apart Campbell's words. So what else is left for me? Aha, I must win a "decisive victory." I do that every day by getting out of bed. Okay, I can't minimize, I've done some pretty awesome things these last four years.

I'll make a list of my victories someday. They are, in many ways, the treasures I noted but I don't have the mental strength to write them down now. As jet lag crept in, I yawned and returned to Timmy before going to bed.

So the hero, Anne Marie, has come back from her adventure with my boon to pass on to others. I believe I'm helping my widowed peeps by volunteering time and lending an ear and a shoulder. I'm helping many families through my renewed collaboration with my boss. What else must I do? I need to contemplate this noble quest another day. Sweet dreams, my Love.

PARADOX

55

*The curious paradox is that when I accept
myself just as I am, then I can change.*

— Carl R. Rogers

The rest of summer and into the fall, I focused on writing, continuing my Jungian classes and just being. Solitude was my guiding light and *La Dolce Far Niente, "the sweetness of doing nothing"* became my mantra. This new rhythm felt softer, with fewer hard edges of sadness cutting into my existence.

My weekday gym routine, part-time work, Sunday gatherings at the Spring, twice monthly widowed support groups along with an occasional lunch date with a friend, was as social as I wanted to be. I started each day with a reading and meditation from *The Book of Awakenings* by Mark Nepo. The subtitle, *Having the Life You Want by Being Present to the Life You Have* fit well with where I was in the arduous process of accepting my reality.

I spent a lot of time walking outside to be close to nature and cuddling Lucca and Vivi when I returned home. I often found myself looking into their eyes. *Lucca's almond-shaped, blue eyes remind me of yours. Do you see me through his eyes? You come to me in animals. Why not in our cat?*

I thought of a Rumi quote given to me by my teacher, Kaye. I love Rumi's writings and learned of this famous Sufi poet's spiritual practice of gazing into the eyes of his beloved, as Tim and I did so often:

"The first time I saw you,
My soul heard words from your soul,
And when my heart drank the water
From your fountain
It drowned in you.
And the river swept me away."

Kaye also taught that Rumi recited his poetry while in a transcendent state of joyful dance. I thought of our nightly dancing ritual that I continued as a way to heal and connect with my Tim.

When Kaye recited my favorite Rumi poem, *The Guest House,* I resonated with accepting all that comes into your house, both positive and negative:

"This being human is a guest house. Every morning a new arrival.
A joy, a depression, a meanness, some momentary awareness comes as
an unexpected visitor.
Welcome and entertain them all!
Even if they are a crowd of sorrows, who violently sweep your house
empty of its furniture,
still, treat each guest honorably.
He may be clearing you out for some new delight.
The dark thought, the shame, the malice, meet them at the door
laughing and invite them in.

Be grateful for whatever comes, because each has been sent
as a guide from beyond."

Kaye explained the "guide from beyond" is within our own psyche, both conscious and unconscious. We all fluctuate from one state of feeling to another and therein, our truth is revealed in the contradiction of opposites, like when we experience sadness and yet have hope. My pervasive grief was always underlying but I found that joy in the moment and anticipation for the future could exist simultaneously.

When we live within these painful paradoxes, Jung said, "holding the tension between the opposites" without identifying with one feeling or the other, leads to a transcendent place of being, the individuated sense of Self. Living within the paradox of my intuitive self — loving the messages from Tim, alongside my skeptical self — testing a logical solution for each, I saw how they held their own tension. I'd learned to live with both selves quite comfortably.

I also went back to using the word "signs" for Tim's symbolic messages since that word is more recognizable to the rest of the world, or at least the world that believes in them. Plus, my skeptical self liked it better, it sounded more logical when I told people that Tim sent me *signs* versus *symbols*. Okay Ms. Skeptical, Ms. Intuition will give you this, happy now?

As my psychic, Lisa Fox and astrologer, Alex predicted, Tim's signs waned over time. They said he had to move forward in his soul path and wouldn't visit me as often. That used to piss me off but I was more at peace, so my desperate pleas for Tim's signs diminished.

As the fourth anniversary of Tim's transition neared, unlike previous years where I needed to be with others, I decided to spend the evening alone at home and welcome whatever entered my world and "guest house." I knew that no matter what happened, I'd be fine. Such was the realization of having survived each sad yet reflective time.

A cool but sunny November 7, 2013 morning arrived and I leaned over to touch Tim's empty bedside.

How is it possible four years have passed without you breathing next to me? At times, I miss you beyond words and feel as if I can't survive another minute, but my body doesn't accommodate. I think of the movie "Castaway," when stranded alone on an island, Jack said all he could do was to keep breathing, then when he was rescued, he lost the love of his life, anyway. So I keep inhaling and exhaling. I've left the island of despair and found my way to hope for the future. Thank you for being with me in my darkest moments. Your continued love and signs have rescued me. As Jack said in that movie, "Tomorrow the sun will rise and who knows what the tide will bring?"

After spending the morning writing, I opened the library closet and blankly stared…widow brain was in full force and I couldn't remember why I was there. As I started to close the door, not finding what I wasn't looking for, I noticed my binoculars and camera on a shelf. What the hell were these doing in here and not in the chest drawer? I had no memory that I'd moved them. Only Goddess Mama knows for sure.

I walked into the kitchen and my eyes were drawn outside to movement. I saw a flutter, then a bird landed in the tree. I grabbed my binoculars and focused my view. What kind of a hawk is *that*? I took his picture then he flew into a nearby bush.

Thank you, Boo! It means so much for you to visit me today. You're much smaller than a red tail. I'll Google you later; I've got to leave now.

Even though being alone was my plan for today, I'd accepted Amy's massage offer, as she always did on our special anniversary dates. I drove five minutes to her house and burst in, "Hey Amer, Timmy was just in the backyard tree!"

Amy, grinning ear to ear, handed me a card to commemorate Tim's anniversary. When I opened the envelope, I couldn't believe my eyes. "Amy this is the *EXACT* hawk that was just in my backyard!"

Still grinning, Amy said, "I know."

"What the hell! How do *you* know?"

"Timmy told me. Two months ago when I was on a hike in the Adirondacks, I came upon a gift shop, walked in and saw this card. Timmy told me to buy it and give it to you from him today!"

I leaped in the air! "Amer, that's freaking amazing! Look, both of their faces are turned sideways as if to say, I'm watching you!"

"Yup, that's our Tim, he's always watching over you, Annie!"

"Thank you, Boo! Thank you, Amy!"

November 7, 2013—Timmy Hawk in our backyard tree.

After a relaxing massage, I geared up and returned home to my Google search that revealed Tim had come in a broad-winged hawk.

Aha! Now I know why you looked vaguely familiar, that's the same species I saw in St. Bart's last year!

I was especially amazed at this particular sighting because Wikipedia said they usually stay in forested areas away from humans and most broad-wings migrate south for the winter. So why was this one here in the Northeast in November?

Okay Boo, how did you get this bird to fly here today and pose like on the card you told Amy to buy? Why am I asking you this? You obviously can get an animal to do anything you want, you've done it many times before. So how about transforming back into fantabulous YOU? Okay, you knew that was coming, can't blame me for trying!

As I stirred marina sauce on the stove, the smell of garlic, basil and tomatoes took me back to the sensuous first anniversary of our meeting. Now, on the fourth anniversary of our heart-breaking yet sensual parting, I drifted back to that day.

I remember your skin was so warm and soft as I bathed your body one last time. Your scent filled my nostrils. You were food for my heart and soul. How I was able to leave you that day is beyond me.

A tear ran down my cheek as I continued, *I can see my finger tracing the deep wrinkle in your right cheek I called your Clint Eastwood crease. Whenever you cried, the tears would follow that trail down your face. After burrowing my nose in your pubic hair, I can still feel the shudder as my desire was smacked back into my body hitting a brick wall. When I climbed on top of you, your arms, unable to envelope me one last time, lingered for a moment where I put them. My back still bears the weight. I still want to feel you, touch you, smell you but I must be content with what remains: your signs that help fill my yearning and your love that will always fill my heart.*

As the sauce simmered, I closed my eyes and pulled out a CD for my nightly ritual. Tim didn't disappoint and gave me the perfect song. As Bruce Springsteen crooned *Human Touch,* I danced and swayed, joyfully spinning around the kitchen to an anthem for that universal and natural body yearning. The lyrics speak to the need for human touch and the safety it may bring, but feeling safe can only come with the price of risking pain. As Bruce belted out,

"*We're all riders on this train,*" I thought, there's no way around it, we all ride the same train of life: touch, love, live and risk loss.

After my candle lit dinner served on our best gold-rimmed china, silver place setting and embroidered linens, I glanced at Tim's empty chair, my new TWH photo and Amy's card.

Your visits have brought me such comfort. Feeling joy amidst my sorrow was confusing but I've learned to live with both. I've found the ability to accept that pain and joy are travelers on the same path, co-existing. In the end, the pains of life, the joys of life, are all we have. One must risk being open to all life has to offer. I'll keep riding on this train as I strive to create another full life with your love that remains.

SUSPENSION OF DISBELIEF

56

Faith is believing what we do not see,
and the reward for this kind of faith is to see
what we believe.

— Saint Augustine

F or two years, I'd been asking SSI's founder, Michele, if I could do a roundtable discussion on "signs from loved ones." She was finally able to fit it into the schedule for Camp Widow East the following March.

She titled it *Signs and Synchronicity* and composed this description: "Do you feel sure that your loved one has sent you a message after their death? Are you wondering if other widowed people see the same animal repeatedly, and whether they assign any meaning to the sightings? Did your opinion shift about how thin the curtain may be between life and death after your loved one died? Join other widowed people for a chance to talk through your thoughts on the messages you might take from personal signs that matter to you."

A week before we were to meet, I was told over half of the widowed attendees had signed up for our roundtable! Clearly a need for this discussion was evident. Michele asked widower, Jerry Weinstock to co-lead with me. I'd met Jerry at Camp Widow West last year and was moved by his memoir *Joyride* in honor of his beloved first wife Joy, who also came to him after her transition.

We only had an hour to share stories so Jerry and I kept our personal experiences to a minimum. He then highlighted an important point about the topic: Most ancient cultures believed in afterlife signs but in recent history where scientific, evidence-based research has become mainstream, signs have been refuted as falsehood and fantasy. We widowed know differently. I explained that "synchronicity" is when a sign comes at a time most needed: a difficult emotional situation, an anniversary date, or in relation to something known only to you and your loved one.

We asked who had experienced a sign from their loved one, and the majority of people raised their hands. When we asked who had not, four raised theirs and admitted they were skeptical. I understood and said, "My skepticism emerged with each new sign, but when logic couldn't explain it and after there were too many to ignore, I became convinced."

We asked for a show of hands if anyone had experienced the more common signs such as orbs in photos, feathers, coins, visits by animals acting strangely or appearing out of season, familiar smells like a loved one's cologne or vivid dreams of their loved one. All of these were met with smiles and nods confirming many had had these experiences.

With so many attendees, we then broke into smaller groups so everyone would have a chance to tell their story. With 20 minutes left, we asked each group to pick one story to share. We found that the overriding commonality was that each sign and synchronicity was unique, meaningful and recognizable to the bereaved person.

The most amazing story came from a petite woman named Susan who began in a hushed tone, "We both knew my husband was going to die soon from his cancer and I asked him to send me a sign afterwards. He agreed he would send one *BIG* sign and I would know it was him."

We waited as she paused and took a deep breath, "My husband died later that day at home and I went outside while the funeral director did his thing. As I sat on the porch swing, I heard a noise and glanced across the street"...petite Susan grew taller as she finished her story with a flourish of her hands above her head..."and suddenly, my neighbor's garage burst into flames!"

The audible gasps from the group was followed by my whimsical question, "Didn't your husband like your neighbor?"

Susan chuckled and said, "They were friends actually; the fire was put out quickly, the garage was saved and I *KNEW* my husband had fulfilled his promise."

It was heartening to hear so many diverse and convincing signs that reaffirmed the "knowing" that our loved ones are still with us. We ran out of time with lots of chatter still going on. As we ended I said, "You've heard each other's stories; please continue to share them this weekend and beyond. And whether you've had a sign or not, invite your loved ones to come to you in your daily lives and in your dreams. Be open to the unexpected and trust your intuition, it is your best and truest guide."

Lisa, who'd never experienced a sign in the eight months since her husband, Joe died, stopped on her way out to ask us about orbs. I took a chance, borrowed a camera, snapped the picture and four orbs and aqua colored auras circled her head!

Lisa's huge brown eyes grew even larger as tears spilled down her cheeks, "OMG, Joe really is with me! I'm so happy, thank you both so much!"

"You're welcome, and be sure to thank your husband!" I said. Lisa glanced upward and blew him a kiss. Then Jerry and I posed for a picture and there were large orbs and colorful auras by our sides. "Jer, your Joy and my Tim are here cheering us on!" It was the perfect ending to our roundtable.

That night in the bar several of us had our own informal roundtable. Jerry shared stories about his wife also coming to him through other people. I told about when Tim had come in dreams to our friend Lorraine, to Amy in her home and on that hike in the Adirondacks and of course, to Zak so many times.

Other people shared stories about their loved ones coming in hawks, hummingbirds, crows and butterflies. I explained about the common theme of loved ones coming in beings that fly through air. According to animal symbolism, they are considered to be messengers between the physical and spiritual worlds.

More unique stories evident only to the widowed person were shared but no one could top Roseann's story about her Michael leaving evidence of one his favorite things, a bazooka bubblegum wrapper in the middle of their kitchen floor.

"Is he still chewing gum in heaven, Roseann?" I asked. We all chuckled and toasted the after-life humor of our loved ones.

Throughout the rest of the weekend, people told us our roundtable was their favorite. With my sixth Camp Widow and a successful roundtable under my belt, I felt deep satisfaction that my healing journey was not only beneficial to me but to others as well.

TIME FOR PEACE

57

*Peace does not mean to be in a place where
there is no noise, no trouble, or hard work,
It means to be in the midst of those things and
still be calm in your heart.*

— Author Unknown

Six months later, I found myself at my seventh Camp Widow in Toronto, co-leading another Signs and Synchronicity roundtable with my friend, Abigail Carter. The stories people shared were as compelling as in the first roundtable.

One widow said her husband had told her to watch the sky when he died, and as she looked upwards, a spontaneous fireworks display appeared. Through our laughter and tears, this universal need to share our stories added a measure of hope to our widowed journeys.

The next day, after co-leading my second, exhilarating Widowed Flash Mob at Toronto's Eaton Center Mall to a crowd of appreciative shoppers, several of us toasted our fun with Prosecco at the hotel bar. "How long has it been now Anne Marie?" Dianne West, SSI volunteer coordinator asked; knowing I'd understand what she meant with her widowed shorthand.

"Tim's five-year anniversary is coming up in November. I've honored the day with various memorial ceremonies but I need to do something different this time. I want to honor him but also myself for all I have done to heal."

"That sounds like a good inspiration for yourself. Speaking of November, I'm going to an inspirational event with Oprah Winfrey called "The Life You Want Weekend" where she and various speakers like Elizabeth Gilbert and Mark Nepo share their stories and words of wisdom about life."

"I'm not a follower of Oprah or Elizabeth Gilbert, but I start each day with readings and meditations from Mark Nepo's *Book of Awakening*, so it might be interesting to see him. When is it?"

"November 7th in Seattle."

"Wow, that's Tim's anniversary date. I can honor him and do something for myself at the same time. Thanks much Di for this lovely synchronicity."

When I asked my friend, Abigail Carter to join me, she invited me to stay at her house in the city and since I was going to be in Seattle, I decided a reading with Lisa Fox would be a second way to celebrate Tim's milestone. I hadn't felt the need to consult a psychic since I began to feel more at peace with my life, but I still had a few questions I hoped Tim could answer.

Fast-forward six weeks and Lisa was at Abby's front door a few hours after my cross-country flight. Her hazel eyes sparkled, "Tim is so excited you're here for his anniversary, it's tomorrow isn't it? He's been patiently waiting in his loving way and has much to say."

I was surprised she knew the date without me mentioning it but then again, not really. "Yes, it's tomorrow. It's good to see you again. I had a list of questions but I don't know where I put them — widow brain still persists. Maybe I'll remember or Timmy can remind me. So, what are his words of wisdom?"

"I see he's gone up a few levels, a choice he made to continue to grow as a soul spirit, closer to the divine. He spends a lot of time in the Akashic records, the library in the sky, with super intelligent souls. He just keeps growing."

"Yup, that would be heaven to Tim being in a library surrounded by books but Lisa, I didn't think there was *time* over there."

"You're right, it's not like the time that we know in this realm. It's weird, there is no *time* where he is, it's hard to describe."

"Speaking of where he is, *Timmy where are you*?" I blurted out one question I could remember.

Lisa closed her eyes and began to speak as Tim. *I'm in a place that transcends time and space. I'm with family and friends who have crossed but I miss being with you so much.*

I will miss being with you until I draw my last breath, I said.

And then we'll be together. I know I told you to find new love but I see a lot of things have impacted that choice: your health, stressful events, and emotional stuff...you weren't ready.

I could be ready to share my life again with someone. He will never be you but I so miss physical touch and sharing my life.

Lisa interrupted, "Tim is gently touching your neck. He says you've had health concerns with your entire back but mostly where you had your neck surgery."

"Yes, I've been having increased pain and numbness in my hands and arms on and off since mid-summer. I had another MRI that found spinal stenosis, several herniated discs, some spinal cord compression and progressive degeneration. I guess this body just keeps getting older and the grief has weighed heavy."

"Of course it has. Louise Hay says that physical problems correlate with emotional issues in life. The neck represents flexibility and stability. It holds your head up, the seat of your intuition and emotion. No wonder you're having problems, your neck has had a lot of work to do."

"I'm getting tired of all this work. I always end up feeling better after a while but this has been worrisome. Will it pass without more surgery?"

"Tim said surgery is not needed but you spend too much time at the computer."

"Yes, my job is Internet-based. I'm on my computer much of the day and often into the night. Even though I strive to be ergonomic, it's been a strain." (Skeptical me didn't want to give away that I was mostly working on my memoir.)

"The flexibility in your neck is tied to your heart and a lack of support. You had love and support when Tim was taking care of you. Now that is gone. There will be more freedom of movement when you have someone to support you in your realm."

"That would be nice. It's draining, supporting myself in everything I do. But I feel a sense of accomplishment too."

Lisa returned to speaking as Tim, *You've done a wonderful job and have accomplished so much. I'm so sorry I died so quickly. I didn't want to leave you but I'm still with you.*

I know Timmy, I know. I do feel you, less and less but I do feel you.

You're beginning a new chapter in your life. Keep going. I'm there with you even if you don't feel me.

Hey Boo, was that you when I heard my caller ID say, "Call from Anne Marie Higgins and my name and our home number appeared on the phone screen?"

Lisa interrupted and said, "I told you spirits can do fun things using electrical energy!"

"Yeah, I just wished he'd been on the line when I picked it up. I heard nothing so I pressed the call back button and of course, there was a busy signal trying to call myself. But I do still hear him in my mind.

Lisa smiled and said, "He was there, Anne Marie and always is. He said he's coming in scents — pay attention to smells you would recognize. Now he's showing me another kind of energy in the air, he's the wind beneath your wings."

"Hawk wings?" I said with outstretched arms.

"Yes, definitely. Please don't be discouraged by the lack of signs because Tim is very much with you. He's been with you the entire time, writing your book."

"Ah, is that my new chapter Tim talked about? Actually there are many chapters. I definitely felt him with me as I was writing, we composed it together." (My intuitive self silently scolded my skeptical self, *See silly, I wasn't surprised when Lisa mentioned the book since, of course Tim knows about it.*)

"He says he is very proud of you. Your book will give people hope and bring healing."

"I'm glad. My intention is to show others their loved ones are still here and can come to them." *Hey, are you still there, Boo?*

I am, my love. I'm just watching you. I adore you.

I say that to you every day when I kiss your urn.

I know. I hear you.

Lisa was silent and I was pensive as I thought about Tim adoring me from afar — a bittersweet reality. Another question popped into my mind. *Timmy, what is it about Zak?*

Lisa continued replying as Tim, *I didn't realize until I passed over that we were in the same soul group. In life those things aren't always obvious.*

Soul group. I've heard that before and meant to Google it, what does that mean?

Lisa volunteered, "You travel through many lifetimes with your soul group to learn from each other. They can be the family you are born into or friends you meet along your way."

"Oh that's the reincarnation thing that's hard for me to wrap my brain around. But it's amazing the connection Zak has with Tim; he only met him once when he was four years old but now he sees him in his dreams and speaks with him."

"They were definitely connected in a previous life and that bond continues," Lisa said.

"Wild. I feel very close to Zak and his family. His mother is one of my dearest friends and our bonds were strengthened even more after Timmy died."

"Yes, Tim wants them to help you. He sends messages through Zak so you won't feel so alone."

I thought about all that Zak had told me about Tim over these five years and his realm being "bluer than the deepest blue you can imagine," plus the amazing coin he gave me. "This all makes sense now. I hope I can help Zak like he has helped me."

"Zak will need you. He has challenges ahead. You will help each other."

"I guess that's what we do in this life, help those we love."

"So true Anne Marie, it's what life is all about. Tim's telling me about another close friend…you help each other a lot, her husband is there with him, it's an M name, is it Mike?"

"Yes! That's Roseann's husband. He transitioned two months before Tim. Roseann and I met through our widowed support community and have become very close. She joined me at the lake over Columbus weekend. I go there every year as a memorial for Tim's stubbed toe anniversary that led to his diagnosis."

Hey Boo, that's one of the questions I wanted to ask you about the photo Roseann took that weekend. Who was it in that fabulous orb at sunset on the lake?

Lisa said, "Tim said it was both of them. He and Mike were there together."

"How lovely. It reminded me of when Tim put himself in the sunset on my laminated memorial card. Patsy, my Reiki master, said

Tim was showing me his spirit is now in the sun lighting my way. So I guess both Mike and Tim are lighting the way for Roseann and me."

"Yes they are."

"That evening after sundown, Roseann and I launched memorial lanterns from the beach for Mike and Tim. Even though there was a South wind blowing, both lanterns followed the exact path of where the sun had set, and there was a wide glow line on the water as if the sun was still out. It was so strange. Once the lanterns disappeared, the glow line slowly faded. It was amazing."

"Tim and Mike truly are lighting the way for you and your friend."

I pulled out my iPad, "See Lisa, here's that sunset picture with the orb; that's the wide glow line that appeared again when we sent the lanterns up into the moonless sky. I've launched many lanterns on this lake and they rise too quickly to cast a shine upon the water. Certainly none have duplicated a sunset glow line like this."

October 12, 2014— Lake Ontario Orb and Aura at Sunset

"That's because Tim and Mike made sure this was different. What a beautiful way to show their love."

I realized Lisa and I were doing all of the talking. *Hey Boo, are you still there?*

I'm right here. I'll never leave you. Shall we dance?

Oh mine, I'll dance with you through eternity, I said as I felt warmth envelop my body. I closed my eyes. Tim's palm kissed mine and our fingers folded together one by one, the touch of familiar skin took my breath away. His other palm gently caressed the small of my back as we moved in circles, spinning to the beat of our hearts.

I was lost in another world when Lisa gently said, "Tim adores you. Your heart and soul are connected more so than I've seen with other couples. You are true soul mates. Even though you will meet another to give the support you need in this lifetime, your relationship with Tim goes beyond this human existence. He will always be a part of you. Your soul, mind and body are all connected. He is in every cell, in your bones, in your DNA. You two are certainly *one.*"

Later that evening, I fell asleep in Abby's comfortable guest bed feeling Tim's arms caressing my waist.

At the hint of dawn, I stood gazing at the gorgeous view from the living room window. As the sun rose over Lake Washington, beams of light washed over my face.

Five years Boo. I was glad to hear you're still growing and learning in your realm. I've had five years of learning a lot about pain and sorrow, waiting and yearning, hoping and resigning, slowly letting go while I embrace what has come. I've not felt the depth of joy we shared in our life together, but there's a different kind of joy that I feel in my new beginnings. Like the flower that survived beneath the broken pot in St. Bart's, my new life has sprung from the seeds planted in the deep soil of my grief. Death must come before there is a rebirth; it is the cycle of life. I'm making my own path now with each step. I take your love with me.

Three days later, as I reminisced on the flight home, I laughed at Abby's perfect renaming of our time as, "The Oprah Backseat Weekend." We agreed the two full days of events and speakers was kind of like being at a rock concert with tons of adoring Oprah fans. The first day, before Oprah's evening appearance, we meandered through "O town," a highly commercialized village of tents built outside the arena where we got free head massages and make-up along with mostly "use once then throw away" samples from the event's sponsors.

Eager to escape the hype, we found a great oyster bar nearby that became our weekend haunt during meal breaks. Many glasses of Prosecco put us in the right frame of mind to be "inspired."

It was fun to see Oprah, Mark Nepo, Elizabeth Gilbert and all the other speakers but after we listened to everyone's stories about how life had done them wrong and they overcame adversity, Abby and I agreed the weekend only reached the level of Inspiration 101; our complex widowed lives called for something more.

Thankfully, we have our Soaring Spirits community and Camp Widow to provide us with what we need. In the end, talking with Timmy and hanging out with Abby enjoying yummy food, good wine, and great conversation fulfilled my desire for "The Life I Wanted Weekend."

The evening before I left, while Abby was preparing spicy Indian Dal for dinner, she and I were talking about how Arron's and Tim's signs had lessened over time.

"Lisa told me that would happen. I miss the frequency but I can still feel my Tim."

"I miss the magic," Abby said wistfully.

"That is a beautiful way to look at it. Their signs have added magic to our lives. And now we are left to figure out how to make our own. Writing this memoir has been a magical experience for me. You are such an accomplished writer Ab, with two published books and one in the making, does it do that for you?"

"Definitely. While the life of a writer has its ups and downs, it has a magical, mystical quality."

"I've loved the solitude and depth of feeling creating something from deep inside of me. I recently found a list of things I wanted to accomplish in my lifetime that I wrote for a class in graduate school. I was surprised to read that I wanted to write a book by the time I was 60 years old."

"That's cool," said Abby.

"Yeah, especially since my 60th birthday is in two months!" We clicked our wine glasses as I declared, "Another accomplishment checked off my burning desire list!"

REALITY CHECK

58

What if this life is all a dream and when we die, we wake up?

— Zak, 10-years-old, many years wise.
(Heard in a dream about Tim, Fall 2014)

Back home again, I reflected over the last five years. What had happened to reality as I knew it?

My career has been devoted to science and human relations. My husband was a lawyer and a judge. We were two logical people living in our rational world. We also appreciated nature in its mind-boggling splendor. Even though we realized there was something "bigger" than us out there, we let the mystery be. We didn't think about what else there could be beyond our own existence.

After Tim's death, I was propelled into a world I knew nothing about. My Catholic upbringing taught me that life after death meant going to heaven, hell or purgatory...done deal. As far as I knew, death was the end of communication between the departed and loved ones left behind. I've been truly shocked and delighted to come into the knowing that the end is not the end. But then what? I did what I usually do and asked Tim.

Boo, I still don't understand how you do it. How is it possible that I feel you and know you are here? Everything that has happened since you transitioned to the next realm has skewed my reality. I'm floating between two worlds, yours and mine, mystery and logic.

I've had so many philosophical questions that Tim didn't answer — at least not in the same way he used to, so when no immediate answer came, I wondered where to go from here. Then I remembered something I'd read from an alternative healing website that confused me early in my widowed life, but my intuition told me to hang onto this quote; now I know why:

"What Is a Metaphysical Journey? Metaphysics are about transcending the physical nature and limitations of our daily lives and exploring consciousness, alternate states of existence, and our identity as spiritual beings. Metaphysical journeys, then, are transformative experiences that cause people to perceive themselves and the world profoundly differently. This in turn alters their values, priorities and appreciation for the purpose of life. Individuals who have these kinds of experiences are able to see reality in two ways, normal day-to-day reality, and also in a more life-confirming way, full of potential for growth and enlightenment" (http://www.meetup.com/Metaphysical-Journeys/).

Well Boo, that sums up this wild and crazy ride we've been on. You're safely on your after-life path and I'm figuring out how to move forward in my "transformed" earthly journey. Like Dorothy, I've traveled my own yellow brick road and found friends and foes along the way. Each has helped in my quest for healing and finding my "new normal" reality. I've run into obstacles, undergone perils, often frightening, and yet all of these hardships guided me back home. My home will always include you but my life is forever changed in a way I never could have imagined when you first left. I had no clue what to expect from widowhood other than pain and missing you. Then you showed me there was something more to believe in, an existence beyond this physical realm.

Another memory popped into my head. Years ago, when Tim and I watched *The Power of Myth*, on PBS, something Joseph Campbell said prompted us to have a conversation about the mysteries of nature and the divine. Campbell talked about a dimension of the universe that is not available to our senses, but when we look at a sunset or something powerful in nature and are overcome with wonder — *that* is participation in divinity. In that experience, one knows there is something much bigger than the human dimension. Even though Tim wouldn't entertain the thought of "life" after death, we both agreed on the mysteries in our everyday experiences.

When I've gone out on a limb and told people about Tim speaking to me or coming in hawks and their reaction was skeptical, I'd ask, " So where is the Internet, where are radio waves, how does your cell phone work? You use those things everyday but you can't see them and yet, you believe in them."

I thought about all I've done to seek answers: Reiki, meditation, qi gong, intuitive readings, vibrational healing, aromatic therapy, hypnosis, shamanic journeying, psychic and astrological readings. I've gone to lectures on power animals, angels and near-death experience, explored past life regression, taken a course on shamanism and another on spiritual and psychic development, all to glean more information about after-death communication.

I haven't just drunk the Kool-Aid on any one of these ways of explaining the afterlife. And as much as I've wanted to believe what each practitioner was telling me, my skeptical self chimed in, "they haven't died so how would they know — after all, they're still human."

My intuitive self then interrupted, "Remember what we learned at The Spring that we are all spiritual beings having a human experience. And what about reincarnation and wisdom passed down through the ages like we discussed in our Jungian classes about the collective unconscious, our innate knowledge as human beings?"

Skeptical self shook her head, thought for a bit, then said, "Yes, but I don't have an innate knowing about signs from the beyond and I'm not sure about this reincarnation thing. No matter what people say, death is a done deal and no one comes back, unless you believe in near death experiences and religious stories."

Intuitive self smiled and spoke with her hands (my Sicilian half is clearly this part of me), "That's where faith comes in, and I don't mean religious faith. I mean a belief in what can't be seen or understood; an acceptance of the mystery. "

And yet, *both* sides of me agreed each alternative healing modality and conceptual framework helped me, gave me food for thought, stretched my imagination beyond anything I ever considered possible, left me reeling, humbled, happy, sad, angry, and mostly comforted. I tried each one on like new clothes, kept what fit, and put back the others.

I thought about when I began my memoir and told my writing coach, Cynthia that I wasn't sure if I'd ever publish. Part of me was afraid that people would think I was crazy and I wasn't sure that Tim's intimate communications were meant to be shared with others.

In response, Cynthia told me about a trip to Africa where she'd met an "elephant whisperer" who'd said elephants spoke to her telepathically about their plight in the world (i.e., poachers and losing their open space.) There was a time when this woman, who was a highly respected scientist, kept the communication to herself until the matriarch elephant stepped forward and said, "We did not reveal this to you just so you would tell other people." In other words: "Do something with this information and help us."

Those words stayed with me. Not that Tim needed my help, but by telling other people, it may help open their minds to the connection between nature and the infinite unknown. I thought about when Tim came to me, it was like he was communicating like elephants do — telepathically — only from somewhere in the great beyond. We certainly communicated telepathically in life, like so many couples do, but this was different than anything I'd ever experienced.

After my conversation with Cynthia, I heard Tim say, *Write for yourself first, then share.*

Okay, my Love but I'm not gonna share EVERYTHING! I'll keep our special secrets between us, always in my heart.

The belief in after-life communication is certainly nothing new. Some Eastern religions believe and scientific theorists have tried to prove that our brain does not house our conscious self and consciousness survives after death of the body. I thought that must be what happens when the soul or spirit or life force separates from the body and continues on, but where?

Looks like I'm back to you, Babe. Where the hell are you? Actually I don't believe in hell — yes I do — it's right here and I've had a big slice of it. I don't believe in heaven either, at least not what I learned in Catholic school. But I had a lovely slice of heaven on earth with you. Damn I miss you! Okay, I'll stop my pity party, put away my violin and cut the drama; there are zillions of people who've suffered way more than I have. But we all must come to terms with our own pain and life experiences and I'm still getting the hang of it. I'll keep plugging along and trust you'll continue to guide me from wherever you are. Logical brain will just have to chill. Intuition rules.

When Lisa, the psychic, told me that Tim was now part of my body's DNA, it gave me comfort. I live with him inside of me and take him wherever I go. He is a part of me that cannot be altered. I'll continue to live this life missing his physical presence but knowing that he is telepathically communicating with me like the elephants — except we prefer hawks.

In the end, I realized my most *profound* validation didn't come from psychics or healers or books or Google but from my own experiences with Tim: hearing him, smelling him, feeling him, seeing him in dreams, hawks and other animals, the heart on the shower door, his spot in the sunset on the laminated card, the orbs and auras in pictures. I loved receiving his gifts: silver wings, feathers, coins, the right music at the right time, flickering lights and other signs, especially on anniversary dates.

I believe my own eyes, ears, intuition and heart and have an enduring *knowing* that Tim is with me. Because this has been my deepest transformation, I no longer feel a compelling need to seek wisdom about the afterlife outside of myself. While I've explored others' truths along the way, I trust what I *know* is true for me.

Before Tim died, I'd never seen an orb or an aura. I was never visited by birds or animals doing uncharacteristic things, or had coins and feathers appear out of nowhere. After he died, these signs, symbols and strange phenomena were everywhere. They are an afterlife manifestation of his love. In many ways, Tim saved my life and I know his love will sustain me until I die.

UNTIL FOREVER...
59

Time is too slow for those who wait, too swift for those who fear, too long for those who grieve, too short for those who rejoice, but for those who love, time is eternity.

— Henry Van Dyke

Two weeks later, on our 30th wedding anniversary, I woke up at my usual time, 4:50am, feeling despondent. I got up and walked into in our dressing room. My hands grasped a garment bag; as I unzipped it, silk ruffles edged in organza gently spilled out and memories floated to the surface.

I remember putting on my plum rose lipstick after my long dark brown hair was pulled into a French braid; white phalaenopsis and alstroemeria orchids were carefully woven into one side. Then I slipped into my cream silk gown and ran my fingers down the flowing ruffles. My mother hugged me as the photographer clicked away. I was anxious to get to the church.

The limo driver was cheery. "Do you believe this weather? Sixty-eight degrees and sunny in November! You and Tim really lucked out!"

"That we did! Keep that luck coming please, whoever is in charge up there!" I looked skyward as the driver held the limo door open.

I climbed out of the car, smoothed my gown and walked into my childhood past. I saw my 29-year-old self standing in the back of my church where I'd spent hours waiting in line for the confessional each week to tell my recycled sins to the priest: "I disobeyed my mommy three times, I was mean to my brother six times, I made my daddy mad at me four times."

I now recognized that my survival skills learned from nine years of Catholic school began my training for coping with life's difficulties. Thank you, Sister Agony and snotty Nancy Purdy for helping me find my voice. Being the youngest of six children also honed that skill, along with a measure of resilience that has served me well. I thought how much I've drawn on and added to that resilience, having survived so much loss with Tim, and now on my own.

I took a deep breath and my mind returned to the bustling vestibule as last-minute wedding guests were ushered in and seated. Then Purcell's *Trumpet Voluntary* grandly heralded the procession of our attendants. As the traditional wedding march began, I kissed my father's cheek, looked down the aisle and from that moment forward, only saw the face of my beloved Tim.

Returning to my present reality, my mind drifted to a quote I'd recently read in Joseph Campbell's *The Hero with A Thousand Faces* from the Hebrew Zohar: "Each soul and spirit, prior to its entering into this world, consists of a male and female united into one being. When it descends on this earth, the two parts separate and animate two different bodies. At the time of marriage, the Holy One, blessed be He, who knows all souls and spirits, unites them as they were before, and they again constitute one body and one soul, forming as it were the right and left of one individual."

My love, you and I were born into this world, two different families, far apart. We each found our way to our unique selves on our own, until that magic night we met and our lives were forever changed. Slowly, our love bond joined our two separate selves with all of our earthly baggage and accomplishments, until this day, when we again became One.

I pulled out Tim's tuxedo and hung it next to my wedding gown. Thirty years later, side-by-side, as we were on that day and forever forward.

LOVE NEVER DIES

60

Seeing into darkness is clarity.
Knowing how to yield is strength.
Use your own light and return to the
source of light.
This is called practicing eternity.

— Lao Tzu

Anne Marie Higgins

A few weeks later, close to midnight, I clicked to close my computer tabs thinking I'd written my memoir's final chapter and saw a word on a widowed friend's Facebook page that I'd never seen before. Normally I would have ignored it because I didn't want to end my momentous night with Facebook, but this word pierced my heart:

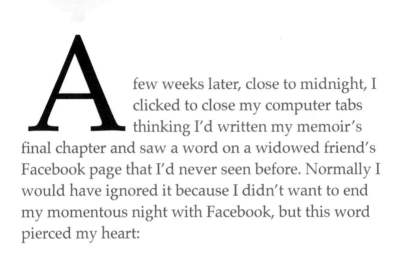

saudade

(n.) a nostalgic longing to be near again to something or someone that is distant, or that has been loved and then lost "the love that remains"

pronunciation: 'sau-"da-dE

My hand reached for Tim's picture. Tears rolled down my cheeks. *Boo, this is exactly how I feel right now, and often throughout each day. Even with the signs of your love that remains, your physical absence still overwhelms my heart.*

Despite my exhaustion, I needed to know more about this fascinating word of Portuguese origin that has no direct translation in the English language. Wikipedia to the rescue: "Saudade is the recollection of feelings, experiences, places or events that once

333

brought excitement, pleasure, well-being, which now triggers the senses and makes one live again. Saudade can be described as an emptiness; like someone or something that should be there in a particular moment is missing, and this absence is keenly felt. It brings sad and happy feelings all together, sadness for missing and happiness for having experienced the feeling."

I went to bed repeating the word over and over, letting it drip off my lips — Sau-da-deh — not wanting to forget this one perfect word that spoke volumes.

The next morning, I thought about the process of how I'd decided to write our memoir three years into Tim's afterlife presence. Having documented his signs, I accepted them as gifts to soften my yearning for all I'd lost. Each time one occurred, I told a few trusted friends to validate the reality of my experience. Adding breath to my written words further soothed my pain. I realized my grief wounds needed air to heal after they cut deeply into every fiber of my being and bled out of every pore. When I wrote and spoke

(Picture from Google Images:Sanfbleu.com)

about my incredible journey, each laceration's scab began to fade. While there are scars left behind, they are evidence of our love that lives on.

My scars reminded me of something my artist friend Annie told me. There is a beautiful Japanese art form called Kintsugi where broken pottery is fixed with lacquer resin dusted with powdered gold. As a philosophy, Kintsugi speaks to breakage and repair becoming part of the history of an object and adding to its beauty. Not only is there no attempt to hide the damage, the repair is highlighted by the new glowing color.

My love, I was a broken vessel and your signs were the gold that helped repair me. They added color and light to heal my wounded body, heart and soul. Your mending has illuminated and forever changed my life story. Healing myself in all that I've done to move forward has added more gold resin and light to my repair. As I surrendered into brokenness and the heart-wrenching abyss of sorrow that burned with such intensity, I found strength and resilience within. From the fiery pyre of my grief, writing our story has been like a bellows that kindled hope from the dust of my despair. I rose like the mythical phoenix from the ashes. In that emergence, I see that my Hero's Journey has come full circle: "**...the hero comes back from this mysterious adventure with the power to bestow boons on his fellow man.**"

My quest since Tim left has been filled with profound mystery that still endures. And yet, I've relished each sign and moment of synchronicity as Tim's boon that helped ease my way. My gift, my boon, is to share what I've been blessed with, to show grieving people that their departed loved ones are still with them. Whether you receive signs or not, know that our loves live on in our hearts, our stories and our memories that carry within "the love that remains."

My thoughts returned to how my life started: My life began with a death. I learned that losing loved ones is an inescapable part of life. So the path I followed was to love deeply, with all of my being. Joyously, I found my Tim, who followed the same path of loving. Once our love in this realm reached its culmination, his death began *my new life*. Now, our two souls are traveling separate paths until we reunite and dance again as *one* through eternity.

AFTERWORD: ENLIGHTENMENTS

In the depth of winter, I finally learned that within me lay an invincible summer.

— Albert Camus

Please, dear reader, travel along with me to the end because I have a few important things left to tell you.

My Hard Won Widowed Truths or Wisdom Borne Of Suffering

When I started my bereavement journey, I was desperate to learn as much as possible about what happens following the death of a loved one. Much wisdom as well as a lot of misinformation was gleaned along the way. Here are *my* grief truths. Take from them what you will because as universal as it is, everyone grieves in their own way.

1. The first year is horrific and the second year is even more horrific.

I had purpose in surviving each "first" with the goal of taking all of our planned and several unplanned trips all over the world to spread Tim's ashes. When Tim didn't come back after the first anniversary of his death, I was truly shocked and implored him, *Boo, I did everything I was supposed to do this past year, now you're supposed to come back to me!*

It was then I knew I was crazier than I had realized. That "year of magical thinking" thing really resonated with me as it did with the author Joan Didion. And as the second year unfolded, I saw our shattered future dreams as a couple lying lifeless at my feet.

Bereavement years three and four have been no picnic, either. Now that I've reached year five, I understand an article I read somewhere that said it takes an average of five to seven years to work through and "integrate" the loss of a loved one. I can't find the exact article; I probably ripped it up in shear terror. But now that I realize it's true, my terror has been replaced by acquiescence. And speaking of time...

2. Time does *NOT* heal all wounds; it just adds more moments to the pain.

Yes, the pain does wax and wane over time, but you have to be *doing* something with your time. And often what other people thought I "should be doing" did not fit for me at all.

Everyone must find their own way through grief. I learned to trust my intuition. When I didn't listen to that inner voice was when I suffered the most. I felt this most keenly while I was working at the hospital with others who thought my grief process was going on "too long." In truth, it was too long for *them* to tolerate. My gut told me I didn't belong there anymore. In the end, losing the job was a gift, and the timing was perfect.

I read an article from Legacy.com's grief support column about two kinds of time: "chronos" that is measured by clock or calendar and "kairos," the time within which personal life moves forward." Kairos time can't be measured like chronos time can, i.e., it's been five years since Tim died. Kairos is "a process through which we are drawn inside the movement of our own story."

Telling my story to anyone who would listen, and in this memoir, has been essential to my healing journey. My grief path will continue to evolve, "all in good kairos time."

3. "Widow brain" is a physiological phenomenon where the bereaved brain ceases normal cognitive function.

My therapist, Linda, warned me a few months after Tim died that my "executive functioning" would be compromised, which is how the brain deals with the loss. More accurately, I thought my brain had become a sieve. Most of what went in leaked right out. This was particularly difficult when trying to deal with financial issues and complete tasks at work. Once the initial shock and numbness wears off, widow brain takes over your life and can go on for years.

You also can lose half your mind. Research done at Harvard by David Wegner found that a couple in a close relationship develop "cognitive interdependence" where each stores different bits of memory about a shared experience and depend upon the other to fully function. This isn't about who does the laundry and who does the gardening, it's much more complex. The dyad develops "transactive memories" where you discuss your experiences and reach a shared understanding. When you lose your partner, it's like losing the other half of your brain and therein, the grieving person becomes disoriented and incapable of remembering and doing what each of you did for the other.

I didn't need my therapist or research to confirm that forgetting more than usual, walking into a room and not knowing why I was there, stopping in mid-sentence because my train of thought was derailed, and feeling like I lost any vestige of control over my life were all slices of this widow brain. Discovering the myth that I had control over my own life was another sad reminder that brutalized me and did not relent.

Hey Boo, I see now we've been snowed into thinking that if we did the right thing, lived a moral life, ate right, exercised, got enough sleep, saved enough money, and were kind to others, we could grab the brass ring on that big ol' merry go round and all would be okay. As you know, it's a freaking lie. And I don't feel any better for saying it. And on top of it, I have widow brain and can't remember why the hell I started this conversation!

And please don't be pissed, but my latest manifestation of this craziness was leaving Lucca and Vivi outside on the upstairs deck all night long. Thankfully they didn't jump off and break their necks from the second floor fall. I'm such a bad kitty mommy but you're worse, you've left us for longer than one night! Damn, I hate this! Okay, now I feel better.

4. People say stupid things.

They say people mean well. You would hope people speaking to you about your loss would have good intentions. Most often people don't know what to say once they get past, "I'm sorry for your loss."

I honestly never liked those particular words because they didn't make sense to me. Why is it that people say they're sorry, when they didn't do anything? But then Timmy died, and "I'm sorry for your loss" felt just fine. It was what followed that sucked. So here are a few of the **"best of the worst"** things that people said to me:

— **"At least you had so many years together and had such an intense love, no one can take that away from you."**

Excuse me but I think you're missing the obvious; death just *did* take the love of my life away. This comment was particularly hard to hear early in my widowed journey when Tim's physical absence was still shocking. And any comment that begins with the words "at least" or "but" is bound to be unhelpful.

— **"I know you didn't have the privilege of having children, but a mother hurts worse than a wife because she's hurting over her own flesh and blood's pain."**

Stab my heart and twist the knife! So let me get this straight, a mother of a widow is in more pain than the widow is over losing her husband because the mother can't bear to see her child in pain?

I'm Sicilian and understand a lot about the flesh and blood connection but that reasoning ranks in the beyond mind-boggling realm. Let's just say, this person was lucky I didn't call one of my Sicilian relatives to help her re-think her wacko rationale.

— **"At least you don't have children to take care of so you can spend all the money on yourself."** Another stab reminding me I've lost my children *AND* my husband but I'm gonna have a real blast spending all the money on me!

The assumption that all widowed people have a lot of money left to them because their partner died is ridiculous. I've met many financially strapped widowed people with and without children. This is just an insulting and wounding remark.

I could go on with stupid phrases about comparing widowhood to divorce, i.e., "at least you loved him when he left you" and crap like "at least he didn't suffer long" or "he's in a better place" but I'll wrap it up with the all time **best of the worst:**

— A woman who works at Wegmans grocery store stopped me in the organic cereal aisle, touched my arm, shook her head, took a deep breath and with downturned eyes said, **"I know exactly how you feel...my horse died."** Without skipping a beat, I looked directly into her clueless eyes and responded, "Yeah, I miss riding him too."

5. Dreaded Compliments

— **"You're so strong!"** Most of the time I hated hearing this: it essentially said to me that if I was weak, I was not okay.

This "compliment" often came when people saw me out in public doing what I needed to do to survive: working or buying groceries or household items needed to fix something I had no clue how to fix. If I was stone-faced instead of crying, I guess that meant I was being strong even though I was crying inside.

Initially I said, "I honestly don't feel strong, I'm exhausted, just trying to get through each moment." After a few months of grief under my belt, my reply changed to "you never know how strong you are until you have no choice."

— **"You look so good!"** This always came with an inflection of surprise in their voice. I sometimes said, "Am I supposed to look like crap?" This "compliment" held an expectation of how I was supposed to be and if I looked good, then everything must be okay, right?

In the old days, when I was told this after a surgery or infertility procedure, I would parody Billy Crystal and say, "It is better to look good than to feel good." When I used this phrase after Timmy died, I wanted people to understand that even if I looked good, I felt horrible inside.

If someone then meekly smiles and asks how I'm doing, my reply is, "I don't recommend widowhood. It's horrible and much worse than you can possibly imagine." Sometimes I'll get a chuckle. I guess they think I'm trying to be funny. Often it leaves them at a loss for words, but words aren't always needed.

When people honestly don't know what to say — and I was one of those people before Tim died — it's best to admit, "I don't know what to say to you." I always welcomed those words with "Thank you, no need to say anything, just stay with me a little while or give me a hug."

Janine Teague Eggers, whom I met at Camp, often used the acronym T.A.N.W. in her SSI Widow's Voice blog. It means, "There are no words." Many in our widowed community use those letters in their blogs and on Facebook. I've added my own acronym that sums up a lot of situations in our widowed existence: T. J. S., "This just sucks."

Sometimes I use T.J.F.S, "this just fucking sucks," when only a swear word could adequately describe a situation. Swear words are quite common in my memoir, as you may have noticed, but what you may not know is behavioral studies have found that people who use a lot of swear words are more honest and trustworthy. I often use them to emphasize my feelings, as many people do, but I've used them a lot more since Tim died because T.J.F.S.!

I understand people mean well. But then I can be blatantly honest and believe educating someone when they've said something stupid or insensitive is better than letting it go because it may prevent future pain inflicted on someone else. I'm not always flip. I thank people for their concern, but not without mentioning it when their remark was painful to me.

If you feel you need to say something, *never* and I mean *never* say, "Call me if you need anything." I didn't know what the hell I needed from one moment to the next. I had no energy to pick up the phone. At times, breathing was about all I could accomplish. Early in my widowhood, I did call people when I was scared during my panic attacks. But as time wore on, I sat alone feeling awful that I had to take the initiative when all I really needed was for someone to call me, most often just to have a shoulder to cry on. My advice — if you want to help — is to pick up the phone and check in, offer to do something if you have the time, or simply listen and be that shoulder to cry on.

6. Dreaded Advice and Bad Cliches
—"You have to move on, Tim would have wanted you to."
Gee, thanks for two bits of stupid advice wrapped into one ridiculous comment. First of all, "moving on" connotes so many things but surviving each day and putting one foot in front of the other was about all I could do for awhile.

Often this misguided advice meant I needed to start dating. One clueless person called me a month after Timmy died offering a blind date with a recently divorced friend because "Timmy wouldn't want you not to have someone to kiss at midnight on New Year's." It never ceased to amaze me how many people knew what Tim wanted! My reply was *always* and continues to be, "Actually Tim would have wanted to be here by my side instead of being dead."

— **"You need to stop speaking about Tim as if he were alive."**
No one ever said those exact words but it was implied by uncomfortable silences, sighs or raised eyebrows when I would speak about Tim or share a memory in response to someone speaking about their living family member. I used to say, "My Tim is still alive in my heart and it helps me to speak about him."

Recently I heard a beautiful quote from a rabbi saying Shiva prayers at a widowed friend's home, "A man dies twice when we stop talking about him." I use that quote now and people usually get it. It is so important to say your loved one's name aloud, speak of your memories, keep them in your daily life and make it a part of your healing ritual.

—**"You need to reach closure."**
This is part of the "moving on" dreaded advice but it's much worse, implying that people are objects to be closed up and discarded. "You close windows; you don't close people," I'd reply. I didn't use the word "door" because someone might then follow up with the other stupid comment, "When one door closes, another opens." That trite slice of optimism never takes into account that the next door might really suck: ask my widowed friend who got remarried and is now getting a divorce. Or another widowed friend whose new love of four months died suddenly from heart failure after they'd just texted good morning. T.J.F.S.!

All of the re-partnered widowed people that I've met through SSI agree, their new love is not a replacement and they still grieve for their departed partner despite being in a new relationship.

Often people give advice because they are uncomfortable just listening to someone in mourning — when that is what's needed most. No amount of advice will change what happened. A joke among my widowed peeps is "death is not contagious." We've all felt like pariahs when people see us and go walking in the other direction or stop inviting us to events we used to attend with our loved one. We already feel like social misfits without our partners but this just adds to our isolation.

Even though everyone is going to die, people don't like talking about it because it's a taboo subject in our society. Most people avoid it. The majority in our culture could learn from other world cultures that accept death as a part of life.

Mexico and other Latino countries have a "Day of the Dead," a national holiday dedicated to gatherings of family and friends to remember those who have died. Many Eastern cultures have similar traditions of a day set aside to visit the graves of deceased family members. Often included in these traditions are celebrations with food and dance, along with prayers and remembrances of the departed. Japanese and Chinese cultures honor their departed ancestors and ask for their continued help in their daily lives.

Yes, we do have Memorial Day in May but many people think it is only to remember those who died in the line of duty and don't view it as a day to reflect on all departed loved ones.

In many parts of the world, because of poverty, disease or war, death is accepted because it is seen everyday. While there are exceptions, most of my contemporaries haven't had to face death other than losing their grandparents. Just a generation ago, before vaccines and life-saving medicines, death was seen as a part of life here as well. A lesson could be taken from what my Sicilian grandfather said when anyone he loved died, "Ah, well, that is *the* life."

Sadly, "the life" is what most of our workplaces expect the bereaved to focus on when typically so little time is given off after the funeral or memorial service of a loved one. Life must go on even though the bereaved have no clue how. I could talk about religions that allow time for grieving, like sitting Shiva in the Jewish tradition. And Buddhism, that teaches the impermanence of life and the reality of suffering; but the subject of religion is too broad and complex to tackle here. Suffice it to say, American culture has much to learn about death, how to honor it, speak about it and allow for adequate time to grieve.

7. Grief advice that resonated with me
—"What's Your Grief?" (www.what'syourgrief.com) is a blog written by mental health professionals, Litza Williams and Eleanor Haley. These women share wisdom from their personal losses and counseling experience as well as informative articles about grief.

In a post about closure, they cited a book called *Continuing Bonds: New Understandings of Grief* by Klass, Silverman, and Nickman. The authors question the dominant models of grief, which end in detachment from the person we've lost. These models deny a reality of how many of us grieve. Instead, the authors suggest a new paradigm that doesn't resolve by detaching, but by creating a new relationship with the departed loved one.

It's amazing to me that this book, copyrighted in 1996, slipped totally under the radar while the Kubler-Ross Five-Stage model — denial, anger, bargaining, depression, acceptance — continues to be erroneously recommended as a guide for grieving people, when in fact, it was originally written as a guide for what the terminally ill go through prior to death.

Litza and Eleanor followed up with another post giving sixteen specific suggestions for how to continue bonds with your loved one. I was pleased to read I'd done a majority of them — talking with Tim, keeping his photos and personal objects around, honoring our anniversaries, enjoying our favorite comfort foods.

I particularly resonated with this one: "It is common to experience the presence of your loved one — it may just be a feeling, a specific type of wind or bird, or countless other things that seem to be a sign they are here. Unlike the studies about simply keeping something that belonged to your loved one, feeling your loved one's presence has been shown to ease the sadness that accompanies grief. So feel them without apology or any worry that you're crazy! This is a normal and helpful way to continue your bonds."

—"The only way out is through, the only way to heal the pain is to embrace the pain." I heard this quote by Fritz Perls, early in my widowed journey and kept it at the tip of my tongue ready to fire off at the appropriate time, which was often.

The horror of losing Tim was the most debilitating emotional and physical pain I've ever experienced. My adrenal glands' fight or flight response was fully activated and the pounds just melted off of my body. Every cell of my being ached, my arms were heavy, my legs did not want to function, my stomach churned, my head was foggy, at times it hurt just to breathe. I was exhausted from the hard work of grief and thought my heart would burst from the deep, relentless suffering that couldn't be soothed.

I found out it is actually possible to die from a broken heart. The Japanese first described this physical anomaly *"Takotsubo cardiomyopathy"* or broken heart syndrome. The heart muscle can be weakened by the stress of mourning enough to be life threatening. The name comes from their pot-shaped octopus traps that resemble a stricken heart when the muscle is compromised (Wikipedia). Yup, my heart felt like it was being crushed by the grasp of octopus tentacles. Now I understand why many older people die within months of one another, their bodies can't withstand the crushing pain.

From the moment Tim died, I knew I couldn't escape the pain so I didn't try. This is not to say I was a blubbering mess 24/7, I simply refused to squelch my feelings or apologize for them. I needed to live in my own skin even though it felt battered and bruised. I functioned as best as I could from day to day (sometimes one moment to the next), went to see my therapist weekly (sometimes frantic phone calls in-between), and took "mental health" time off when I needed to.

Keeping our old rituals and developing new ones helped me begin to heal. I learned as much as I could about grief, alternative healing practices and then found Soaring Spirits International and Camp Widow where I shared my experience with like-minded people. While everyone's grief and how they handle it is unique to each person, sharing our common bond of loss eases the way.

And yet, even when my grief was shared with others, I alone bore the brunt of the gut-wrenching pain of life without Tim. At times, I didn't want to go on but somehow I did, as so many other bereaved people have done. I've learned to look outside myself at others in pain and see the world in a different way. While surviving the death of a loved one may not be considered impressive on the grand scale of life achievements, it was a personal accomplishment for me and for many people I've met. Witnessing the everyday pinnacles of ordinary men and women has been truly inspirational. Now, as I listen to other's stories, I look into their eyes and hear them with ears of experience, gratitude and understanding. Newfound compassion is worth it, even though it comes at a price.

Tim and I loved reading fairy tales and fables. When I hear misguided advice about dealing with grief by pushing it away, I think of an Aesop's fable called *The Oak and the Reed* where the mighty oak tree trusts its strength to withstand a storm and is blown over but the reed bends with the wind and survives. I was a reed in a windstorm of emotions and allowed my feelings to surface as I felt them. If you pretend they aren't there, the feelings will come up eventually and your oak-like façade will be blown away.

Sadly, I've seen widowed people with children who needed to 'be strong" and postponed their grief to attend to the tasks of single parenthood and helping their children cope. That's a slice of the grieving process I cannot speak to, but I shudder to think how difficult it must have been for my grieving widowed father, a busy physician left with four children to raise.

On the other hand, some people (usually parents) suggested my grief was worse because I didn't have a living reminder of Tim. I'd long since accepted that was not to be. Some parents have envied our travels and the many years we shared alone. We worked hard for what we had and felt fortunate we were to be able to do the things we did. But there was a time I would have traded all of that for having our baby.

But comparing grief is not useful. We all have our own story of pain. I do believe that without a child, other than taking care of myself and Lucca and Vivi, I had the "luxury" of being able to spend time with my grief, get to know it, feel it, and learn from it.

I resonated with the advice of Tom Zuba, life coach and grief expert I met at Camp who lost his wife and two children over a fifteen-year span. Tom teaches the "New Way to do Grief" by facing it, living with it, healing through the pain. Stuffing it down, denying it, being strong, keeping busy, avoiding grief is the "old way" and it simply does not work without negative health and relationship consequences (www.tomzuba.com).

Post Traumatic Stress Disorder (PTSD) is finally recognized in the mainstream of our post 9/11 society for those who have suffered trauma in horrific tragedies, war, abusive relationships and the like. But people often don't equate widowhood with trauma; however, there is a body of research about "traumatic grief."

While there is a measure of trauma whenever a loved one dies, there are difficult situations that can either delay or prolong the healing process such as traumatic and/or tragic death that results in recurring recollections of the death and inability of the survivor to function. PTSD may be evident soon after the event, or it may develop years later. I realized my trauma early on and sought help, but I'll never forget when my sister said to me in the summer of year four, "Annie, I don't know how you haven't started screaming and not stopped." I told her, "Honestly, I still scream on the inside."

Research has also shown that after trauma, Post-Traumatic Growth (PTG) often occurs. People who grow after trauma can experience increased appreciation for life, enhanced relationships, deepened spirituality, greater personal strength and see new possibilities as a result of their struggles. I definitely see these things in my life, but it has taken awhile.

Wikipedia says: "PTG is not about returning to the same life as it was previously experienced before a period of traumatic suffering; but rather it is about undergoing significant 'life-changing' psychological shifts in thinking and relating to the world, that contribute to a personal process of change, that is deeply meaningful."

As much as I have grown, the pain of loss still lies underneath, ready to spring forth, often without warning. My main point is that people suffer, life can suck and avoiding the pain only leads to more pain so it's important to get help. Don't listen to the chorus of advice givers who tell you to keep busy, check out online dating, pray, drink, start a new hobby, go shopping, move into a new house, get rid of your loved ones things, go on vacation and when all else fails, just *KEEP BUSY*. Believe me, grief will catch up with you and you'll eventually crash. Any of these new experiences can occur when you are ready but not because someone who has no clue tells you how to live your life.

The most outrageous advice I received to "keep me busy" was when someone told me to adopt a child and then I wouldn't be lonely! A relationship with a child is no substitute for a loving partner. My advice to misguided advice givers is to "be grateful for what you don't have that you didn't want and come back to me after you've lost the love of your life; I get it and will be there to listen."

And yet, despite all of the work I've done in my mourning process, when things are relatively calm and I think all is going well, *BAM*, something happens to trigger a memory — a song, a smell, a taste, an animal, a photo — and I'm a sobbing mess. There is no time limit on this, I am sure it will happen the rest of my life.

—**And "the rest of my life,"** were the most helpful and reassuring words I read in Ashley Davis Bush's *Transcending Loss, Understanding the Life Long Impact of Grief.*

"Grieving is not a short-term process; it's not even a long-term process; it's a lifelong process. Having a future now means that although your life will flow again, it will flow differently as a result of the loss. Your grief will become incorporated into your life history, become a part of your identity. And you will continue to redefine your relationship with your deceased loved one. Death does not end the relationship; it simply forges a new type of relationship — one based not on physical presence but on memory, spirit, and love."

After the funeral, a wise widow told me I would develop a deeper bond with Tim in death. I thought she was freaking crazy until I began to feel a depth of love I'd not known while Tim was alive. Despite our intense physical and emotional bond in life, I found my after-death connection to Tim is incredibly powerful. With our physical bond broken, the emotional love became deeper; more evolved; it grew and transformed into a profound inner life with Tim that transcended the physical. I believe much of that transcendence has to do with how I've changed and grown. After reaching outside myself, my personal evolution led me back *home* to Tim and to myself. It was there I found the answers I was looking for all along.

8. The ultimate truth: No matter how much time you have had with your beloved, it is never enough; you'll always yearn for more.

Ironically, the day after my discovery of the word *saudade*, I read a post in "What's your Grief" about nostalgia and yearning for what one has lost. They cited a research study in England that found nostalgia to be very common and the majority of their bereaved subjects had nostalgic feelings multiple times in one week.

Interestingly, they say, "One of the most common triggers of nostalgia is when someone experiences negative emotions. This suggests we are apt to access memories of a happier time in an attempt to counteract feelings like fear and anxiety in the present. This may explain the link between loneliness and nostalgia because when we feel lonely or lost due to life events and transition, nostalgia helps us feel more connected. One can counteract feelings of isolation by remembering important relationships from the past and bringing them into the present."

This made sense. When I'm particularly down, I choose a special memory — a wonderful meal, a great vacation, a shared sunset — and I feel better. Counting my blessings and having gratitude for all we shared for 31 years pulls me forward.

It is comforting to know that a moment spent reminiscing is healing and serves the need to stay connected to those we love. I read on an alternative healing website that when you simply *think* of a lost love, it is a visit from them; all consciousness is energetically connected from the spiritual dimension to the human mind. So rest assured, even if you experience nothing else, your love is sending a sign with each thought.

Signs or no signs, death is not fixable. I live with that cold reality day in and day out, and that does not change: Tim is not in my bed at night, he is not kissing me good morning, he is not here to share my joys or sorrows. My life goes on and it has been horrendously painful but it has also been glorious. There is intimacy in pain from loss that can't be reached by those who've not been there.

If I find myself drowning in despair, I take a breath, swim underneath the surface and eventually break through my waterfall of tears, cleansed, able to keep going. I have no doubt I will persevere. I've survived the worst thing that has happened in my life. I honestly can say, in many ways since, I have thrived.

I chose the word *Trust* as my white stone intention for 2015. I've learned to "trust the process" that I am where I need to be. Accepting the flow of each new day, even if there is pain, has helped me learn to trust that somehow, I will be okay.

I'm no longer afraid to die since I learned it is a transition to another existence. Tim's love signs from his realm were so vivid and real, I *know* there is something yet to come. I don't know what that will be but I look forward to my continued adventure and each new awakening.

IN GRATITUDE

To my devoted family and dear friends who stayed by my side and supported me through the dark times and the good times; I'm not listing names for fear of leaving someone out — I'm claiming "widow brain" and trust you'll understand. Please accept my undying gratitude for being with me while Tim was hospitalized, or emailing or calling or bringing food to sustain me when he was in a coma. For those there on the day of his death, I could never have gone through it without you. Afterwards, whether you stayed with me, brought food or wine, shopped for me, helped me plan and be a part of Tim's memorial service, walked with me, spread flowers in the backyard, drew pictures to make me feel better, took care of our cats or delivered cat food, cleaned and did chores around our house, traveled with me, invited me to your homes and special events, surprised me with a visit, kidnapped me for fun, got me through the holidays and special anniversaries, called me over and over and over, hugged me, danced with me, laughed with me, cried with me and listened when I needed to talk about Tim over and over and over… your patience and love has been boundless. I thank you all from the bottom of my heart and the depths of my soul for being an integral part of my healing journey.

No matter how far into my grief process, my mental health became a barometer for how I coped day to day. To Linda, my therapist and weekly lifeline, thank you for your wisdom and comfort.

To Alex, Patsy Scala, Lisa Fox, Pat Floyd, Katrin Naumann and all of the "alternative healers" who showed this western medicine practicing, skeptical gal that there is much more to this infinite universe than meets the eye or science can explain. I am in awe of your openness to the *truth* that we are all spiritual beings having a human experience. I have learned so much from each of you and my gratitude is eternal.

To my "body healers" and dear friends, Amy and Sandi, you soothed my aching neck and back but you soothed my heart even more.

To Zak, your amazing connection to Tim and your sweet way of sharing your stories — and Tim's special coin — gave me hope and joy. Thank you for your courage to talk about things that others might not believe, but that you know in your heart are real. You have given me so much comfort.

To Soaring Spirits International and my fellow widowed friends, especially dearest Roseann, thank you for opening your hearts, sharing your stories and being an undying inspiration to keep *HOPE* alive.

The creation of a book is like a gestation, a process of development and growth over time. I carried this precious baby inside of me until I needed help to see me through to its birth. To my writing coach and copy editor, Cynthia Kling who has become a friend, I have much admiration for your expertise and patience to guide me over two and a half years while I freaked out at the length of time and amount of pain-staking work this would take. Sharing your wisdom as an accomplished writer and passionate student of life inspired me to keep moving forward, learn from my mistakes and grow through the intimate process of writing. My heart is full of gratitude for you.

To my cover designer, "widda sista" and friend, Sarah Treanor, your beautiful artistry and sensibility about the pain of loss and the depth of undying love created what my mind's eye envisioned and so much more. Your imaginative and exquisite flair is much admired and deeply appreciated.

To my book designer, Tim Atseff, thank you for sharing your impeccable expertise and artistic creativity. Your design added beauty and depth to enhance my words and shape a visual work of art. I am deeply grateful for your time, talent and friendship. And to Karen Sherwood, I am so grateful for your patient meticulousness and help with production.

To my Beta readers, Kasey Mathews, Laura Shabott, Candice Collins-Boden and Mrs. Collins, my heartfelt thank you for your generous time, hard-work and immensely helpful feed-back. Your insights were paramount in my process of editing and re-writing this manuscript countless times.

To Christine A. Krahling, thank you for your attention to detail in proofreading and copyediting. I so much appreciated your time and expertise.

To my web designer and cherished friend, Abigail Carter, your talent, wisdom and mostly your ability to give of yourself has moved my heart time and time again. I am so grateful you are in my life.

To Laura Ponticello, I am deeply grateful for your marketing and publication expertise, and your belief in the creative force in all of us speaks to my heart and soul.

To my precious Lucca and Vivi, I truly would not have survived this ordeal without you. Thank you for giving me the chance to be a mother and keep love growing in my heart.

To my Tim — from conception to birth, as we co-created our love story beyond death, my life has been transformed. You opened my heart to infinite, eternal love and my soul to the mysteries of the universe. My gratitude is boundless and my love is forever.

Resources: These include a combination of websites and social networks created by amazing, talented people who have supported and inspired me along my widowed journey. Each author or group speaks to the universal experience of loss and life's struggles while sharing their unique ways of helping others.

Grief and Widowhood
Abigail Carter- www.abigailcarter.com
Taryn Davis- www.americanwidowproject.org
Megan Devine- www.refugeingrief.com
Carol Brody Fleet- www.widowswearstilettos.com
Eleanor Haley and Litza Williams- www.whatsyourgrief.com
Janine Teague Eggers- www.mysecondplanA.com
Kim Hamer- www.100actsoflove.com
Michele Neff Hernandez- www.micheleneffhernandez.com
Rachel Kodanaz- www.rachelkodanaz.com
Matthew Logelin- thelizlogelinfoundation.org
Kelley Lynn- www.ripthelifeiknew.com
Elaine Mansfield- elainemansfield.com
Kim Kluxen Meredith- listenforthewhispers.com
Christina Rasmussen- www.secondfirsts.com
Soaring Spirits International www.soaringspirits.org
Michelle Steinke- www.onefitwidow.com
Tanya Villanueva Tepper- www.projectrebirth.org
Sarah Treanor- www.streanor.com
Dianne West- amyelomawidowsjourney.blogspot.com
Tom Zuba- www.tomzuba.com

Alternative Healing and Inspiration
Deborah DeRusha- www.thedreaminggypsy.com
Pat Floyd- www.dancingdrumha.com
Lisa Fox- www.lisakfox.com
Katrin Naumann- innerbalancelifeworks.com
Laura Ponticello- lauraponticello.com
Roseheart Center- www.theroseheartcenter.com
Patsy Scala- Patsy@mysticwaters.info
Robert Schwartz- www.yoursooulsplan.com
Upstate NY IANDS- www.unyi.org
Virginia Waldron- www.GateKeeperGuidance.com
Beth Wright- www.energyhealingteacher.com

Sources: Quotes at the beginning of chapters were found on brainyquote.com, goodreads.com, and google quotes/images.

About the Author

Story telling is in our family's DNA.

Raised on the tradition of enjoying good food and great tales at the family table, Anne Marie learned at an early age about sharing intimacy through the spoken word. Her large family often "loved loud" and even though everyone spoke at the same time, all were understood. She has fond memories of her Italian father starting most conversations, then her older siblings and their children shared their own stories of the day or memories of years past. Anne Marie also inherited the potential skill for the written word from her mother's Irish roots being distantly related to famed novelist, James Joyce.

I asked a friend to take a family portrait for the book's author page. Here I am with struggling Lucca and Vivi who don't like holding still for the camera, but obviously Tim liked it since he joined us, as usual, on my left side. What a perfect gift to wrap up this chapter in our book of eternity.

The love of family and sharing stories about life was a perfect springboard for Anne Marie to become a writer. But not until Tim died and gave her convincing "food for thought" and experiences beyond her imagination, did she feel compelled to document their history. Writing this memoir has been an incredibly healing experience with peaks and valleys along the way. As her life continues in this realm, she looks forward to the next chapter in her journey, with hope for whatever it may bring.

Anne Marie Higgins is a writer, nurse practitioner and family therapist who lives with her two cats, Lucca and Vivi in Syracuse, NY. Anne Marie is also is a confirmed "Hawkaholic." From early spring through summer, she can be found watching the Cornell University Lab of Ornithology's hawk nest cam as Red-Tailed Hawks Big Red and Ezra raise their yearly brood.

Made in the USA
Lexington, KY
19 November 2015